The Moral Evaluation
of Emergency
Department Patients

ANTHROPOLOGY OF WELL-BEING

Individual, Community, Society

Mission Statement

Well-being is central and important in people's daily lives and life history. This book series brings about understanding of what the complex concepts of well-being include. The concepts of quality of life, life satisfaction, and happiness will be explored and viewed at the individual level, the community level, and the level of society. The series encourages and promotes research into the concept of well-being, how it appears to be defined culturally, and how it is utilized across levels and across different social, economic, and ethnic groups. Understandings of how well-being promotes stability and resilience will also be critical to advances in understanding, as well as how well-being can be implemented as a goal in resisting vulnerabilities and in adaptation. Series books include monographs and edited collections by a range of academics, from rising scholars to experts in relevant fields.

Advisory Board Members

Carlos Garcia, Cynthia Isenhour, and Kathleen Galvin

Recent Titles in the Series

The Moral Evaluation of Emergency Department Patients: An Ethnography of Triage Work in Romania, by Marius Wamsiedel

Well-Being as a Multidimensional Concept: Understanding Connections among Culture, Community, and Health, edited by Janet M. Page-Reeves

Boundaries of Care: Community Health Workers in the United States, by Ryan I. Logan

Clinical Anthropology 2.0: Improving Medical Education and Patient Experience, edited by Jason W. Wilson and Roberta D. Baer

Living with HIV in Post-Crisis Times: Beyond the Endgame, edited by David A. B. Murray

The Moral Evaluation of Emergency Department Patients

An Ethnography of Triage Work in Romania

Marius Wamsiedel

LEXINGTON BOOKS
Lanham • Boulder • New York • London

Published by Lexington Books

An imprint of The Rowman & Littlefield Publishing Group, Inc.
4501 Forbes Boulevard, Suite 200, Lanham, Maryland 20706
www.rowman.com

86-90 Paul Street, London EC2A 4NE

British Library Cataloguing in Publication Information Available

Library of Congress Cataloging-in-Publication Data Available

ISBN 978-1-6669-1654-6 (paperback)
ISBN 978-1-66691-655-3 (electronic)

Contents

Acknowledgments   vii

Introduction   1

Chapter 1: The Need for Moral Evaluation   21

Chapter 2: Moral Evaluation Criteria   45

Chapter 3: Patient Types   67

Chapter 4: Credibility Work and the Assessment of Legitimacy   95

Chapter 5: Manufacturing Responsibility and Worth   117

Chapter 6: Producing Exclusion, Reproducing Racism   139

Conclusions   159

Bibliography   169

Index   183

About the Author   187

Acknowledgments

This book is the result of a long, arduous, and rewarding journey that started more than a decade ago. At that time, I was both a graduate student in the Department of Sociology at the University of Bucharest and a researcher at the Roma Center for Social Intervention and Studies (Romani CRISS), where I was documenting the access to health services of the Roma in Romania. The idea of studying the social categorization of patients and its consequences stemmed from an interest in symbolic interaction and the desire to understand the subtle mechanisms through which social exclusion was accomplished in healthcare settings. I had talked about this project with my supervisor, Puiu Lăţea, and my colleagues and friends Margareta Matache, Marian Mandache, and Ionuţ Sîrbu. Their encouragement and support at this early stage were invaluable.

I conducted the fieldwork as a doctoral student at the University of Hong Kong. My heartfelt gratitude goes to my supervisor, Cheris Shun-ching Chan. Her splendid intellectual guidance, unceasing support throughout the ups and downs of my doctoral journey, and mentorship during and after completing the Ph.D. have meant a lot to me. I fondly remember our discussions about ethnography, post-socialism, informal practices, and medical sociology. The members of the examination committee—Patrick J. Williams from Nanyang Technological University in Singapore, and Xiaoli Tian and David A. Palmer from the University of Hong Kong—provided insightful comments and suggestions, many of which made their way into the book.

Over the years, I have presented preliminary findings at various conferences, including the annual meetings of the American Anthropological Association, the American Sociological Association, the Society for the Study of Symbolic Interaction, the Council for European Studies, the Society for Romanian Studies, and the Gypsy Lore Society. The feedback received from Margaret Beissinger, Therese Gerstenauer, Anna Klepikova, Borbála Kovács, Abel Polese, Anamaria Ross, Dumitru Sandu, Carol Silverman,

Sabina Stan, Marko Stenroos, Valentin-Veron Toma, and many others has enriched my understanding of moral evaluation as a social process.

A brief teaching spell at the University of Bucharest in the fall of 2016 and a summer fellowship at the Research Institute of the University of Bucharest (ICUB) three years later provided me with the opportunity to further document the transformation of the healthcare system in Romania. I am grateful to the Department of Sociology and Social Work faculty, and particularly to Călin Cotoi, Liviu Chelcea, and Gabriel Jderu, for both their trust in me and their support. I also vividly remember the conversations with the other ICUB-Social Science research fellows—Frank Elbers, Ioan-Mihai Popa, and Gaby Ramia.

Preparing and revising this manuscript would have been much more difficult had it not been for the institutional support from the two international universities with which I have been affiliated—Xi'an Jiaotong-Liverpool University (XJTLU) and, starting from July 2022, Duke Kunshan University (DKU). At XJTLU, Elmer Virgil Villanueva kindly allowed me to go on research leaves in Romania in the summers of 2017 and 2018. Johannes Knops reduced my teaching workload and relieved me of service duties during the semester when I was drafting the book manuscript. My colleagues Richard Carciofo, Don Prisno, Stephen Pan, and Zhengfeei Ma have always been supportive of my research endeavors. At DKU, the co-directors of the Global Health Research Center, Yunguo Liu and Shenglan Tang, and my colleagues Qian Long, Chenkai Wu, and Lijing Yan provided me with unwavering support and encouragement during the revision of the manuscript.

Publishing a first book is never easy. I can count myself lucky to have received precious advice on how to prepare, submit, and revise a manuscript from Erica van der Sijpt, Péter Berta, Sam Beck, and Radu Umbreş. The two anonymous reviewers provided excellent suggestions on how to strengthen the argument and make the text easier to read. Incorporating their feedback into the revised version of the manuscript was a great pleasure. Parts of this book have been previously published in "Credibility work and moral evaluation at the ED," *Social Science & Medicine*, 248:112845 and "Reasonableness: Legitimate reasons for illegitimate presentations at the emergency department," *Sociology of Health & Illness* 40(8): 1347–60. I deeply appreciate the editors and reviewers for their comments and suggestions. I also thank the Lexington Books acquisition editors Kasey Beduhn and Alexandra Rallo, who believed in this project and offered me guidance throughout the publication process.

Many friends have accompanied me along the way: Martina Bristot, Owen Fung, Tawanda Nyawasha, Vincent Cheng, Chen Yang, and Man Yee Tai in Hong Kong; Liviu Fetic and Anemona Constantin in Romania; Cristina Ivanovici, Gergely Horváth, and the wonderful Sherry Qiang in Mainland

China, to name a few. During difficult times, their optimism uplifted me and gave me the power to get through.

I want to also thank Thomas Willard, my mentor during the undergraduate years at the University of Arizona and the supervisor of my first independent research project. I have long admired his intellectual brilliance and generosity.

The book could not have been completed without the support of the numerous people whose work makes the object of this study. I am grateful to the nurses and clerks at the emergency departments of two public hospitals in Romania who kindly allowed me to observe their practice and shared with me their ideas, experiences, concerns, and expectations. In return, they asked me to provide an honest account of what was going on at the emergency department. I have done my best to honor that promise.

I dedicate this book to my parents, Nela and Erwin Wamsiedel, and to my grandfather, Petre Mihăilă, with gratitude for their relentless support and unabated confidence in me over the years.

Kunshan
November 14, 2022

Introduction

Fifteen years ago, a Romanian dark comedy took the movie world by storm. *The Death of Mr. Lazarescu*, directed by Cristi Puiu, received wide critical acclaim and an award at the Cannes International Film Festival for realistically depicting a tragic and absurd tale. Its plot was simple, linear, and, after some time, predictable. One evening, the protagonist, an elder Bucharest denizen, calls the ambulance after experiencing excruciating pain. The ambulance arrives late, and the man is rushed to a nearby hospital under suspicion of a life-threatening illness. The doctors at the overcrowded emergency department (ED) confirm the severity of the condition but refuse to admit him. Mr. Lazarescu is then carried from one hospital to another throughout the night before finally getting admitted and receiving the needed intervention. In an ironic plot twist, the surgery succeeds, but the patient dies of another, previously undiagnosed disease.

The story is highly plausible. The protagonist, a retired engineer living on a meager pension and barely making ends meet, medicates his loneliness by drinking. With his wife dead and his only daughter living eight thousand miles away, Mr. Lazarescu does not find solace in a society radically different from the one he has spent most of his adult life in. He becomes reclusive, disengaged, and hopeless. The years of isolation and drinking have taken a heavy toll on his appearance. On the fatidic night that makes the object of the movie, he carries to the ED not only his old, frail body but also the discrediting characteristics of a socially alienated man. Doctors at three hospitals regard him as a superfluous individual who is undeserving of care, and this harsh moral evaluation contributes to his preventable death.

In fact, *The Death of Mr. Lazarescu* dramatizes a real-life case that took place four years earlier. Florin Nica, a fifty-one-year-old male with end-stage liver disease, died after being shuttled from one ED to another in a comatose state. Unlike his fictional counterpart, Nica had had no family and was not an engineer. The media described him as a "social case," which is a widely used bureaucratic euphemism for "homeless." Moreover, he was deaf, intellectually disabled, and with a record of psychiatric hospitalizations.[1] Similar cases of patients being denied access to the ED and carried from one hospital to another have been reported in the Romanian media over the years, many of them involving people of low socio-economic status or belonging to the Roma minority.

In 2018, the remains of Devon Freeman, an Indigenous teenager living in a group home in Hamilton, Ontario, were accidentally found in a nearby wooded area.[2] At that time, the adolescent had been missing for seven months. His death was ruled a suicide. The family accused the charitable organization operating the group home of multiple failures that contributed to Devon's untimely demise: not reporting the previous suicide attempt, not informing the family about it, and not providing him with qualified mental health assistance despite being aware of his ongoing suicidal ideation. They also criticized the police for paying lip service to the investigation into Devon's disappearance, which initially had been treated as that of a runaway.[3] In an official complaint to the regional supervisor coroner, the family requested that the investigation be made public, arguing that it was in the general interest to expose the systemic flaws of the Canadian child welfare system and their disproportionate impact on Indigenous children.[4] A thorough journalistic inquiry[5] found out that at least 102 Indigenous children connected to the child welfare system died over a period of five years (2013–2017) in the province of Ontario alone.

In 2020, the brutal killing in Minneapolis, Minnesota, of George Floyd by a police officer on duty sparked nationwide protests and global outrage. The victim, a black man in his prime, was suspected of passing a counterfeit $20 bill at a local grocery store. He was restrained by the police, handcuffed, forced into the patrol car, and, after a struggle with one of the law enforcement officers, pulled out of the car. He ended up on the pavement, facedown. What happened next made headlines: security camera footage and cell phone video records of passersby show one officer kneeling on George Floyd's neck for seven minutes and forty-six seconds, during which time he repeatedly made it clear that he could not breathe and desperately called for mercy. Eventually, Floyd died from lack of oxygen due to asphyxiation, as the post-mortem revealed. The massive protests erupting across the country denounced the systemic racism and called for police accountability and reform.

At first glance, these events have little in common. However, closer scrutiny reveals at least three commonalities. First, they all involve ordinary individuals failed, with tragic consequences, by the very institutions meant to serve and protect them: the hospital, the child welfare agency, and the police. Second, the victims belong to communities that are economically marginalized and socially excluded (e.g., racial minorities and Native peoples) or have characteristics that make them vulnerable (e.g., poverty, homelessness, mental illness, and physical disability). Third, these events are neither unique nor new. These stories have generated media attention and public outcry precisely because they epitomize patterns of violence and exclusion perpetrated by the state against its least fortunate citizens. Racial profiling, unwarranted brutality, denied access to care, and neglect are common and recurrent practices through which street-level bureaucrats discriminate against the powerless.

What is the institutional logic that makes such practices possible in public organizations? To answer this overarching question, in this book, I delve into the everyday interactions between triage workers and clients at the EDs of two public hospitals in Romania, which I refer to as City and County.[6] More specifically, I deconstruct analytically the moral evaluation to which legions of Messrs. Lazarescu—ordinary individuals with distressing symptoms—are subjected every day at the ED. By moral evaluation, I understand the social process whereby triage workers place patients in procedurally relevant categories based on non-clinical considerations.

MORAL EVALUATION AND THE CRISIS OF THE ED

The origins of moral evaluation as an object of social science investigation can be traced back, albeit indirectly, to the heyday of functionalism. Writing from the normative standpoint of the sick role model, Talcott Parsons[7] advances the idea that sickness is a peculiar form of deviance: although unintentional, it prevents people from accomplishing their social roles and hence has the potential to disrupt the orderliness of the society. To mitigate such risks and prevent malingering, the society engages in a moral assessment of the sick based on their illness behavior. Only those who acknowledge sickness as undesirable and look for medical help are granted the privileges of being temporarily exempted from the performance of daily tasks and not being hold responsible for their sickness. The assessment is moral in nature, but it takes place outside clinical contexts.

The sick role implies the patient role, in the sense that the provisional legitimation of sickness by family and friends requires medical validation. Parsons does not spell out the rights and obligations of physicians and patients but emphasizes affective neutrality as a prerequisite for the success of the therapeutic relationship: "whether [the physician] likes or dislikes the particular patient as a person is supposed to be irrelevant, as indeed it is to most purely objective problems of how to treat a disease."[8] In other words, he argues that moral evaluation is neither intrinsically evil nor completely avoidable. It becomes pernicious only insofar as patients' perceived likeability interferes with clinical reasoning and informs medical decisions.

Interactionist studies conducted in the 1960s, albeit critical of Parsons's grand theory, accept the norm of affective neutrality and bemoan its transgression in a variety of healthcare settings, including tuberculosis wards,[9] pediatrics, geriatrics,[10] and emergency rooms.[11] Practitioners in these settings fail to maintain a neutral stance toward the clientele, and their non-clinical judgment impacts the handling of patients and the care they receive. The studies conducted in this period document a coherent and pervasive moral evaluation process that is more complex than Parsons envisaged. Through it, physicians and nurses order users based on their putative value, delineated in terms of personal characteristics and actual or potential contribution to society.[12] Moral evaluation leads to differences in treatment ranging from minor privileges and sanctions during hospitalization[13] to significant clinical decisions such as the performance of cardiopulmonary resuscitation,[14] which unwittingly contribute to "the social inequality in death and dying."[15] Barney Glaser and Anselm Strauss[16] criticize moral evaluation in unambiguous terms, regarding it as a threat to medical professionalism brought by the penetration of lay values in settings presumed to be scientific and rational par excellence.

Further works abandon this skeptical stance as they delve deeper into the practice. Omnipresent as it is in healthcare settings, they argue, moral evaluation is only a part of a more extensive process of patient categorization, whose aim is to make the delivery of care consistent with the mission of the medical unit. In emergency wards, which become the setting of choice for unveiling the informal handling of the clientele, this means that establishing a patient's presumed worth goes hand in hand with assessing the legitimacy of the case,[17] that is the degree of resemblance between the condition of the patient and an acute illness requiring immediate assistance. While the initial categorization is informed by social as well as medical criteria,[18] the latter have precedence.[19] In these studies, the social categorization of the clientele appears as a reasonable attempt on the part of hospital workers to cope with situations in which the demand for medical assistance exceeds the available resources. The ensuing rationing of care permits healthcare practitioners to concentrate their efforts on patients with severe acute illness while discouraging illegitimate patients from making inopportune visits again.[20]

Moral evaluation is, thus, inextricably related to organizational concerns, which, in turn, are ways to make sense of and respond to the structural factors impacting emergency care. By categorizing patients on non-clinical grounds, triage workers attempt to tweak a dysfunctional emergency system. The current crisis of emergency medicine across the world[21] makes revisiting the topic worthwhile and necessary.

Two interrelated and partially overlapping factors contribute to the crisis of the ED. The first is the considerable disagreement among practitioners and health authorities about the occupational jurisdiction of emergency medicine and the scope of the ED. Some regard emergency medicine as a highly technical specialty whose exclusive or primary focus should be on acute care. To them, medically non-urgent problems are a serious threat to professionalism and reputation,[22] and, consequently, should be discouraged at all costs. Others argue in favor of extending the scope of the specialty to include the public health functions of screening, brief intervention, and referral to treatment (SBIRT). This measure would benefit the patients who do not receive preventive care services elsewhere, and in the long run may also reduce their visits to the ED.[23] Still others propose that the ED go even further and also attend to the social needs of the disadvantaged,[24] including homeless people[25] and victims of intimate partner violence.[26] In this way, the ED can work together with other institutions to address the broader determinants of health.

The second contributor to the crisis of the ED is the mismatch between the demand for care and the available human and material resources. The number of visits to the ED has increased over the years for a combination of reasons, including population growth and aging, patients' difficulty in setting up appointments with primary care physicians, and managed care problems.[27] As this was not paralleled by a proportional increase in resources allocated to emergency medicine, it led to overcrowding of EDs and heavy workloads for doctors, nurses, nurse aides, orderlies, and other staff. The frequent bottlenecks in the flow of patients, long waiting times, and brief examinations of patients without urgent conditions engendered animosity between practitioners and their clients. In many parts of the world, the verbal and physical violence perpetrated by patients and visitors against ED healthcare workers has been soaring,[28] further exacerbating the crisis and leading to poor patient care outcomes.[29]

In short, EDs operate in a context of structurally induced scarcity that has to be dealt with locally, through informal ways of apportioning care. This situation makes the moral evaluation of patients particularly salient an issue.

THE ETHNOGRAPHY OF A SOCIAL PROCESS

The last decade has seen a resurrection of interest in the moral evaluation of patients in emergency care settings. Two monographs of pre-hospital emergency services in the United States[30] and Canada[31] examine the informal categorization of the clientele as a central part of ambulance work. Building upon the theory of street-level bureaucracy and Armando Lara-Millan's[32] study on the interplay between emergency medicine and the criminal justice system, Josh Seim provides a much-needed integration of the moral evaluation into the wider institutional context in which it occurs. His book *Bandage, Sort, and Hustle* shows that ambulance crews' moral orientation to and handling of patients are influenced by their ongoing interaction with bureaucrats from two other institutions, the ED and the police. At the same time, a host of vertical forces, ranging from standardized protocols and supervision practices to the more abstract relation between government and capital, impact ambulance workers' approach of the clientele. In a similar vein, Michael K. Corman's *Paramedics On and Off the Streets* considers the impact of new public management reforms on ambulance work. The book demonstrates, inter alia, that the introduction of detailed protocols has failed to standardize paramedics' practice. Instead, it has unintendedly facilitated exclusionary practices directed against vulnerable groups, such as the elderly and the racial minorities.

In Europe, the recent works draw upon fieldwork conducted in hospitals and emergency primary care clinics, examine the work of triage nurses and clerks, and take a more interactional perspective. Alexandra Hillman in the UK, Lars Johannessen in Norway, and I in Romania pay ample attention to the accomplishment of moral evaluation and the active role of patients therein. Hillman[33] documents the identity work through which patients and relatives explain and justify their attendance of the ED, showing that it is instrumental to the prioritization of patients. Inspired by the negotiated order approach proposed by Anselm Strauss, Johannessen examines the various attempts of nurses and patients to reach a common definition of the situation. This negotiation impacts the access to emergency care[34] as well as the initial assessment of the case.[35] In another work, Johannessen[36] scrutinizes nurses' gatekeeping narratives to identify how they orient to patients who fail to meet the threshold level for being categorized as an emergency. My papers delve into the joint accomplishment of patient credibility during triage encounters[37] and triage workers' criteria for classifying ED patients,[38] the latter documenting the often-neglected inclusionary dimension of the gatekeeping.

This book is the ethnography of a social process. It complements and extends the extant scholarship, providing a holistic analysis of the moral evaluation of ED patients. In doing so, it uncovers the underlying logic, practical accomplishment, and consequences of the informal categorization of patients. The first question guiding this study is related to the social logic behind the moral evaluation process: Why do nurses and clerks go beyond formal procedures to morally assess their clients? To answer it, I explore the narratives through which triage workers make sense of moral evaluation, as well as the unfolding and content of their interactions with prospective patients. The systematic examination of triage encounters allows me to dig into the tacit, implicit, but consequential reasoning of nurses and clerks. To investigate the actual production of moral evaluation, I adopt a similar approach. I start from the premise that a separation needs to be drawn between how triage workers see their patients and how they handle them. Triage interactions reproduce and make visible staff's assumptions about patients and cases, but they also constitute the interactional arena in which patients and staff co-construct understandings of the situation and representations of each other. Rather than being static and unilateral, moral evaluation is a dynamic process to which patients and companions actively contribute. Therefore, the analysis breaks down the production of moral evaluation into a pre-interactional and an interactional component. The former considers triage workers' assessment criteria and general orientation to patients, which are stable a priori concerns that shape the organization of the admission interview. The latter exposes the negotiation of patient credibility and patients' performance of legitimacy, responsibility, and worth, based on which they are assigned to different priority categories. The final part of the book attends to the consequences of the moral evaluation, from the rationing of access to emergency care to the making of social exclusion in healthcare settings.

IN THE FIELD

I decided to conduct this study at the ED because ot its characteristics: the eclecticism of the clientele, the practical need to prioritize patients, and the relatively high volume of daily presentations. By design, the ED caters for people experiencing a sudden deterioration of health. As such changes are unanticipated, and no other services provide urgent medical assistance, the ED attracts a diverse range of patients. This diversity constitutes an opportunity for analyzing how patients' social characteristics impact their handling. The staff's practical need to prioritize patients in conditions of scarce objective data about the case provides a fertile ground for the mobilization of non-clinical judgments. Finally, the high number of patients and the wide range of medical conditions for which they seek medical help provide ample data for the analysis. These characteristics made the ED act as a magnifying glass for the study of moral evaluation.

In selecting the first research site, I was primarily interested in its ordinariness. Thus, I excluded military hospitals, which are special medical structures providing service to a narrow category of people, and private hospitals, which in Romania only attend to minor emergencies and are used predominantly by the affluent urban population. With these considerations in mind, I opted for doing fieldwork at County, the main hospital servicing an administrative unit of about half a million people. The county where the hospital is located fares slightly above the national average in terms of population size, land area, and contribution to the country's budget. Altogether, I conducted five months of ethnographic data collection there: the first round between March and June 2013, and the second one in June 2014.

One of the things that raised my interest while doing fieldwork at County was that people lacked emergency care alternatives, as the hospital was the sole provider of complex emergency services in the entire administrative unit. As I was about to complete the first round of data collection, I started wondering whether this structural condition influences the process of moral evaluation and its outcomes. To find out, I decided to extend the data collection to an ED located in a larger city. I was looking for an ED similar in size, number of daily presentations, and general profile of the clientele to County. Based on these criteria, City Hospital seemed the most appropriate option. Two doctors at County who were well acquainted with City because they had completed the residency there confirmed to me that the hospital would be a good match. I ended up doing another month of fieldwork at City (July 2014).

I relied on personal connections to get access to both hospitals. At County, I approached the medical director through a person who was well connected to the local medical world, albeit not personally acquainted with the director. The use of an informal connection established my request as legitimate and my status as trustworthy. During the meeting, I talked about my academic trajectory, the purpose and design of the doctoral research, and the intended period of stay for data-gathering in the hospital. The deputy director, whose son also pursued a graduate program overseas, was sympathetic toward my project. After checking my research proposal and the ethical approval letter,[39] he granted me permission to conduct fieldwork at ED. Then, he introduced me to the head nurse and asked her to support me in my research. I was given a gown and presented to the rest of the ED staff.

I followed the same approach to enter City hospital. I looked for a reliable person to introduce me to the general manager. Through informal connections, I was directed to the director of one of the most prestigious hospitals in the area. I met her and briefly presented my project and my data collection plan. She then called the manager at City and arranged a meeting with him on the same day. The meeting was brief and successful. The manager asked me to write a formal request letter and enclose relevant documents in order to obtain formal access. I did so, and a few days later I could start data-collection.

The top-down approach and the use of informality were instrumental in securing access to the two EDs. Nonetheless, access was an ongoing process of negotiation with participants.[40] I asked every doctor, nurse, and clerk whose practice I wanted to observe for permission to do so. Because the ED brings together a wide variety of practitioners from other hospital sections, including surgeons, orthopedists, and neurologists, the negotiation of access became a fieldwork ritual.

SETTINGS, PARTICIPANTS, AND
TRIAGE ARRANGEMENTS

Both hospitals are urban. County Hospital is in a medium-sized town of about 100,000 inhabitants, while City Hospital is in a much larger municipality that is also an important university center.[41] The hospitals were founded in the early 1970s through the reorganization of several healthcare facilities. The buildings hosting them date back to the same decade, as it is the case with most large hospitals in Romania.[42] The ED at City was created in the early 1990s, whereas the one at County opened five years later.

Erected in a period of massive infrastructural development and urban reconfiguration, the two buildings carry the imprint of the dominant ideology of the time—a strive for uniformity[43] and standardization. Both hospitals can be considered architectural palimpsests, as the remnants of the socialist style coexist with more recent design tendencies. City, whose structure is quadrangular, has undergone major yet incomplete renovation work recently. To the observer outside, it looks like a modern building with a pastel blue façade and white double pane glasses. However, the small patio inside reveals how the hospital used to look: the walls are coated with decaying gray roughcast, and some of the windows still have the original massive wooden frames. At County, the original brick façade remained largely unaltered, but the flat roof was replaced by a dual-pitch metal roof whose red tiles give it a more cheerful appearance. The interior conserves socialist-style linoleum floors and cast-iron radiators that can hardly be encountered in ordinary private houses nowadays but adds to them equipment that was unfathomable for a public building a quarter of a century ago, such as air-conditioners and TV sets, along with PVC doors and frames.

In terms of staff, City has more doctors but considerably fewer nurses, nurse aides, and orderlies than County (see Table 1).[44] The management deals with the shortage of nurses by informally delegating a large part of the triage work to clerks, an arrangement that I explain below. Both EDs are gendered organizations. The heads of the department are females; female doctors largely outnumber males (8 versus 3 at County, and 11 versus 3 at City, respectively); and, with one exception in each hospital, all nurses are females. There is no male among the nurse aides, aides, and clerks. On the other side, only males work as orderlies.

Table 0.1. Staff structure at the two EDs in 2014

Staff	*County Hospital ED*	*City Hospital ED*
Doctors	11	14
Nurses, excluding triage nurses	54	41
Triage nurses	8	0
Nurse aides	22	11
Orderlies	22	12
Aides	7	0
Triage clerks	6	6
Social workers	1	1 (part-time)

At County, the head nurse assigns ED nurses to work in the triage for a three-month period. However, the arrangement is flexible and subjected to negotiation. Thus, some nurses spend a longer time in the triage, whereas others manage to avoid it altogether. When I returned to County for a second round of fieldwork in 2014, four of the eight triage nurses were the same as the year before. *Source*: Compiled by the author based on information provided by the staff.

At County, the triage work is divided between nurses and clerks, but the delineation of responsibilities is neat: nurses perform the initial assessment of cases and decide the priority codes, whereas clerks digitize patient records and compile basic statistics.[45] On a regular shift, two nurses get involved in assessing the newcomers. In the triage booth, one of them conducts the admission interview, fills in all relevant paperwork, and enters data into the electronic patient file. The other nurse, stationed in an adjacent room, performs a detailed anamnesis and takes vital signs. Patients are assigned one of the five priority codes—red, yellow, green, blue, or white.[46]

The situation differs at City, where a dual system is in place. The clerk on duty is the only person working in the triage section of the ED. In addition to the formal responsibilities, which are the same as the ones at County, the clerk processes all cases except for those handled by the two pre-hospital emergency units, the ambulance and the Mobile Emergency Service for Resuscitation and Extrication (MESRE).[47] Ambulance and MESRE crews bypass the triage and present patients directly to one of the doctors in the major emergency room unless they consider that the patient's condition does not warrant fast-track admission. If this is the case, the patient is left in the triage waiting room. The existence of a separate entrance to the major emergency room with direct access from the parking lot facilitates this arrangement.

Since clerks lack medical and nursing training, they tend to adopt a defensive tactic. Whenever they suspect a potentially life-threatening condition, they let the patient in to get assessed by a nurse. If the seriousness of the problem is confirmed, the patient gets admitted right away; otherwise, they return to the waiting room. The priority codes assigned by the clerk are tentative and do not carry any practical implications because the admission principle for patients in the waiting room is "first come, first served."

The unanticipated differences between County and City regarding the organization of triage work provide an opportunity to explore the connections between moral evaluation and gatekeeping, an issue that will be examined throughout the book.

THE ED AS A BESIEGED FORTRESS

As a situated activity, ethnographic research cannot be divorced from the peculiar conditions encountered in the field. One of the things that impacted my position in the field and access to data was the dominant perception among staff that the ED is under constant scrutiny and ongoing attacks.

The reform of the healthcare sector and the reorganization of emergency medicine, which will be discussed in Chapter 1, left many nurses and clerks dissatisfied. The reasons for discontentment are many, including a perceived decline in the prestige of the ED, which became a convenient substitute of family medicine for numerous users; the considerably increased workload; the reduced gatekeeping role due to the introduction of an inclusive policy of access that prevents triage nurses from denying access to the service; and the further reduction of autonomy brought by the digitalization of the service and the intense scrutiny of electronic records by health authorities. Clerks at City face the additional stress of performing triage tasks for which they lack training, and of which they were not aware when joining the ED. Another source of frustration for nurses and clerks at both hospitals is related to the media representation of the service. They regard the alleged tendency of TV stations to overreport cases of alleged malpractice and side with patients in controversial situations as utterly unfair, especially since media have largely been silent about the difficult work conditions in emergency care settings. Several triage workers drew a connection between media reporting and the perceived unruly conduct of patients and their families. In short, to most nurses and clerks, the ED resembles a besieged fortress, enduring concurrent attacks from medical authorities, media outlets, and users.

This perception turned out to be an unexpected opportunity for conducting fieldwork. With many stories learned from reading hospital ethnographies,[48] I expected to pass through a tedious and, at times, frustrating accommodation process during which my allegiances would be tested in order to overcome participants' initial reluctance toward me. Instead, to my surprise, I found nurses, clerks, and doctors eager to talk and share with me their experience of working at the ED. They volunteered information about patients, allowed me to consult various reports compiled as part of their duties, and provided me with valuable background information through which I could make a better sense of their conduct in interaction with the patients. I was also invited to observe the "dirty work"[49] of handling inebriated individuals and people with erratic behavior, and I was encouraged to do fieldwork at times when the likelihood of contentious encounters with patients was higher than average. In welcoming me to their workplace, nurses and clerks expressed their hope that my research would provide an accurate representation of what is going on. Moreover, they asked me to also tell "the other side of the story," one that is often obscured in public discussions of the emergency wards—namely, that working conditions are difficult, some of the patients are aggressive and over-demanding, and, despite all the adversities, the personnel strive to accomplish their tasks professionally.[50]

At the same time, the representation of the hospital as a besieged fortress came with a practical downside for my research. In polarized social spaces where sides are so neatly delineated, allegiances are crucial.[51] A hint of suspicion regarding loyalty can lead to a fall from grace, as I would find out—the hard way—during my last few days at City.

Four weeks of smooth data gathering had passed when I started noticing sudden changes in the way participants reacted toward my presence. As I was conducting formal interviews at the time, I asked the head nurse of the ED for a favor. I wanted her to introduce me to the nurses working in the ED sections where I had not done observation so that my request would not come out of the blue. The head nurse, who had been supportive throughout my stay in the department, gently turned my request down. She invoked plausible reasons for not being able to assist me right away the two times when I brought up the issue and argued that such a move was unnecessary given that all members of the department were aware of my legitimate presence there. She encouraged me to approach the nurses directly, assuring me of their wholehearted cooperation. However, when I followed her advice, I faced tactful, polite, yet unambiguous refusals to participate.

Around the same time, a shift in the behavior of a male nurse from the minor emergency room caught my attention as well. The afternoon I first met him, I was intrigued by the conspicuously formal manner in which he accomplished his duties. He started the shift by cleaning the workplace, meticulously arranging medicines and instruments, and inquiring about each patient's condition. Unlike other nurses, he invariantly carried the tray with necessary utensils next to the patient's bed and put on gloves before performing even the most basic procedure. In interaction with patients, he maintained a sober line and always addressed them politely. Everything changed the following day, as soon as he found out that I had nothing to do with the audit of the ED, as he had initially assumed. From that moment, he abandoned the persona of a textbook nurse and many of the mannerisms that supported it and engaged in conduct of a different sort. Diffidence left place to haughtiness and play by the rules to careful avoidance of norms. The air of nonchalant confidence and superiority he put up in relation to patients made quite a few mistake him for a doctor. With me, he was friendly and aloof at the same time. His behavior changed once again during my last week in the field. He became excessively amiable toward me and benevolent toward patients and resumed the habit of scrupulously following occupational norms. Moreover, he refrained from cracking jokes and passing negative judgments on patients in my presence.

There were other more or less subtle changes in my relationship with members of the ED. They culminated with the refusal of two triage clerks to be formally interviewed. I was taken aback by their rejection because I had already spent many an hour observing their practice, talking to them about their work and the people they were interacting with, and every time they shared with me their opinions without hesitation. The interview guide, which I showed them when making the request, did not cover any topics that had not been discussed earlier, so this was not a plausible argument for refusing to participate. One clerk told me that she wasn't sure whether she was permitted to talk to me. This argument confused me, as the situation occurred at the end of my fieldwork at City. By that time, we knew each other relatively well, and there was no secret that I had obtained the management's approval to conduct fieldwork there.

It was only after leaving the field that, in a phone conversation with one of the participants at City whom I befriended, I found the most likely origin of these difficulties. One doctor, who was also the ED spokesperson, raised doubts about the reasons for my presence in the hospital. She insinuated that I might be connected to the secret intelligence service, gathering discreditable data about the work performed there. The doctor admonished the staff for giving too much inside information and advised them to adopt a more cautious approach toward me from that moment on.[52]

In hindsight, the doctor's suspicion does not seem completely out of place. This event took place shortly after I spent an entire night doing observation in the minor emergencies section. My zealous commitment to fieldwork, which was largely due to the relatively short time available at City, had already triggered curiosity among staff members. The broader political context at the time, dominated by campaigns to consolidate the rule of law by eradicating corruption,[53] probably further contributed to raise suspicion about to my presence.

I have mentioned these events to point out my fluid positionality in the field and to draw attention to the contingencies of the empirical context. Participants' assumptions about my role and their representation of the ED as a site of ongoing contention generated a peculiar set of opportunities and constraints for data gathering. Although events of this sort influenced to a certain extent the collection of ethnographic data, they did not compromise the reliability of my study for at least a couple of reasons. First, many of the issues of importance to triage workers had little in common with my theoretical interests. Their impression management efforts focused on projecting a favorable image as competent, industrious, and concerned workers operating in a harsh and sometimes unfair environment. In contrast, my interest was in the organization of the triage work and the social categorization of the clientele. Moreover, the prolonged immersion into the social world of triage workers, the diversity of situations encountered, and the number of participants whose activities I observed allowed me to unravel practical inconsistencies as well as contradictions between verbal accounts of work and actual work performance. Thus, I had access to data that participants were unaware of or not inclined to disclose to me. Second, the 'spy incident' occurred at the very end of my fieldwork, after collecting most of the data at City. If it were to take place earlier, it might have jeopardized my data collection there. By taking place at the end of my stay in the hospital, it only represented an opportunity for me to observe how my status position influenced the access to information.[54]

ORGANIZATION OF THE BOOK

Chapter 1 situates the moral evaluation of ED patients into the general context in which it occurs, exploring the objective conditions of triage work and how triage workers make sense of and respond to them. The reform of the Romanian healthcare system incentivized people to look for care at the ED irrespective of the nature and severity of symptoms, which led to a considerable increase in the number of visits at both hospitals. At the same time, formal regulations and informal work arrangements restricted the gatekeeping function of the triage service. Nurses and clerks work in the context of a clash between mandate and mission, that is, between what the ED is institutionally authorized to do and what staff feel they should do. From a bureaucratic standpoint, the moral evaluation of patients is the informal mechanism through which triage workers attempt to correct shortcomings in the formal organization of emergency care. Nevertheless, moral evaluation also plays an important, yet often neglected, role in the clinical assessment of cases. Facing uncertainty and lacking objective evidence, nurses and clerks use patients' perceived social characteristics and interactional demeanor to establish their credibility as reporters of symptoms and infer the seriousness of the case. The bureaucratic and medical preoccupation are often intertwined, blurring the boundary between moral evaluation and clinical assessment.

Chapters 2 and 3 examine triage workers' concerns and background knowledge about the patients, which inform their approach of the admission interview. In chapter 2, I show that nurses and clerks attend to the degree of fit between the condition and the mission of the ED service (the *legitimacy* of the case), the availability and accessibility of primary care (the *reasonableness* of the visit), and the patient's putative contribution to the society (the *social worth* of the patient). These staff-devised criteria indicate a coherent orientation to patients and an understanding of gatekeeping that is both inclusionary and exclusionary. Chapter 3 shifts the attention to the staff's representation of the patients. Patients are typified based on a master status. Except for Roma, all other types are assigned two tentative configurations of legitimacy, reasonableness, and worth, each carrying a different moral entitlement to emergency care. The criteria and patient types are remarkably stable and consistent at the two ED in which I have conducted fieldwork.

The next part of the book investigates the joint construction of moral evaluation by patients and staff. Chapter 4 is dedicated to the negotiation of patient credibility and legitimacy of the case, whereas chapter 5 documents patients' strategies of manufacturing responsible use of the service and social worth. Together, these chapters emphasize the dynamic, interactional, and performative component of the moral evaluation process and unravel some subtle differences in the handling of patients with similar characteristics and symptoms. They show that far from being deprived of agency in the interaction with triage workers, patients are active contributors to the moral evaluation process. Interactional prowess is a salient resource they can mobilize to support their claim for admission.

Chapter 6 turns the attention from the accomplishment of moral evaluation to its consequences. Building upon the idea of medicine as a social institution, I look into the medical and social exclusion of patients who fail to pass the moral evaluation. The paradigmatic case is that of Romani patients, who have a small but noticeable presence in both hospitals. After discussing the staff's tactics of sanctioning undesirable patients and their impact on the access to emergency care, I focus on the making of racial exclusion at the ED and the consequences it entails. I argue that the micro-aggressions to which Romani patients are routinely subjected are meant to keep them in their place, thus reproducing the broader social order into the ED microcosm. While Romani patients have the means to escape the negative assessment at an individual level, they cannot address the dominant racial discourse, which gets reproduced and reinforced through triage practices.

In the concluding chapter, I revisit the argument and discuss the contribution this book makes to the understanding of moral evaluation as a social process and of social exclusion in healthcare settings.

NOTES

1. Cris Constantinescu, "'My Child Died after Being Shuttled between Hospitals,'" Click.

2. Dan Taekema, "Inquest into Death of 16-Year-Old Devon Freeman Announced," CBC.

3. Kristy Kirkup, "How Devon Freeman Died: An Ontario Teen's Suicide Raises Hard Questions about Child Welfare and Indigenous Youth," The Globe and Mail.

4. CBC, "Family Calls for Inquest into Suicide of Indigenous Teen in Government Care," CBC.

5. Kenneth Jackson, "Death as Expected: Inside a Child Welfare System Where 102 Indigenous Kids Died over 5 Years," APTN News.

6. For the sake of anonymity, both names are fictitious. Participants' names have also been replaced by pseudonyms.

7. *The Social System* (Glencoe, IL: Free Press, 1951).

8. Parsons, 435.

9. Julius Roth, *Timetables* (Indianapolis: Bobbs-Merrill, 1963).

10. Barney Glaser and Anselm Strauss, *Awareness of Dying: A Study of Social Interaction* (Chicago: Aldine, 1965); Barney Glaser and Anselm Strauss, *Status Passage* (London: Routledge & Kegan Paul, 1971).

11. David Sudnow, *Passing On: The Social Organization of Dying* (Englewood Cliffs, NJ: Prentice-Hall, 1967).

12. Barney G. Glaser and Anselm L. Strauss, "The Social Loss of Dying Patients," *The American Journal of Nursing* 64, no. 6: 119–21.

13. Roth, *Timetables*.

14. Sudnow, *Passing On: The Social Organization of Dying*, 103–4.

15. Stefan Timmermans, "Social Death as Self-Fulfilling Prophecy: David Sudnow's 'Passing On' Revisited," *The Sociological Quarterly* 39, no. 3: 454.

16. "The Social Loss of Dying Patients."

17. Julius A. Roth, "Some Contingencies of the Moral Evaluation and Control of Clientele: The Case of the Hospital Emergency Service.," *American Journal of Sociology* 77, no. 5: 839–56; James M. Mannon, "Defining and Treating 'Problem Patients' in a Hospital Emergency Room," *Medical Care* 14, no. 12: 1004–13; Roger Jeffery, "Normal Rubbish: Deviant Patients in Casualty Departments," *Sociology of Health & Illness* 1, no. 1: 90–107.

18. Terry Mizrahi, "Getting Rid of Patients: Contradictions in the Socialisation of Internists to the Doctor-Patient Relationship," *Sociology of Health & Illness* 7, no. 2: 214–35.

19. Nurok and Henckes, "Between Professional Values and the Social Valuation of Patients: The Fluctuating Economy of Pre-Hospital Emergency Work"; Vassy, "Categorisation and Micro-Rationing: Access to Care in a French ED."

20. Some more recent contributions to the study of social categorization at the ED document other factors impacting the moral evaluation of patients. Besides staff's values and beliefs (Nurok and Henckes, "Between Professional Values and the Social Valuation of Patients: The Fluctuating Economy of Pre-Hospital Emergency

Work"), moral evaluation is also shaped by various organizational contingencies (Vassy, "Categorisation and Micro-Rationing: Access to Care in a French ED"; Dingwall and Murray, "Categorization in Accident Departments"), staff's concerns with accountability for errors (Juan M. Rey Pino, Gonzalo Sánchez Gardey, and Ingunn Hagen, "When Staff Create the Organisational Culture: A Case Study in the Spanish Emergency Health Care System," *Journal of Health Management* 10, no. 2: 163–89), the perceived intellectual value of the case (Nicholas Dodier and Agnès Camus, "Openness and Specialisation: Dealing with Patients in a Hospital Emergency Service," *Sociology of Health & Illness* 20, no. 4: 416), inter-institutional arrangements (Armando Lara-Millán, "Public Emergency Room Overcrowding in the Era of Mass Imprisonment," *American Sociological Review* 79, no. 5: 866–87; Josh Seim, *Bandage, Sort, and Hustle: Ambulance Crews on the Front Lines of Urban Suffering* [Oakland, CA: University of California Press, 2020]), and the framing of the problem by patients and their companions (Alexandra Hillman, "'Why Must I Wait?': The Performance of Legitimacy in a Hospital Emergency Department," *Sociology of Health & Illness* 36, no. 4: 485–99; John Heritage and Jeffrey D. Robinson, "Accounting for the Visit: Patients' Reasons for Seeking Medical Care," in *Communication in Medical Care: Interaction between Primary Care Physicians and Patients*, ed. John Heritage and Douglas W. Maynard [Cambridge: Cambridge University Press, 2006], 48–85). Moreover, these studies emphasize categorization as a joint accomplishment by doctors, nurses (David Hughes, "When Nurse Knows Best: Some Aspects of Nurse/Doctor Interaction in a Casualty Department," *Sociology of Health and Illness* 10, no. 1: 1–22), and allied health professionals (David Hughes and Lesley Griffiths, "'Ruling in' and 'Ruling out': Two Approaches to the Micro-Rationing of Health Care," *Social Science & Medicine* 44, no. 5: 589–99). Categorization is thus constructed as a multifaceted process whose outcomes lie at the intersection between staff-devised typifications of the clientele, situational contingencies, workplace power relations, and patients' maneuvers of self-presentation.

21. Wang et al., "Causes of ED Overcrowding and Blockage of Access to Critical Services in Beijing: A 2-Year Study."

22. Given the many visits for non-urgent health concerns, the acronym 'ED' is sometimes jokingly spelled out as 'Everything Department.' Similarly, the British 'A&E' (Accident and Emergency) Department is rendered as 'Almost Everything Department.'

23. Rhodes, Gordon, and Lowe, "Preventive Care in the ED, Part I: Clinical Preventive Services-Are They Relevant to Emergency Medicine?"

24. Gordon, "The Hospital ED as a Social Welfare Institution."

25. Morris and Gordon, "The Role of the ED in the Care of Homeless and Disadvantaged Populations."

26. Elisa A. M. Hackenberg et al., "Victims of Severe Intimate Partner Violence Are Left Without Advocacy Intervention in Primary Care Emergency Rooms: A Prospective Observational Study," *Journal of Interpersonal Violence*, 1–23.

27. Derlet and Richards, "Overcrowding in the Nation's EDs: Complex Causes and Disturbing Effects."

28. Jianxin Liu et al., "Prevalence of Workplace Violence against Healthcare Workers: A Systematic Review and Meta-Analysis," *Occupational and Environmental Medicine* (BMJ Publishing Group).

29. D. M. Gates, "The Epidemic of Violence against Healthcare Workers," *Occupational and Environmental Medicine*.

30. Seim, *Bandage, Sort, and Hustle: Ambulance Crews on the Front Lines of Urban Suffering.*

31. Michael K. Corman, *Paramedics On and Off the Streets: Emergency Medical Services in the Age of Technological Governance* (Toronto: University of Toronto Press, 2017).

32. "Public Emergency Room Overcrowding in the Era of Mass Imprisonment."

33. "Why Must I Wait?"

34. Lars E.F. Johannessen, "Negotiated Discretion: Redressing the Neglect of Negotiation in 'Street-Level Bureaucracy,'" *Symbolic Interaction* 42, no. 4: 513–38.

35. Lars E.F. Johannessen, "The Commensuration of Pain: How Nurses Transform Subjective Experience into Objective Numbers," *Social Science & Medicine* 233: 38–46.

36. "Narratives and Gatekeeping: Making Sense of Triage Nurses' Practice," *Sociology of Health & Illness* 40, no. 5: 892–906.

37. Marius Wamsiedel, "Credibility Work and Moral Evaluation at the ED," *Social Science and Medicine* 248, no. 112845: 1–8.

38. Marius Wamsiedel, "Reasonableness: Legitimate Reasons for Illegitimate Presentations at the ED," *Sociology of Health and Illness* 40, no. 8: 1347–60.

39. The study was approved by the Institutional Review Board at St. Mary's Hospital in Hong Kong, as I was a doctoral student at the University of Hong Kong when I conducted the data collection.

40. Carla L. Reeves, "A Difficult Negotiation: Fieldwork Relations with Gatekeepers," *Qualitative Research* 10, no. 3: 323.

41. Some specific information is not disclosed in order to protect anonymity.

42. Roger M. Battistella, "Health Services in the Socialist Republic of Romania: Structural Features and Cost-Containment Policies," *Journal of Public Health Policy* 4, no. 1: 94–95.

43. Darrick Danta, "Ceausescu's Bucharest," *Geographical Review* 83, no. 2: 172.

44. The staff turnover is relatively high at County, particularly among doctors and nurses. In the space of a year, three doctors resumed work after having completed residency elsewhere, one doctor left for another hospital, one nurse retired, and two nurses and one aide migrated abroad.

45. For this reason, clerks are informally referred to as "statisticians." However, this is a misnomer, as clerks lack any qualification in statistics or actuarial sciences. Most of them are high-school graduates with basic computer skills. The activity reports they compile refer to the number of patients, the distribution of patients by priority codes and diagnostic categories, the number of patients transferred to other medical units, and the number of deceased patients.

46. In Romania, the triage follows an adapted version of the Emergency Severity Index. However, as I will show in the data chapters, formal procedures coexist with

and are often replaced by informal decision-making. The five codes carry different assumptions about the condition of set a maximum waiting time. The red code refers to conditions with an imminent vital risk, in which patients are admitted right away. Next comes the yellow code in which "waiting may be dangerous" as a poster in the triage booth warns. The maximum waiting time for a patient with a yellow code is ten minutes. The third, and by far the most common code, is green, which covers situations where the vital functions are not affected, but the handling of the patient requires multiple resources. In this case, patients can be kept in the waiting room for up to half an hour. The blue code, assigned to cases without vital risks and demanding only one resource, carries a maximum waiting time of an hour. The lowest priority code is the white one, assigned to cases for the handling of which no resource is needed. The white code attracts a waiting time no longer than two hours. In practice, the overwhelming majority of cases receive a green code.

47. In Romanian, *SMURD (Serviciul Medical de Urgenţe, Resuscitare şi Descarcerare).* The arrangement at City contravenes official regulations, which stipulate that only doctors and nurses are allowed to perform the triage assessment. See Romanian Ministry of Health, "Ordinul Nr. 48/2009 Privind Aprobarea Protocolului Naţional de Triaj Al Pacienţilor Din Structurile Pentru Primirea Urgenţelor [Order 48/2009 Regarding the Approval of the National Protocol for the Triage of Patients in Emergency Units]" (2009).

48. Conducting qualitative fieldwork in hospital settings is notoriously difficult (see Shahaduz Zaman, "Native among the Natives: Physician Anthropologist Doing Hospital Ethnography at Home," *Journal of Contemporary Ethnography* 37, no. 2: 137). Managers are often reluctant to let ethnographers collect data on the premises (Sjaak van der Geest and Kaja Finkler, "Hospital Ethnography: Introduction," *Social Science & Medicine*, Hospital Ethnography, 59, no. 10: 1996; Debbi Long, Cynthia Hunter, and Sjaak van der Geest, "When the Field Is a Ward or a Clinic: Hospital Ethnography," *Anthropology & Medicine* 15, no. 2: 71) for fear that empirically grounded research might expose the chasm between the desired representation of the institution and its actual performance, and, thus, challenge the official line (Howard S. Becker, "Whose Side Are We On?" *Social Problems* 14, no. 3: 242–43). Building rapport with members of hospital staff is also, at times, problematic because of the ambiguous status of the researcher in the field and the readily apparent differences in the work routine. As Wind ("Negotiated Interactive Observation: Doing Fieldwork in Hospital Settings," *Anthropology & Medicine* 15, no. 2: 83) notices, ethnographers engage in seemingly nugatory activities, flexibly dispose of their time, and accomplish tasks of no immediate practical use. Staff members in highly specialized medical units, on the other hand, perform technical procedures of various degrees of complexity and make critical decisions fast.

49. Everett Cherrington Hughes, *The Sociological Eye: Selected Papers* (New Brunswick, NJ: Transaction Publishers, 2009), 314.

50. I assured them that I intended to give a fair and objective representation of the events, but I also told them that my primary audience consisted of people with a theoretical interest in the interaction between healthcare workers and patients, rather than the general public. I specified that my purpose was to understand a social process

and that I was neither competent nor willing to assess the service quality or the performance of hospital workers.

51. Nora Dudwick, "Postsocialism and the Fieldwork of War," in *Fieldwork Dilemmas: Anthropologists in Postsocialist States,* ed. Hermine G. de Soto and Nora Dudwick, 2000, 14.

52. Becoming persona non-grata in the field is in itself a topic of ethnographic interest and a potential source of important data. In my case, the increased reluctance of some informants to discuss topics about the routine activities they accomplish was accompanied by the unanticipated willingness of other participants to disclose discrepancies between the idealized accounts of practice and the actual situations. The "segmentation of interests" (see John van Maanen, "The Fact of Fiction in Organizational Ethnography," *Administrative Science Quarterly* 24, no. 4: 545 fn 8) that ensues on this kind of occasions provides access to information that might not be otherwise available.

53. The public debates of the time gave ample space to the various forms of corruption in the medical sector, ranging from petty informal payments to rigged public procurement contracts. Vlad Mixich, a leading health policy analyst, condemned in unambiguous terms the deleterious effects of such practices: "While underfunding is the great sin of the Romanian medical system, corruption is the devil inside it" (Vlad Mixich, "Corupția Din Sistemul Medical - Protejată Sau Exorcizată de Noua Lege a Sănătății? [The Corruption in the Medical System - Protected or Exorcised by the New Healthcare Law?]," Hotnews) The year of my fieldwork at County also coincided with the pinnacle of the anti-corruption campaign (National Anti-corruption Directorate, "Bilanț 2014 [Annual Review 2014].") , many of the cases relying on evidence collected by the Romanian Intelligence Service.

54. Another important contextual peculiarity is the open secrecy surrounding controversial issues, such as ethnicity or informal practices. Instead of talking directly about such topics, nurses and clerks often prefer to use innuendos, knowing smiles, allusive language, and other forms of indirect communication. To break the open secrecy, I strove to maintain a partial insider status, which also gave me the chance to ask questions that would be inappropriate for an insider while getting close enough to the participants not to be treated as a stranger. The triangulation of data-collection instruments (observation of naturally occurring triage admission interviews, casual talk and formal interviews with staff members, and analysis of documents) also helped me get a deeper understanding of what triage workers say and do. I explain my methodological strategy in detail elsewhere (Marius Wamsiedel, "Approaching Informality: Rear-Mirror Methodology and Ethnographic Inquiry," in *The Informal Economy in Global Perspective: Varieties of Governance,* ed. Abel Polese et al. [London: Palgrave Macmillan, 2017], 97–115).

Chapter 1

The Need for Moral Evaluation

It was one of my early days at the County Hospital when a nurse asked me about the reasons for doing research in the emergency department. While briefing her about the nature and purpose of my study, I mentioned the eclecticism of the users: "I'm looking for a place where people from all walks of life interact. I focus on the emergency ward because everybody comes here when needing urgent medical care, from the mayor to . . . " The nurse did not let me finish the sentence. "You'll never find the mayor here!" she replied, an amused and indulgent smile on her face, adding that the profile of the users was far less diverse than I expected: the overwhelming majority of patients were, in fact, poor, old, and uneducated; people who could afford to pay for medical care seldom made an appearance at the emergency department. I would later hear this view echoed many times by other staff members in both hospitals.

The staff used the skewed class distribution of the patients as a compelling argument against the actual organization of the healthcare system in general and emergency medicine in particular. If all cases they handled were "real" emergencies, the profile of the clientele would approximate that of the general population. As this was clearly not the case, it meant that the service was misused, a point on which every hospital informant agreed without hesitation.

Considerations of this sort are difficult to understand without some familiarity with the local context. Therefore, this chapter will provide a brief overview of the healthcare system in Romania before and after the fall of state socialism in 1989, with an emphasis on the major transformations that impacted the access to care. Then, it will examine how nurses and clerks at the two hospitals in this study make sense of and respond to the structural conditions that impact their work. Two narratives encountered in the field will also be discussed—the perceived crisis of the healthcare system, and the perceived mission of the emergency service, respectively. The chapter suggests that the moral evaluation of patients is rendered necessary by the structural problems marring the healthcare system.

THE HEALTHCARE SYSTEM IN ROMANIA

Like other former socialist countries in Central and Eastern Europe, Romania has for decades experienced a model of socialized medicine of Soviet inspiration.[1] The early efforts of the socialist state went in the direction of addressing the wider determinants of health and reducing the health disparities along class lines. The improved nutrition, provision of better housing and sanitation, increased access to education, and immunization contributed to some notable achievements in population health, particularly with regards to infectious diseases.[2] For instance, malaria, a disease that was endemic and had an incidence of 2,138 cases per 100,000 inhabitants in 1948,[3] was eliminated at the beginning of the 1960s. Socialist Romania experienced the epidemiological transition theorized by Omran, with non-communicable diseases replacing communicable diseases as the leading cause of mortality.[4] The life expectancy also increased in the first decades, becoming similar to that of developed countries.

The socialist health system was grounded in the principle of health as a basic human right and characterized by universal coverage, rigid centralization, state planning, and focus on preventive care. Private practice was suppressed in 1948, with the nationalization of hospitals, clinics, pharmacies, and clinical laboratories. The private sector was reintroduced only in 1990, after the change in political regime.

The primary care was greatly improved, through the establishment of polyclinics (community health centers) in urban areas and dispensaries in rural ones. Nevertheless, medical care took place predominantly in the secondary and tertiary inpatient hospitals.[5] Hospitals were prepared to handle emergencies and each of them had an ambulance service that could reach even the isolated regions.[6] While the ambulance service was designed to respond to neurosurgical emergencies, in practice it was widely used to bypass the general practitioners or to get access to care when the primary care facilities were closed. Some health policy researchers[7] claim that "over 90 percent of ambulance visits were for primary care in [late socialist] Romania." The figure is to be taken with a pinch of salt as no empirical evidence is provided to buttress it. However, there is little doubt that pre-hospital and hospital emergency services were often used as a substitute for primary care. The low status of general practitioners, who had received only basic medical training, and the convenience of calling the ambulance are contributors to this phenomenon.

Despite some notable achievements in developing infrastructure, increasing accessibility, and reducing mortality due to acute communicable diseases, the overall performance of the medical system during state socialism was compromised by a string of shortcomings, including underfinancing, poor quality of services, unmotivated staff, and inefficient primary care.[8] The situation worsened during the economic crisis of the 1980s, when the drastic austerity measures adopted in the attempt to pay back the country's foreign debt further affected the already frail healthcare sector. The disinvestment contributed to negative health outcomes.

At the moment of the violent demise of socialism, the health status of the Romanian population was among the worst in the Eastern Bloc. Romania had the lowest life expectancy at birth, the highest maternal mortality rate (fifteen times higher than in neighboring Yugoslavia), the highest mortality rate due to lung diseases, and the second highest mortality rate due to ischemic heart disease.[9] Moreover, a major nosocomial HIV epidemic among institutionalized children, caused primarily by the use of unsterilized medical instruments and the reuse of needles and syringes, led to the highest prevalence of HIV in Central and Eastern Europe.[10]

For almost a decade after the 1989 Revolution, the health system remained largely unchanged. Health services continued to be provided free of charge, with co-payments only required for dental care and admissions without a referral. Prescribed drugs were heavily subsidized, but also required an out-of-pocket payment.[11] The most important transformation of the decade was the development of primary healthcare, for which the government received financial support and technical assistance from the World Bank. This reform consisted in the establishment of general practitioner as a medical specialty, the reintroduction of post-secondary nursing schools, and the upgrading of many rural health centers.[12] Nevertheless, the limited human and financial resources hindered the success of the reform, especially in rural areas. During this period, there was a significant decrease in infant mortality and maternal mortality rates, but an increased incidence of infectious diseases, including tuberculosis and syphilis.[13]

A significant reform of the health system took place in 1997, with the adoption of the social health insurance.[14] The insurance, which became effective two years later, was funded by mandatory contributions from employers and employees and voluntary contributions from the people not formally employed. In addition to contributors, the coverage was also extended to other social categories, including the retirees, the recipients of unemployment benefits or social allowance, the disabled, the minors and the students until the age of twenty-six, the pregnant women, the war veterans, and the participants to the 1989 Revolution that overthrew the socialist regime.[15] The new policy changed the structure of funding for healthcare, generated additional revenues, and established some competition among providers of care, as patients had the freedom to choose the doctors and the facilities that best responded to their needs.[16] The health sector expenditure, which never exceeded 4 percent of the GDP after 1989, increased to 4.6 percent after the adoption of the social health insurance, but remained lower than that of other countries with a similar level of economic development.[17]

The adoption of the social health insurance was followed by a series of policies aiming to increase the efficiency and responsiveness of the healthcare system. The private health sector developed after the primary and secondary care doctors became free professionals, and private clinics and hospitals became eligible for contracts with the National Health Insurance House.[18] Two unintended consequences of this reform were the increased inequities of access along class and residential lines, with the growing urban middle-class getting access to better care and the indigent being restricted to the crumbling public health sector, and the transformation of many small towns and rural areas into "healthcare deserts."[19]

Another major problem affecting the Romanian healthcare sector was the massive migration of doctors and nurses to more affluent Western European countries. This phenomenon started around Romania's accession to the European Union (in 2007) and was accelerated in the 2010s, after the austerity measures adopted by a right-wing government led to a 25 percent cut of the already meagre salaries in the public sector. In a period of only three years, the total number of doctors employed in the Romanian hospitals decreased by over a third (from 20,648 in 2011 to 13,521 in 2014).[20]

BARRIERS TO HEALTHCARE ACCESS

Several factors impact the access to, and the quality of, care, including the health insurance system, the economy of favors, the uneven distribution of healthcare resources and, in the case of vulnerable populations, the widespread discriminatory practices.

As mentioned earlier, the social health insurance system provides generous coverage to contributors and many other social categories deemed vulnerable or meritorious. However, the population coverage is far from universal. More than two million people, many of them agricultural workers or persons in long-term unemployment,[21] lack health insurance[22] and thus are ineligible for free services and discounted medicines.[23] Roma are disproportionately represented among this group, with only one person in two being covered by social health insurance.[24] The lack of insurance is a deterrent to seeking care[25] and a significant contributor to the inequity of access to medical services along class and ethnic lines, but it is hardly the only financial barrier that patients in Romania experience.

Although the social health insurance is supposed to fully cover the most common medical investigations, this does not happen in practice.[26] Every three months, the National Health Insurance House (NHIH) allocates to each medical analysis center in the country, public or private, an amount of money to cover the cost of laboratory and imaging tests ordered by doctors. However, many laboratories exhaust the allocated budget in just a few days, leaving patients with the alternative of paying out-of-pocket for the tests or waiting for days or weeks until public funding resumes.[27] The first option is prohibitive for many. For instance, the cost for an MRI scan in 2016 was about 1,000 lei[28] (US$246.9), which was the equivalent of half the average monthly earnings of a fully employed person.[29] The inability to get laboratory and imaging tests in a reasonable time contributes to delayed diagnosis[30] and unmet health needs, which are more common in Romania than in most other European Union countries.[31]

Informal payments also impact the access to medical care. During socialism, the severe shortage of goods and services led to the development of a complex economy of favors. Gifts were exchanged to foster personal relationships with potentially useful people and to grease the wheels of an otherwise rigid, slow, and inefficient bureaucracy.[32] In the context of a chronically underfunded healthcare system, in which the resources available were scarce, giving gifts to doctors and nurses became not only socially acceptable but also necessary for receiving adequate care.[33] The economy of favors retained its vitality after the change in political regime,[34] with the object of informal transactions in the healthcare sector gradually shifting from gifts to money. The monetization of gifts opened the way to predatory practices, such as restricting care to patients who make informal payments or providing substandard treatment to those unable or unwilling to contribute.[35] While informal payments to doctors and nurses are not uncommon in Central and Eastern Europe, survey data indicate that their prevalence is higher in Romania than in any other former socialist country that is now part of the European Union.[36] Informal payments take a heavy toll on vulnerable groups, such as the urban poor, the retired,[37] and the Roma,[38] impacting their illness behavior. To avoid the informal costs of medical care, many people in dire straits rely on home remedies, folk treatments, or spiritual healing[39] for dealing with distressing symptoms and go to see a doctor only when the symptoms become difficult to bear.

In addition to formal and informal costs, the access to healthcare is affected by the uneven geographical distribution of human and material resources. Although almost half of the Romanian population lives in rural areas,[40] the density of family doctors is 30 percent lower in rural areas than in urban ones, and nine out of ten localities without a family doctor are rural.[41] Moreover, more than half of the family doctors in rural areas report having no access to laboratories and X-rays, compared to one third of their urban counterparts.[42] Rural-urban disparities also exist in the availability of secondary and tertiary care. Two thirds of the medical doctors in Romania are clustered in six cities, whereas all rural communities are serviced by only one fifth of the country's physician workforce.[43] The reforms of the healthcare system aimed at improving efficiency and reducing costs led to a substantial reduction in hospital beds in small towns and rural areas and a concentration of hospital care in large urban centers.[44] The poor road infrastructure further aggravates the problem of rural dwellers' access to quality care. A recent study relying on geographic information system (GIS) data estimates that people in isolated rural areas need to drive on average for more than five hours to reach the nearest hospital that provides multiple services.[45] The disparities in the availability, accessibility, and affordability of care are linked to the much higher[46] mortality rate in the rural areas.

The access to healthcare services is particularly problematic for Roma, the third largest ethnic group in the country,[47] which lies at the intersection of several axes of vulnerability, including poverty, rural residence, and discrimination. A survey by the European Union Agency for Fundamental Rights (FRA) reveals that seven out of ten Roma in Romania are at risk of poverty, a rate that is almost three times higher than that of the general population.[48] Also, only 10 percent of the Roma report no difficulties in making ends meet.[49] A majority of Roma live in rural areas,[50] being grossly overrepresented in the marginalized areas.[51] Romani people have been historically oppressed, and continue to be the most widely discriminated against ethnic group in Romania. The repertoire of discriminatory practices to which they fall victim within the healthcare system is vast, including forced sterilization of women, ethnic segregation in maternity wards, subjection to aggressive medical procedures, use of offensive language during clinical interactions, and insufficient disclosure of information about the side effects of the treatment.[52]

The attempts to improve primary care through family medicine have largely been unsuccessful.[53] Public hospitals continue to be a significant provider of service[54] even for conditions that could have been handled cheaper, and with lower risks for patients, within the primary sector.[55] Particularly important for the purpose of this book is that the scarcity of emergency assistance in the primary health sector increased the demand for hospital emergency services considerably. A review of the health system in Romania[56] bemoaned the misuse of the ED and explained it through the lack of financial incentives for family doctors to conduct home visits and provide emergency care outside the regular working hours. Under these conditions, people in need of primary care rely on the pre-hospital and hospital emergency services. Interestingly, the same report uses the healthcare practitioners' emic category of "real" emergencies and estimates that they account for less than a quarter of all the calls to 112, the emergency telephone number.[57]

Users and beneficiaries alike agree on negatively assessing the functionality of the system. Thus, almost three-quarters (73 percent) of the population in

Romania consider that the overall quality of healthcare is low, as compared to the European Union average of slightly more than one quarter (27 percent).[58] Physicians report dissatisfaction with the general organization of healthcare and the constant legislative changes, the scarcity of human and material resources, the low wages, and the perceived loss of prestige of medicine.[59]

ORGANIZATIONAL CONCERNS

Dr. Costea, a specialist in emergency medicine in his late twenties working at County, told me one time about a patient who showed up at the department to get a second opinion. Prior to the visit, she had been examined by a famous endocrinologist from a top hospital in the capital city of Bucharest, who set the diagnostic and prescribed her four medicines. The patient only took two of them, claiming that the other two were of no use for her problem. To Dr. Costea, this was a textbook case of incorrect use of the service. Not only the medical condition was not acute, but the case had already been diagnosed by a reputed specialist in internal medicine. Moreover, the patient had not followed the treatment scheme to know whether it worked or not. Dr. Costea informed the patient that he wholeheartedly agreed with the initial medical recommendations and counselled the woman to concurrently take all four medicines as prescribed and then go back to the endocrinologist for a control check in a few days' time. Neither the patient nor her companions were content with the handling of the case. They insisted to have her hospitalized for a while, but to no avail.

Both departments are, according to the informants, inundated with cases that are blatantly inappropriate for emergency care, and each staff member has her own stock of "atrocity stories"[60] to recount. Patients with ongoing minor ailments, chronic diseases, or conditions lacking a somatic basis, patients in search of a second medical opinion, or simply looking for temporary shelter are considered to make the bulk of the presentations.

Staff members interpret this as an indication of the profound crisis affecting the healthcare system, a crisis whose origin is only partially related to the organization of the emergency service, but which finds in the ED propitious conditions to manifest itself to the full. To account for the presumed crisis, participants have developed complex narratives that make reference to the reconfiguration of the ED during the reforms, the failure of primary care sector to provide adequate service, along with general structural conditions, and individual flaws.

THE PERCEIVED CRISIS OF THE
EMERGENCY HEALTHCARE SYSTEM

A major reorganization of the EDs took place in 2007 at County and in 2010 at City. Prior to that, the EDs catered only for the critically ill (i.e., persons with life-threatening conditions requiring immediate assistance). All other cases used to be handled by various hospital outpatient wards that were open twenty-four hours.[61] In 2007 and 2010, the hospital outpatient wards have been closed and parts of the services have been transferred to the ED. Surgeons, who used to man the emergency service, have been replaced by young doctors specialized in emergency medicine or family medicine. The services have been integrated, so that a patient could benefit of medical consultation from various specialists and have all the necessary tests and procedures performed without leaving the hospital premises.

Triage workers in both hospitals tend to regard the initial arrangement as more beneficial to everyone involved as compared to the current one. Before—the argument goes—staff members were exposed to fewer demands and could dedicate themselves entirely to patients in critical condition. The work environment was perceived to be less stressful because it was not as prone to conflict as it allegedly is nowadays, after the flow of patients has increased manifold. Patients with less severe conditions, in turn, benefited from being examined by a specialist in the field of medicine under the jurisdiction of which their condition belonged, instead of a specialist in emergency or family medicine, and had to wait much shorter on average before receiving the examination. Triage workers also think that the previous organization was more cost-efficient, since doctors in the ED dealing with a variety of minor ailments tend to compensate for their lower competence in various fields of medicine by ordering more laboratory tests than it would be necessary to determine the nature and gravity of the case.[62]

Another prominent factor contributing to the crisis is, in staff's narratives, the inefficiency of the primary healthcare. The per capita financing constitutes an incentive for family doctors to have as many patients on roll as law permits. However, they are not allowed to examine more than twenty regular and four emergency cases each day. Thus, people have to set appointments well in advance, which might work for chronic patients in need of regular checkup or prescription renewal but prevents many of the acutely ill from getting timely care. This flaw in the design of the general practice is compounded by family doctors' reluctance to conduct home visits or to assist the sick outside office hours, and their alleged propensity to redirect patients they want to avoid to the ED.

Physician shortage emerged as a major contributor to the crisis of the emergency service in the narratives collected at County but was rarely mentioned at City. A well-informed nurse working at County shared with me the grim situation by taking the case of cardiologists as an illustration. The second largest town in the county, which had a population of about thirty thousand persons, was serviced by only one specialist. A smaller town had no cardiologist at all. The only cardiologist in the municipal polyclinic had already been fully booked for two months. Private practitioners also could not cope with the demand. The shortage of specialists, which affects not only cardiology, but also other branches of medicine, constrains people to seek care at the ED. In this case, it is not the convenience or lack of knowledge of the pathway to care that brings people to the hospital. Instead, it is a structural problem for the existence of which patients have no responsibility.

According to the nurse, several factors contributed to the physician shortage in the region where County is located, including current hiring policies in the public sector that render difficult the replacement of staff lost due to attrition; the practice of hiring young doctors who are doing the resident practice in other cities and upon finishing the program refuse to come back; and the limited attraction the hospital has for recent graduates of the medical school.

Triage workers' accounts of the crisis make frequent references to the lack of insurance and the relatively high costs of care for the uninsured. The overall costs of examination and treatment can be a burden for the indigents. The fee for consultation ranges from 20 to 40 lei, the equivalent of 5.6 to 11.2 USD, but the uninsured also need to pay for the more expensive tests and procedures, as well as for the treatment. Medicines have to be paid at their market value, whereas the insured benefit of discounted prices and can receive some medicines free of charge. Additional costs incur in case the patient is referred to a specialist, whose fee is considerably higher.

The crisis is also explained through patient behavior. Lacking proper education with regards to health, many patients are simply unaware of the normative path in case of illness. Familiar with the socialist organization of medicine, which recommended hospitalization even for minor conditions, many of the elderly prefer to make a presentation to the hospital instead of scheduling an appointment with the family doctor. Other patients are held to be lazy and convenient, and to intentionally bypass the general practitioner in order to get speedy examination and prescriptions. Finally, some nurses and clerks talked about the limited set of knowledge that many patients can mobilize to roughly estimate the severity of their condition.

THE PERCEIVED MISSION OF THE
EMERGENCY SERVICE

In this general context, triage clerks and nurses developed a restrictive under-standing of the mission of emergency service. To them, it consists in helping the critically and the severely acutely ill only, a limited group of patients that are commonly referred to as "real" emergencies.[63] The other cases, which representing the vast majority of actual presentations, fall outside the per-ceived mission and are admitted only because of their formal entitlement to examination:

> NURSE VERA: Most of the cases do not constitute emergencies. We have, let's say, a hundred persons showing up during the day shift, maybe fifteen to twenty [of them] are emergencies. The others are non-emergencies. They are cases [suitable] for polyclinic or family medicine, but they don't go there for various reasons: lack of time, lack of money, impatience.

> INTERVIEWER: So, the cases that do not constitute an emergency—are they all accepted or not?

> NURSE VERA: Yes, our protocol [requires] to admit everyone. (Interview, County)

> INTERVIEWER: What kind of patients go to the minor emergency room? What is their profile?

> NURSE FLORICA: Many of them [are] chronically ill. The chronic do not go to the family doctor but come to the Emergency Department instead because they say it's faster this way. [. . .] But this isn't fair. It's not fair. They have to go to the family doctor.

> INTERVIEWER: I see! So many of them should not end up—

> NURSE FLORICA:—should not end up in the Emergency Receiving [Unit], that's right. Because we are looking for accidents, we are looking for all sorts of emergencies. (Interview, City)

This view is consistent with the mission of the ED before reorganization but differs from the broader approach of the current framework regulating the functioning of the service, which extends the understanding of emergency to cover a very large set of symptoms and conditions. Thus, according to the formal protocol for the handling of patients, the ED is in charge not only with life-threatening conditions, but also with "situational emergencies," presented as cases "in which [either] there is a risk of unfavorable evolu-tion if the treatment is not initiated in due time" or the patient experiences "severe discomfort." Moreover, the protocol specifies that eligible for admission are also the "less urgent" cases corresponding to conditions that are chronic or minor.

Triage clerks and nurses consider that their role is to apportion care according to the mission of the ED, by ensuring immediate access to persons in "real" need (the critically and severely ill) and preventing the rest of the users from interfering with the handling of the "real emergencies." In practical terms, this means discouraging patients whose case does not fall under the purported jurisdiction of emergency medicine from coming back to the department with similar problems. To deter their return, triage staff impose sanctions of various sorts, including delayed admission and exposure to moralizing discourse, and socialize them with respect to what constitutes a "real" emergency and what does not.

Members of the triage staff account for the gate-keeping role by regarding it as a practical necessity for the proper functioning of the service. Managing the flow of patients, they argue, is unavoidable in situations where demand exceeds the number of resources available. One clerk at City also invoked the interest of the ill. While a visit to the ED provides some important benefits to the patient, including examination by a specialist and free laboratory tests, it can be detrimental in the long run, particularly if the condition is severe. The brevity of the visit to the emergency ward might bring some temporary relief to the patient but cannot address the deep root of the problem. The family doctor, who is better accustomed to the patient and is knowledgeable of her clinical history, is more apt than the physician at the emergency ward to provide a comprehensive interpretation of the symptoms and to check on the progress toward recovery.

The tension between external demands and staff beliefs regarding the proper organization of the emergency service can be considered as a conflict between "charter" and "mission."[64] "Charter" refers to the official goals of the organization, which impose "limits of legitimizable action"[65] to its members, whereas "mission" defines "members' own notion of 'what we are here for.'"[66]

The charter of the emergency service in Romania is, like in other countries,[67] to provide universal access to persons in need. According to the law regarding the healthcare reform,[68] the provision of emergency assistance constitutes a right of the citizen and a duty of the state. A corollary of this charter is the rule of granting access to examination by a medical specialist to all persons who make an appearance to the ED, regardless of the perceived nature and gravity of the problem. The mission, that is the collective representation of the appropriate scope of the emergency service by members of the two departments, is more restrictive. Triage workers consider that the emergency department should cater only for potentially life-threatening cases and for the severely acutely ill. All other patients, the argument goes, should be redirected to other providers of medical care who are equally prepared to diagnose and treat the problem. The obligation to admit everyone increases considerably the workload of the department, drains unnecessarily organizational resources, and limits the amount of time doctors and nurses can spend with "real" emergencies.

This contradiction between charter and mission is by no means peculiar to the emergency system in Romania. In France, Dodier and Camus talk about the contradiction between "openness and specialization"[69] and Vassy discusses the ideals of equality and equity[70] that orient doctors' handling of the clientele. Similarly, studies conducted in the United States[71] and the United Kingdom[72] around a time when the eligibility to emergency healthcare figured prominently on the public agenda point out staff's reluctance to provide unrestricted access to emergency services for fear that such a move might increase work demands manifold, lead to a fall in prestige of the service, and hinder the specialization of emergency medicine. What is particular in the Romanian case, nevertheless, is that the reorganization of the service and the redefinition of official goals are very recent. Thus, many members of the two departments have worked under a charter closely resembling the current mission of the organization.

The tension between charter and mission shapes to a large extent the triage activities. During fieldwork, I have encountered only four situations of triage workers denying admission to would-be patients, all of them taking place at County.[73] This suggests that triage staff typically follows the rule of granting admission to everyone despite objecting to the logic that makes it possible and being unhappy with its consequences. In doing so, they acknowledge a gate-keeping role limited to controlling the flow of patients rather than deciding who gets in, determining the conditions of access rather than the access per se. Triage workers attend to the mission of the organization in the non-clinical evaluation of the clientele.

SORTING PATIENTS OUT

The moral evaluation of patients is inherently related to the practical problem of safeguarding the mission of the organization. To prevent the ED from becoming a substitute for primary care and to keep the flux of patients manageable, nurses and, to a lesser extent, clerks need to set apart the people who are perceived to actually need emergency care from those who can find a solution to their medical issues at the family doctor's office or in the polyclinic and dissuade the latter from making use the emergency service.

However, the current regulations impose limits on triage workers' decision-making power, the most important of which is the impossibility of denying access. "If a fly gets in, we need to create a medical record and examine it," nurse Andra at County told me in exasperation during an interview,[74] adding that she was trying to "diplomatically" redirect patients with minor health concerns to other healthcare facilities. Her persuasive efforts, albeit rarely successful, point out to an important aspect of the triage work: the freedom to subvert rules without technically breaking them. Like other street-level bureaucrats, nurses and clerks are not deprived of agency even though the formal rules under which they operate are strict and binding. Thus, they find creative ways of aligning service provision to the dominant beliefs, values, and norms in the ED. In the process of admitting patients, the discretionary power of nurses and clerks manifests itself through the use of three strategies, whose unstated, yet transparent, purpose is to restrict access to the service: socializing patients, managing waiting times, and scolding perceived misusers.

SOCIALIZING PATIENTS

At the beginning of fieldwork, I was puzzled to notice that in the case of patients with ongoing ailments or minor acute symptoms, the triage admission interview—an otherwise brief and relatively standardized affair—veered toward issues without any clinical or bureaucratic signification, including the reasons for choosing the ED over the family doctor's office. When I brought this up, triage nurses explained to me that many people of good faith[75] "abused" the emergency services just because they were unfamiliar with the pathways to care or did not know how to make sense of and handle their symptoms. "Educating them" was not only a mantra to lament the crisis of emergency service but also a local solution to this crisis.

Nurses and clerks believe that providing the insured patients with information about the functions of emergency medicine and the symptoms that warrant a visit to the ED is a win-win strategy. It has the potential to reduce the unnecessary demand for emergency care, avoiding the bottlenecks that represent a source of frustration for personnel and patients alike. At the same time, the non-medically urgent patient is spared a long waiting time and gets a more complex and accurate examination, as the family doctor interprets the current symptoms against the past medical history, follows up on the progress of the treatment, and amends it if necessary or redirects the patient to a specialist.

In addition to familiarizing patients with the pathway to care, nurses at County often give them practical advice on how to navigate the healthcare system. This usually happens in the triage examination room, where the interactions tend to be longer and less structured than those at the admission booth. Nurses pick up from patients' stories hints about the difficulties they encounter in primary care and address them. For instance, they explain to patients eligible for the social health insurance where to go and what documents to bring with them in order to receive the proof of being insured that would entitle them to free consultations and lab tests and discounted medicines. They also advise patients who are dissatisfied with the quality of care they receive at the family doctor's office to opt for another practitioner. Such ad-hoc awareness-raising actions show triage workers' concern with patients' access to quality healthcare[76] but are also attempts to remove the barriers to primary care that make people rely on emergency services for minor or chronic problems.

At County, another dimension of patients' socialization has to do with the triage process itself. Although the color-coded triage algorithm is prominently displayed on the waiting room walls, where other posters explain that the emergency service does not use the principle of first come-first serve, most patients ignore them. Nurses and clerks also rarely take time to mention the priority coding system during the admission interview. However, when challenged by patients disgruntled by the long time spent in the waiting room, they explain that priority codes are assigned based on the perceived severity and urgency of the case. Many patients remain unconvinced about the arguments and question the fairness of the triage process, much to the exasperation of triage workers: "They don't understand these things, and they accuse us of receiving *șpagă*[77] to admit people faster, or [think that] we know some patients, we have some connections with them,[78] and that's why we get them in ahead of others" (Nurse Vera, County). Patients have good reasons to be suspicious. While the informality of access is much less common than they suspect, nurses have considerable leeway in deciding the order of access and, implicitly, the waiting time.

MANAGING WAITING TIMES

Patients whose condition is considered potentially life-threatening or requiring immediate medical attention receive a red or yellow code and are admitted right away. This happens irrespective of the social characteristics of the patient or the circumstances in which the health problem occurred. However, cases of this sort are relatively few. Also rare are the situations at the other end of the priority spectrum, in which patients receive a blue or a white code. According to the triage protocol, the blue code corresponds to minor acute cases such as diarrhea, tonsillitis, cold, or flu, whereas the white code describes situations that do not require any specialized intervention, such as refilling a prescription or issuing a medical certificate. Although minor acute conditions are relatively numerous, nurses have strong bureaucratic reasons[79] to assign the blue code sparingly. When they use it, there is a strong likelihood that they want to sanction the patient by extending their wait indefinitely. Hence, a blue code indexes not only a banal condition but also what nurses interpret to be a gross misuse of the service, a socially unacceptable demeanor, or, more often than not, both.

The overwhelming majority of cases, including many that, based on a restrictive understanding of 'emergencies,' fall below the threshold for admission, are assigned the green code. Among these cases, the order of entry is not fixed. Usually, the nurse in charge of the triage examination places the patients' files in a pile, with the more severe cases on top and the trivial ones toward the bottom. At regular intervals, she brings the patient files to the doctor, who is the one to have the final say on the order of admission.[80]

At first glance, this arrangement suggests that nurses have little power in managing patients' waiting time. They are constrained, on the one hand, by the informal requirement to reduce the number of blue and white codes and, on the other hand, by the authority of the doctor to change the tentative prioritization. Actually, this is not the case. Doctors and nurses share the same beliefs about the mission of the emergency service and have a common orientation toward patients,[81] and it is this alignment of views that gives nurses a firm hold on handling cases. During my time in the field, I have observed a high degree of overlap between the tentative hierarchy of precedence set by the triage nurse and the order in which calls in the patients.

In short, patients whose visit is inconsistent with the staff-devised mission of the ED are subjected to protracted waiting to discourage them from coming back with similar health concerns. The underlying logic is simple: if people are using the emergency service out of convenience, an inconvenient and unpleasant experience at the ED should deter their return. The third strategy, reprimanding undesirable patients, goes along the same lines.

SCOLDING MISUSERS

Triage interactions are often contentious. Nurses and clerks routinely challenge patients to check on the credibility of their stories. Some patients retort when challenged, and others deliberately transgress the rules of behavior in public places in an attempt to cut short the waiting time. The instrumental role of verbal confrontations in the practical accomplishment of moral evaluation is a transversal theme of this book, and it will be explored in more detail in the second part of the book.

For the moment, it suffices to mention that doctors, nurses, and clerks sometimes adopt toward patients and their companions a stance that, for lack of a better term, I will refer to as "interactional despotism." This is a form of interaction that reflects and reinforces the asymmetry of power between the participants through various maneuvers that, intentionally or not, are conducive to status degradation. Ignoring for long stretches of time the patients queuing at the triage booth, abruptly ending verbal exchanges, refusing to answer questions or providing deliberately ambiguous responses, shouting, mocking patients who make incoherent statements or rely on lay theories of disease causation, or making negative comments about patients in their presence are all indicative of interactional despotism. This treatment is usually reserved for the least valued emergency service users and those whose demeanor is considered blatantly inappropriate.

Reproofing is a less extreme and far more common way of sanctioning alleged misusers. It can take various forms, from gentle admonition to harsh criticism, but, unlike interactional despotism, it doesn't cause patients to lose face. It is used primarily to emphasize that the visit to the ED is clinically unjustified from the staff's point of view. For instance, after a patient discloses ongoing coughing as the reason for presentation, triage nurse Alice comments: "It just doesn't make sense to me: you've been coughing for seven days, you are registered with a family doctor, but now, on Friday, you decide to come here for a check-up."

CONCLUSION

The deep changes that Romania has experienced during the passage from state socialism to market economy included the health system and the organization of the hospital emergency care.

I have shown in this chapter that triage workers are deeply discontent with the way in which the ED is organized and the policy of admitting every person seeking care, irrespective of their health condition. In staff's narratives, the overcrowding of the service and the alleged misuse of human and financial resources has three major sources. The first one refers to the structural problems affecting the health system in general. The inability of the primary sector to attend to the needs of everyone who needs basic care, the scarcity of healthcare practitioners, and the costs of care, especially for the uninsured, make people prone to use the ED as a substitute for primary care. Secondly, some patients are blamed for either not knowing where to look for medical care or being complacent and choosing the hospital emergency service for getting complex investigations in a short time and without costs. Thirdly, the policy framework that prevents triage workers from denying access to people whose health concerns do not coincide with what staff regard as being a "real" emergency drastically limits their decision-making.

Nevertheless, nurses and clerks aim to protect the mission of the ED by socializing patients with regards to the scope of the emergency service and the pathways to care, managing the waiting times, and making the hospital experience of people falling the moral evaluation unpleasant. Although these strategies do not restrict the access to emergency care of people who come to the ED, they aim to deter future visits for problems that are not consistent with what staff regard as "real" emergencies. The next chapter will delve deeper into the moral evaluation criteria.

NOTES

1. Mark G. Field, "Noble Purpose, Grand Design, Flawed Execution, Mixed Results: Soviet Socialized Medicine after Seventy Years," *American Journal of Public Health* 80, no. 2: 144–45; Mark G. Field, "The Health Crisis in the Former Soviet Union: A Report from the 'Post-War' Zone," *Social Science & Medicine* 41, no. 11: 1469–78.

2. Shirley Cereseto and Howard Waitzkin, "Capitalism, Socialism and the Physical Quality of Life," *Medical Anthropology* 11, no. 2: 161.

3. Raul Neghina et al., "Malaria and the Campaigns toward Its Eradication in Romania, 1923–1963," *Vector Borne and Zoonotic Diseases* 11, no. 2: 107.

4. Roger M. Battistella, "Health Services in the Socialist Republic of Romania: Structural Features and Cost-Containment Policies," *Journal of Public Health Policy* 4, no. 1: 92.

5. Cristian Vlădescu, Silviu Rădulescu, and Sorin Cace, "The Romanian Health Care System: Between Bismark and Semashko," in *Decentralization in Healthcare: Analyses and Experiences in Central and Eastern Europe in the 1990s,* ed. George Shakarishvili (Budapest: Open Society Institute, 2005), 455.

6. Battistella, "Health Services in the Socialist Republic of Roman," 92.

7. Vlădescu, Rădulescu, and Cace, "The Romanian Health Care System: Between Bismark and Semashko," 456.

8. Cristian Vlădescu, Gabriela Scîntee, and Victor Olsavszky, "Romania: Health System Review," *Health Systems in Transition* 10, no. 3: 21.

9. The maternal mortality rate in Romania was 148.8 deaths per 1,000 live births (as compared to only 10.6 deaths in Yugoslavia). Diane Rowland, "Health Status in East European Countries," *Health Affairs* 10, no. 3: 202–15.

10. UNAIDS, "Romania: Epidemiological Fact Sheets."

11. William C. Cockerham, *Health and Social Change in Russia and Eastern Europe* (New York and London: Routledge, 1999), 205.

12. Vlădescu, Rădulescu, and Cace, "The Romanian Health Care System: Between Bismark and Semashko."

13. Ibid., 443.

14. Bernd Rechel and Martin McKee, "Health Reform in Central and Eastern Europe and the Former Soviet Union," *The Lancet* 374, no. 9696: 1186–95; Dimitri A. Sotiropoulos, Ileana Neamtu, and Maya Stoyanova, "The Trajectory of Post-Communist Welfare State Development: The Cases of Bulgaria and Romania," *Social Policy & Administration* 37, no. 6: 665.

15. Law 95, "Legea Nr. 95/2006 Privind Reforma În Domeniul Sănătății [Law 95/2006 Regarding Healthcare Reform]" (2006).

16. Sabina Stan, "Neoliberal Citizenship and the Politics of Corruption: Redefining Informal Exchange in Romanian Healthcare," in *Economy, Crime and Wrong in a Neoliberal Era*, ed. James G. Carrier (New York and Oxford: Berghahn Books, 2018), 172–94.

17. Vlădescu, Rădulescu, and Cace, "The Romanian Health Care System: Between Bismark and Semashko," 468.

18. In Romanian, *Casa Națională de Asigurări de Sănătate (CNAS)*, the body that administers the national social health insurance.

19. Sabina Stan and Valentin-Veron Toma, "Accumulation by Dispossession and Public–Private Biomedical Pluralism in Romanian Health Care," *Medical Anthropology* 38, no. 1: 85–99; Stan, "Neoliberal Citizenship and the Politics of Corruption: Redefining Informal Exchange in Romanian Healthcare."

20. Șoimita Mihaela Suciu et al., "Physician Migration at Its Roots: A Study on the Emigration Preferences and Plans among Medical Students in Romania," *Human Resources for Health* 15, no. 1: 1–9. The same authors reported the finding of a survey conducted between 2013 and 2015 among the graduates of a medical university in Romania. Eighty-five percent of the respondents stated that they had contemplated migrating abroad.

21. Stan and Toma, "Accumulation by Dispossession and Public–Private Biomedical Pluralism in Romanian Health Care," 88.

22. Huihui Wang et al., "Generating Political Priority for Primary Health Care Reform in Romania," *Health Systems & Reform* 7, no. 2: 1.

23. The medically uninsured are only eligible for a basic package of services comprising emergency care, family planning, pregnancy and postnatal monitoring, and care for communicable diseases.

24. The 2011 Regional Roma Survey conducted by UNDP, World Bank, and the European Commission showed that 49.3 percent of the Roma in Romania (versus 14.7 percent of the non-Roma) lack health insurance. The ethnic difference remains significant after statistically adjusting for gender, age, marital status, and employment status. Charlotte Kühlbrandt et al., "An Examination of Roma Health Insurance Status in Central and Eastern Europe," *The European Journal of Public Health* 24, no. 5: 709.

25. George Siân, Katy Daniels, and Evridiki Fioratou, "A Qualitative Study into the Perceived Barriers of Accessing Healthcare among a Vulnerable Population Involved with a Community Centre in Romania," *International Journal for Equity in Health* 17, no. 1; Marius Wamsiedel, Eniko Vincze, and Iustina Ionescu, *Roma Health: The Perspective of Actors Involved in the Health System—Doctors, Health Mediators and Patients* (Bucharest: Romani CRISS, 2012).

26. Iuliana-Claudia Mihalache, Felicia-Cătălina Apetroi, and Mihaela Tomaziu-Todosia, "Equity in Financing the Health Sector: An Important Aspect in Reducing Inequalities in Accessing Health Services. Romania in the European Context," in *European Union Financial Regulation and Administrative Area*, ed. Mihaela Tofan, Irina Bilan, and Elena Cigu (Iași: Alexandru Ioan Cuza University Press, 2019), 571.

27. Mirabela Tiron, "Anomaliile Din Sănătate: Spitalele de Stat Sunt Gazde Pentru Laboratoare Private, Fondurile Casei Se Duc La Privați, Dar Pacienții Sunt Plimbați de La Un Laborator La Altul Pentru Că Nu Există Fonduri Pentru Analize Gratuite [Anomalies in the Healthcare S," Ziarul Financiar.

28. "Fondurile Pentru Analize Compensate, Epuizate În câTeva Zile. Explicațiile Medicilor [The Funds for Subsidized Lab Tests, Exhausted in a Few Days. The Doctors' Explanations]," Digi 24.

29. The average net earnings per month in 2016 was 2,046 lei (US$ 505.3) National Institute of Statistics [Romania], "Earnings since 1938—Annual Series."

30. Călina Ana Buțiu, "Healthcare Policy in Romania. Frameworks and Challenges," *Social Change Review* 14, no. 1: 14–15.

31. The Eurostat data reveal that 4.7 percent of the people in Romania had unmet healthcare needs in 2017 and 4.9 percent in 2019. While the situation improved as compared to 2011, when one person in eight (12.2 percent) reported unmet medical needs, the rate is the third highest in the European Union. OECD and European Observatory on Health Systems and Policies, *Romania: Country Health Profile 2021* (Paris: OECD Publishing, 2021); OECD and European Observatory on Health Systems and Policies, *Romania: Country Health Profile 2019* (Paris: OECD Publishing, 2019).

32. Marius Wamsiedel, "The Meanings and Consequences of Informal Payments in the Romanian Healthcare Sector," *Economic Sociology*; Marius Wamsiedel, "Accomplishing Public Secrecy: Non-Monetary Informal Practices and Their Concealment at the Emergency Department," *Journal of Contemporary Central and Eastern Europe* 24, no. 3: 307–20; Steven Sampson, "Muddling through in Rumania (or: Why the Mamaliga Doesn't Explode)," *International Journal of Rumanian Studies* 3: 165–85.

33. Steven Sampson, "Bureaucracy and Corruption as Anthropological Problems: A Case Study from Romania," *Folk. Dansk Ethnografisk Tidsskrift Kobenhavn* 25: 63–96.

34. Cătălin Augustin Stoica, "Old Habits Die Hard? An Exploratory Analysis of Communist-Era Social Ties in Post-Communist Romania," *European Journal of Science and Theology* 8, no. 1: 171–93.

35. Sabina Stan, "Neither Commodities nor Gifts: Post-Socialist Informal Exchanges in the Romanian Healthcare System," *Journal of the Royal Anthropological Institute*, no. 18: 65–82.

36. According to the 2014 Eurobarometer Survey, 28 percent of the Romanians who used healthcare services in the year preceding the interview made informal payments. This was by far the highest proportion among post-socialist EU members, whose average was only 9 percent. Colin C. Williams, Ioana Horodnic, and Adrian Horodnic, "Who Is Making Informal Payments for Public Healthcare in East-Central

Europe? An Evaluation of Socio-Economic and Spatial Variations," *Eastern Journal of European Studies* 7, no. 1: 53. The percentage of Romanian patients who reported making informal payments during the 2020 Eurobarometer Survey went down to 19 percent, but was the highest in the entire European Union. Adrian V. Horodnic, "Trends in Informal Payments by Patients in Europe: A Public Health Policy Approach," *Frontiers in Public Health* 9: 1–9.

37. Gerard A. Weber, "Forsaken Generation: Stress, Social Suffering and Strategies among Working-Class Pensioners in Post-Socialist Moldova, Romania" (The City University of New York, 2009); Gerard A. Weber, "'Other Than a Thank-You, There's Nothing I Can Give': Managing Health and Illness among Working-Class Pensioners in Post-Socialist Moldavia, Romania," *Human Organization* 74, no. 2: 115–24.

38. Siân George, Katy Daniels, and Evridiki Fioratou, "A Qualitative Study into the Perceived Barriers of Accessing Healthcare among a Vulnerable Population Involved with a Community Centre in Romania," *International Journal for Equity in Health* 17, no. 41: 1–13.

39. Gerard A. Weber, "'Please Ask the Priest to Pray for Dana, the Sick One': Health-Seeking, Religion and Decline of the Public Sector in Post-Communist Romania," *Transylvanian Review* 25: 77–90; Ágota Ábrán, "'I Was Told to Come Here in the Forest to Heal': Healing Practices Through the Land in Transylvania," *Transylvanian Review* 25: 91–106.

40. Forty-six percent of the Romanian population lived in rural areas in 2020, the highest percentage in the European Union. World Bank, "Rural Population (% of Total Population)—European Union," World Data Indicators [Data file].

41. The density of family doctors in 2016 was 0.49 per 1,000 people in the rural areas and 0.69 in urban areas. Adanna Chukwuma et al., *Provider Payment Reforms for Improved Primary Health Care in Romania* (Washington, DC: World Bank Publications, 2021), 12.

42. Of the rural family doctors, 53.9 percent lack access to laboratory facilities, and 52.3 percent of them lack access to X-ray facilities (versus 33.2 percent and 33.2 percent, respectively, in the case of family doctors working in the urban areas.) World Health Organization, *Evaluation of Structure and Provision of Primary Care in Romania* (Copenhagen: World Health Organization, 2012), 12.

43. Liliana Dumitrache et al., "Contrasting Clustering in Health Care Provision in Romania: Spatial and Aspatial Limitations," *Procedia Environmental Sciences* 32: 290–99.

44. Giorgian Guțoiu, "Development Inequalities of Romanian Physical Public Healthcare Infrastructure: The Case of Hospital Beds," *Human Geographies* 15, no. 1: 37–52.

45. The estimated average time is 308 minutes. The actual time may be even higher given that the study takes into consideration the traffic time outside rush hours. Liliana Dumitrache et al., "Modelling Potential Geographical Access of the Population to Public Hospitals and Quality Health Care in Romania," *International Journal of Environmental Research and Public Health* 17, no. 22: 12.

46. In 2015, the mortality rate in rural areas was 15.4 per 1,000 population, compared to 11.7 in the urban areas. Chukwuma et al., *Provider Payment Reforms for Improved Primary Health Care in Romania*, 10.

47. According to the 2011 Census, there are 621,573 Roma people in Romania, accounting for 3.3 percent of the country's total population. National Institute of Statistics [Romania], "The Stable Populations (Residents)—Demographic Structure," Final results of the 2011 Census of Population and Households.

48. The at-risk-of-poverty rate is defined as falling "below 60 percent of the median equivalized income after social transfers." In 2014, the rate was 70 percent in the case of Roma and 25 percent in the case of the general population. FRA, *Second European Union Minorities and Discrimination Survey Roma—Selected Findings* (Vienna: European Union Agency for Fundamental Rights, 2016), 14.

49. FRA, 15.

50. According to the most recent Census (2011), 62.9 percent. National Institute of Statistics [Romania], "The Stable Populations (Residents)—Demographic Structure."

51. Over a quarter (27 percent) of all the residents of rural marginalized areas are self-identified Roma. Emil Teşliuc, Vlad Grigoras, and Manuela Sofia Stănculescu, *The Atlas of Rural Marginalized Areas and of Local Human Development in Romania* (Bucharest: World Bank, 2016), 33.

52. Wamsiedel, Vincze, and Ionescu, *Roma Health: The Perspective of Actors Involved in the Health System—Doctors, Health Mediators and Patients*; European Roma Rights Center, *Ambulance Not on the Way: The Disgrace of Health Care for Roma in Europe.* (Budapest: European Roma Rights Center, 2006).

53. Marek Oleszczyk et al., "Family Medicine in Post-Communist Europe Needs a Boost. Exploring the Position of Family Medicine in Healthcare Systems of Central and Eastern Europe and Russia," *BMC Family Practice* 13, no. 1: 15.

54. Claus Wendt, Lorraine Frisina, and Heinz Rothgang, "Healthcare System Types: A Conceptual Framework for Comparison," *Social Policy & Administration* 43, no. 1: 85.

55. Gabriela Scîntee and Cristian Vlădescu, "Primary Health Care in Romania after 20 Years of Reforms," in *Health Reforms in South-East Europe*, ed. William Bartlett, Jadranka Božikov, and Bernd Rechel (Houndmills, Basingstoke, Hampshire: Palgrave Macmillan, 2012), 135.

56. Vlădescu, Scîntee, and Olsavszky, "Romania: Health System Review," 121.

57. The authors do not provide any evidence to support the claim that three quarters of all the calls are not, in fact, "real" emergencies.

58. European Commission, "Patient Safety and Quality of Care," Eurobarometer, 1.

59. Florina Spânu et al., "What Happens to Health Professionals When the Ill Patient Is the Health Care System? Understanding the Experience of Practising Medicine in the Romanian Socio-Cultural Context," *British Journal of Health Psychology* 18, no. 3: 5.

60. Julius A. Roth, "Some Contingencies of the Moral Evaluation and Control of Clientele: The Case of the Hospital Emergency Service.," *American Journal of Sociology* 77, no. 5: 846.

61. This model was inherited from the socialist era and entertained a restrictive definition of emergency, which covered very serious conditions only.

62. A high-ranking official in the Ministry of Interior who initiated the reorganization of the emergency service firmly rejects such an interpretation. To him, the previous arrangement represents "one of the most baleful systems that could be imagined." (Interview) The advantage of the current organization lies in providing a comprehensive evaluation of the medical condition, which spots possible life-threatening elements and addresses them immediately. The former organization created the conditions of possibility for doctors of various specialties to "play table tennis, using the patient as a ball." By this, he refers to sending the patient from one specialist to another. This practice was not only time consuming, but also prone to medical errors. Moreover, the official argued, the overall cost of paying a highly competent medical team is exaggeratedly high as compared to the volume of work if they only handled critical cases.

63. I will explain this emic concept in the next chapter.

64. Robert Dingwall and Phil M. Strong, "The Interactional Study of Organizations A Critique and Reformulation," *Journal of Contemporary Ethnography* 14, no. 2: 205–31.

65. Dingwall and Strong, 216.

66. Ibid.

67. Ruth E. Malone, "Heavy Users of Emergency Services: Social Construction of a Policy Problem," *Social Science & Medicine* 40, no. 4: 472.

68. Law 95, Legea nr. 95/2006 privind reforma în domeniul sănătății [Law 95/2006 Regarding Healthcare Reform].

69. "Openness and Specialisation: Dealing with Patients in a Hospital Emergency Service," *Sociology of Health & Illness* 20, no. 4: 424.

70. "Categorisation and Micro-Rationing: Access to Care in a French ED," 629.

71. James M. Mannon, "Defining and Treating 'Problem Patients' in a Hospital Emergency Room," *Medical Care* 14, no. 12: 1004–13.

72. Roger Jeffery, "Normal Rubbish: Deviant Patients in Casualty Departments," *Sociology of Health & Illness* 1, no. 1: 90–107.

73. I refer here only to cases for the handling of which the ED was properly equipped with staff and equipment. Although the overall number of patients denied admission is much higher, the other situations reflect the inability of the emergency unit to cater for their needs rather than the discretionary decision of triage workers. For example, in both hospitals, cases involving eyes and teeth were redirected to other healthcare facilities, since neither department provided ophthalmology and stomatology services. There were also numerous cases in which triage workers recommended patients to go to another facility in order to cut short the waiting time. I would not consider them as cases of denied access because all patients who refused to go elsewhere got admitted.

The four cases comprise an elderly woman with high blood pressure, a victim of domestic violence that took place six days prior to the presentation, an elder man who returned to the ED several days after being treated for a tick bite because of skin rash, and a young woman who had tonsillitis and claimed not to have enough money to pay for examination at her family doctor (the woman was also uninsured). All four cases fell blatantly outside the mission of the ED, but so did numerous other cases that had been admitted. Therefore, it is difficult to explain nurses' differential behavior.

74. Nurses resent this constraint that limits their autonomy and power.

75. That is, people who have medical insurance and are not inclined to misuse the healthcare system.

76. I will discuss the inclusionary dimension of triage gatekeeping in the next chapter.

77. Informal payment. See Stan, "Neither Commodities nor Gifts: Post-Socialist Informal Exchanges in the Romanian Healthcare System."

78. The concerns are related to the ubiquity of informal practices of access in Romania. I document the use of connection work at County in a separate paper.

79. The County Health Insurance House does not fully reimburse the hospital for the expenses incurred in handling blue code cases.

80. Nurses also have other ways of conveying the undesirability of some patients, from briefing the doctor about the case to including unambiguous cues about the inappropriateness of the visit in the patient file. For instance, quoting patient's grammar mistakes or inconsistent remarks in the description of the case sends a clear signal that the patient is misusing the service.

81. The homogeneity of the ED culture stems in part from the fact that triage nurses have the experience of working alongside doctors.

Chapter 2

Moral Evaluation Criteria

Protecting the mission of the ED, a task of utmost importance for nurses and clerks, requires distinguishing between "real" emergencies and cases that are subthreshold for admission. While this may appear as a simple task, its practical accomplishment is complicated by the variety of clinical, bureaucratic, and moral aspects of each case. In this chapter, I will examine how triage workers situate cases in terms of "legitimacy" and handle the patients without alternatives for care.

The moral evaluation is concerned not only with the features of the case, but also with the characteristics of the patient. Nurses and clerks acknowledge that triage work is permeated by emotions and feelings. Nurse Andra explains this to me during an interview: "We can't be objective, let's face it. We do our best to treat everybody the same, but [sighing] no matter how hard we try, we're still subjective. Because we're humans. The computer is not, a machine is not, but we're humans." She gives me the example of some elderly patients for the saving of whom "one struggles until the very end, and pours all their heart and soul, and do whatever they can." The elderly who trigger the sympathy and mobilize the entire team's efforts are "nice, loveable, and one can tell that they are good people who deserve help." The staff also go the extra mile for young patients who stand out through their personal characteristics. The nurse shares with me the memorable case of a seventeen-year-old boy who got electrocuted while taking part in a cousin's wedding preparation. The adolescent, whose life could not be saved despite a titanic four-hour struggle, is remembered with lots of affection: "such a beautiful, tall, handsome boy, and an only child, one who said that he always wanted to help others, a very good child." His youth, innocence, and altruism, together with his mother's excruciating pain at losing him concur in setting this tragic event apart from the other untimely deaths that took place at the ED. The subjectivity of staff and the efforts they put in saving patients are also influenced by the origin of the health problem: "One is not going to do as much for someone who attempted suicide as for one who had an accident."

All these examples refer to life-and-death situations, and the nurse makes it clear that the staff does everything by the book no matter how they subjectively assess the patient. However, the assessment of worth also applies to the mundane, ordinary cases that make the clear majority of the presentations to the ED and object of this book. I will focus on these cases to show how nurses and clerks construct and determine social worth. The chapter will conclude with a discussion of the inclusionary and exclusionary dimensions of moral evaluation.

LEGITIMACY OF THE CASE

Previous studies acknowledged the legitimacy of the case as an important factor in the handling of patients in emergency wards, but tended to frame it in medical, rather than non-clinical, terms.[1] In the hospitals where I have conducted fieldwork, triage workers talk about the legitimacy of the claim for admission[2] in clinical terms but operationalize it through a string of non-clinical considerations, including the trustworthiness of the user, the timing of the presentation, the frequency of visits to the ED, and the patient's demeanor during and after the admission interview. Only the critically ill escape judgments of this sort, partly because their situation falls within the perceived mission of the ED, and partly because the severity of the condition precludes a detailed examination at arrival. As many of the critically ill are brought by ambulance, they have no direct encounter with triage staff at all. Nurses and clerks make sense of legitimacy by referring to the degree of congruence between the characteristics of the case and the characteristics of "major" and "minor emergencies," as defined by the current protocols for handling patients.

The use of non-clinical considerations to determine the legitimacy of the case is related to the reputation of dishonesty surrounding a large part of the clientele. Nurses and clerks frequently talk about the inclination of people showing up at the department to make everything they can in order to shorten the waiting time. The repertoire of deceptive maneuvers includes exaggerating symptoms, providing inaccurate information during the admission interview, or pretending that the situation worsened after a period of waiting to the point where vital risks incurred. Rectification of statements is also common: "There is a high discrepancy between what patients say here [at the admission room], what they say during the consultation, and what they say at the lab. And one doesn't even know which version to believe" (Nurse Tatiana, County). The construction of users as untrustworthy until proven otherwise carries the implication that their accounts can never be taken at face value.

Therefore, triage agents feel obliged to examine any cues that might help them determine the accuracy of the information the user presents.

In my early days in the field, when I felt comfortable with assuming the naïve newcomer role, I often asked triage workers to share with me "what actually happened" during the admission interview. Very often, their interpretations went beyond the encounter with the patient, as the following passage indicates:

> NURSE NINA: Don't I explain clear enough? I think I'm clear enough.
>
> RESEARCHER: She might not be aware of how the emergency works.
>
> NURSE NINA: It's not that. She probably went to the doctor who rejected her, and that's why she came here. (Field note, County)

The case that makes the object of the verbal exchange refers to is that of a young female who claimed to have been referred by the family doctor to the ED to get a pulmonary X-ray. She could not provide the referral letter stating that she left it at home by mistake. The nurse did not buy the story and asked her to go back home and pick the document. After some heated discussion, the nurse reluctantly agreed to fill in the admission form, but assigned her the blue code, which corresponds to a low priority rank.

Nina's interpretation of the case is that the account of the patient was to some extent plausible. She had mentioned the name of the doctor and the location of his office, and had described the encounter in rich detail, which meant that "she probably had been to the doctor." However, the absence of a referral letter and the patient's angry reaction when asked to return home to bring it were read as signs that the doctor had refused to comply with her request, making her show up at the ED. By including the patient into the "untrustworthy" or "dishonest" category, the triage nurse also established the illegitimacy of the claim to receive care.

In addition to trustworthiness, the assessment of legitimacy relies on the duration of the problem and the timing of arrival. Triage nurses tend to consider that problems lasting for more than twenty-four hours fail to qualify as medical emergencies, unless a sudden deterioration of health has taken place in that time frame. Although duration stands as an objective indicator of the medical problem, in practice it also serves as a pointer to the personal characteristics of the patient. Thus, patients failing to report to a healthcare practitioner for more than twenty-four hours after the onset of the disturbing symptoms are questioned during the admission interview about the reasons for doing so. If the justification is not convincing enough, she is labeled as "careless," "negligent," or "lacking preoccupation for health" and her claim for assistance within the ED is deemed illegitimate.

The connection between timing of arrival to the hospital and the perceived legitimacy of the case is so strong that some nurses construct complex temporal typologies. According to these typologies, the elderly tend to come very early in the morning, whereas the young adults are more prone to make a visit to the ED in late evening; the homeless people come to the ED when the weather conditions make living on the streets uncomfortable and risky; and unfilial children dump their elderly parents to the hospital just before major holidays, so that they can have a good time.[3]

The use of timing of presentation as a proxy for legitimacy originates in the belief that a severe acute illness is disturbing enough to bring the patient in without delay. If the person comes to the hospital at a convenient time, it means that the condition does not qualify for immediate examination, irrespective of the way in which the patient frames it during the admission interview. The triage worker's conviction that the demand is illegitimate is reinforced when the arrival at a convenient time combines with a long duration of the problem and some disreputable characteristics of the person making the visit.

Frequency of visits to the ED represents another criterion on which legitimacy is appraised. Occasionally, the triage agent recognizes in the would-be patient a familiar face. More often, the electronic registry reveals the patient's history of visits to the hospital. The frequent visitor usually triggers negative reactions from the staff because she is suspected of misusing the system by bypassing the therapeutic agency more suitable to handle the case. Persons with chronic illness, psychiatric cases, and people refusing or being unable to see the family doctor are most likely to make repeated appearances at the ED in both hospitals.

The negative assessment of frequent visitors is also due to their acquaintance with the modus operandi of the triage. They are more likely than first time visitors to know what qualifies as an emergency, what questions are usually asked during the admission interview, what responses tend to be accepted, and this stock of experiential knowledge often translates into irreproachable presentations of the case. In reply, triage workers go to great length during the interview to spot inconsistencies or anything that could discard the patient's story. Even when such flaws do not occur, they tend to maintain a cautious stance toward the frequent visitor and to regard the presentation as a forgery.

Legitimacy is also inferred from the patient's talk during the admission interview and demeanor in the waiting room. The interactional strategies through which nurses and clerks assess the credibility of the patient as a reporter of symptoms and the severity of the case will be discussed in chapter 5. For the moment, it suffices to mention that patients who look and act out of ordinary and have little vigor in responding when challenged have the highest chances to be considered in a state of genuine distress that is compatible with the staff understanding of a medical emergency.

In the literature on non-clinical evaluation, legitimacy has been commonly equated with life-threatening cases that require doctors' "heroic technical efforts"[4] and with acute cases that can be handled expeditiously[5] through focus only on physiological aspects of the problem.[6] Legitimacy has also been extended to cases, be they acute or not, that provide emergency doctors with some practical benefits, including the opportunities to expand knowledge and improve technique, learn new skills and prepare for examinations, demonstrate prowess and maturity, perform uncommon interventions, and engage in research.[7] The tendency to associate legitimacy with clinical condition and the variegated opportunities arising from it assumes a straightforward determination of the condition. This might be the case in studies focusing on doctors but is not necessarily so when the staff members categorizing patients have no medical training, like nurses and clerks.

My findings indicate that the assessment of legitimacy at triage is clinical in orientation rather than in actual content. Although triage workers aim to set apart acute conditions from non-acute ones and severe problems from trivial ones, they go beyond objective indicators of health and reported symptoms. Their evaluation incorporates non-clinical considerations that pertain primarily to the credibility of the patient and the plausibility of her accounts.

Determining trustworthiness represents a key issue in ordinary encounters with a stranger for it allows one to define the situation and decide upon the due course of action.[8] In medical contexts, the credibility of patients is a matter of controversy not only because of "the presumptive attribution [to the ill] of characteristics like cognitive unreliability and emotional instability,"[9] but also because individuals might claim sickness in order to avoid performing regular activities.[10] When secondary gains are at stake, credibility becomes particularly salient. Suspected opiate abusers[11] and reporters of potentially factitious conditions such as medically unexplained disorders[12] become the object of intense scrutiny from healthcare practitioners with regard to trustworthiness.

The legitimacy of the claim for admission, to which the assessment of patient's credibility plays an important part, indicates the perceived degree of congruence between the features of the case and the mission of providing timely care to the severely acutely ill. Since the nature of emergency medicine makes it partially overlap with other specialties[13] including family medicine, many patients might be confused about the therapeutic agency under the jurisdiction of which their problem belongs. Therefore, triage agents consider the socialization of would-be patients with regard to the functioning of the healthcare system an important work duty. During admission interviews, they frequently point out features of the case that contradict the typical representation of "real" emergencies and invite would-be patients to seek assistance for the problem from general practitioners or outpatient clinics.

REASONABLENESS OF THE VISIT

Legitimacy refers to the degree to which the condition of the patient matches the perceived mission of the emergency service. Even if the assessment relies on numerous conjectures unrelated to clinical manifestations, its scope is focused on the health problem itself. In the assessment of reasonableness, nurses and clerks also attend to the context of the presentation, by examining if the visit to the ED could have been reasonably avoided.

For a visit to be considered reasonable,[14] it has to concurrently satisfy a couple of conditions: first, the patient should have no immediate responsibility for the onset of the problem; second, the patient should have no practical alternative to obtain healthcare for reasons beyond her control.

The first condition is broken by most cases of aggression, self-harm, and intoxication, and by all problems deemed to have been caused by negligence. Although aggressions are evaluated on a case-by-case basis and victims have the opportunity to produce exculpatory accounts of the incident, nurses and clerks tend to manifest caution toward such representations and to consider that "there is no smoke without fire." Nonetheless, patients who manage to put on a favorable presentation of self and who do not display the most common characteristics of participants to fights tend to be exempted from blame.

Domestic violence represents a sui generis case of aggression in that responsibility is constructed in relation to the conduct of the victim *after* the battery took place. The victim is held unaccountable for the situation only if she agrees to report the case to the authorities by filing a complaint against the aggressor. This is related to the beliefs that domestic violence is recurrent, and that victim's passivity creates favorable conditions for its escalation. Particularly blameworthy are considered women who fail to present the problem as a case of domestic violence but admit to it after being challenged by the staff.

Accidents are never discussed in terms of personal responsibility, regardless of the circumstances in which they occurred. Victims of car accidents are usually brought to the department by ambulance, and the crew can provide triage workers with reliable information about the collision. Driving at high speed, falling asleep, failing to respect street-traffic signs are sometimes mentioned as cause of the accident. However, this does not lead to attribution of blame, probably because of the unintentional character of the mistake.

Triage workers tend to operate a distinction between immediate and general responsibility for the onset of the problem, and to restrict the assessment of reasonability to the former. Thus, drunks are commonly considered to make unreasonable use of the emergency service, whereas patients in the acute phase of cirrhosis caused by alcoholism and patients with alcohol withdrawal symptoms are not. Similarly, patients whose condition deteriorated after failing to respect dietary restrictions imposed by a physician are considered to make unreasonable visits, but this is not the case with patients having acute problems related to conditions whose etiology includes unhealthy lifestyle. Triage workers adopt such a distinction because of their concern with assessing the context of the current visit only. Thus, reasonableness is denied to those whose voluntary action contributed to the emergence of the health problem for which assistance is requested. The cirrhotic might be deemed responsible for the chronic disease but is not accountable for its acute manifestation that brought her to the hospital, unless there is a strong reason to suspect this.

The second condition that must be satisfied in order for the presentation to be regarded as reasonable, the lack of practical alternatives for obtaining healthcare for reasons beyond patient's control, takes into consideration the structural problems affecting the delivery of healthcare. Despite the general representation of clientele in negative terms, triage workers acknowledge that many of the visits to the ED that could have been avoided are primarily caused by deficiencies in the provision of primary and secondary care:

INTERVIEWER: I want to ask you, why do you think that patients [prefer to] come here instead of going to the family doctor?

CLERK CRINA: Because you have to schedule appointments in advance with the family doctor, I learnt it to my cost. So, you call today, and they set the appointment two or three weeks later for an acute problem, right? I think the system should be changed so that the family doctor also admits emergency cases. Although I've heard such provision already exists.

INTERVIEWER: There are twenty cases a day [the doctor is allowed to examine] and four emergency cases.

CLERK CRINA: I had problems, and I went [to the family doctor] as an emergency for gall bladder dyskinesia and for high blood pressure. The doctor admitted me, I cannot deny, but with many rebukes, [telling me that] I should set an appointment, I should . . . Wait a minute: how can I know the time when I get sick in order to book an appointment in advance? So, if family doctors saw more emergency cases, there wouldn't be as many people showing up to the emergency [department] for problems that don't constitute emergencies. (Interview, City)

As discussed in chapter 1, numerous factors are potentially involved in patients' decision to make an appearance to the ED, including long waiting lists at family doctor's office, family doctor's leave, lack of specialist in the locality, high costs of examinations in the private healthcare system, and lack of insurance. However, triage nurses and clerks are unwilling to consider all of them as reasonable motives for coming to the ED.

Presentations are assessed on a case-by-case basis, but some regularities can be found. Thus, claims of being unable to access a general practitioner tend to be accepted in most cases if the person resides in a hamlet or in a small village, particularly if the region has a low population density; occasionally if the person lives in a large rural area or a small town; and only exceptionally if the place of residence is in a city. The importance of the territorial criterion comes from the organization of family medicine. Because each doctor needs a minimum number of patients on roll, which is currently set at eight hundred but used to be higher, it is common for one doctor to serve several communities scattered across a large area. The family doctor's presence in each community is sometimes limited to only one day a week. Moreover, the monitoring of the activity by healthcare authorities is rather perfunctory in remote areas, which creates the conditions of possibility for work absenteeism. Therefore, when persons living in isolated areas come to the ED, their visits tend to be accepted as reasonable. This is ostensibly not the case for persons residing in large urban areas, where the availability of physicians is considerably higher.

In assessing the reasonableness of the visit, moral considerations about the patient are frequently used in conjunction with the availability of alternative venues for treatment. The person with trivial symptoms at the moment of arrival, such as headache, might not have other choices available if the presentation takes place during nighttime, given the family doctors and polyclinics operate only during daytime. However, the decision to seek immediate assistance is considered to be originated in the impatience of the patient, since other options would become available in the morning. Also, lack of health insurance is an important deterrent for seeking help outside the ED. The uninsured are nevertheless held accountable for their situation, which is predicated upon presumed moral flaws, such as laziness or ignorance.

In most cases perceived as legitimate, the visit is also considered reasonable. However, legitimacy does not necessarily imply reasonability. Intoxicated patients, for instance, are considered legitimate users (because they have an acute problem that requires timely competent assistance), but their presence in the hospital is also deemed unreasonable since they are held immediately responsible for the problem.

Reasonableness constitutes an acceptable departure from the mission of the ED that offsets the negative evaluation in terms of legitimacy.[15] Thus, patients with legitimate reasons for making illegitimate claims for admission tend to receive favorable treatment from triage nurses and clerks: they are neither verbally reprimanded nor sanctioned through delayed admission for the decision to come to the ED.

Reasonableness has not been recognized in the literature as a criterion for the non-clinical evaluation of patients, albeit several works address issues related to it. For instance, Roger Jeffery mentions in passing the staff's concern "with the ascription of responsibility and reasonableness"[16] in the case of patients regarded as a nuisance, but, in the wake of Parsons, his analysis focuses on the overall responsibility for the condition,[17] dismissing altogether the social context of the visit. Other authors point out the tendency of staff to grant special treatment to patients in situations of vulnerability even when they fail to meet the clinical features of a typical emergency case. Dodier and Camus discuss the impact of patient's social problems on doctors' willingness to treat them,[18] showing that the homeless occasionally manage to get more than perfunctory examinations for trivial conditions. However, their findings indicate that practitioners harbor divergent views with regard to the proper handling of vulnerable patients. Similarly, Carine Vassy[19] argues that emergency practitioners' approach to indigent patients varies from complete ignorance of their social and economic conditions to the prioritization of such cases on the grounds of the social mission of the hospital. In a different study, she finds that in apportioning care, the emergency staff attends to the social situation of the patient by devising "an informal system of positive discrimination."[20] The system benefits those who have a poor understanding of how the medical system functions, stand low in terms of economic capital, experience domestic problems, are not registered with a general practitioner, and lack health insurance.[21] Some recent contributions to the scholarship on healthcare deservingness[22] also provide conclusive evidence on the favorable treatment vulnerable persons, particularly undocumented migrants, receive in medical settings.

Positive discrimination is similar to reasonableness in the sense that both extend the entitlement to emergency healthcare to individuals whose condition falls outside the mission of the medical service. Thus, they counterbalance the assessment in terms of legitimacy in a way that is advantageous to the patient. Moreover, they incorporate considerations pertaining to the social characteristics of the individual and the practical obstacles she faces in accessing primary care. However, the reasonableness criterion is concerned less with the vulnerability of the patient and more with the issue of personal responsibility for the situation. Triage workers attend to the immediate responsibility of the individual for the onset of the problem for which she seeks assistance, as well as to her general responsibility for lacking practical alternatives, if this is the case. For instance, homelessness is not in itself sufficient to grant the incumbent of the status the assumption of reasonability. What matters is the social construction of the homeless person as either victim of unfortunate life circumstances or as a person predisposed for a life on the streets. Only the former category of homeless qualifies for reasonableness.[23] By the same token, staff tends to consider visits made by Roma, one of the most vulnerable populations,[24] as unreasonable on the grounds of their alleged responsibility for the situation.

Reasonableness is a composite criterion, encompassing different degrees of responsibility with regard to two situations that have little in common: the onset of the illness and the availability of alternative venues for diagnostic and treatment. What brings the two sub-criteria together is their orientation to the mission of the service. As compared to legitimacy, whose approach focuses on the clinical features of the problem, reasonableness takes into consideration the possibility that the visit to the ED could not exist in the first instance and links it to the patient's responsibility for the situation. A visit can be avoided if (1) the health concern did not exist or (2) the health concern could be addressed by a different therapeutic agency. The assessment in terms of reasonableness serves to protect patients who cannot be hold accountable for the existence of any of these conditions.[25]

By virtue of reasonability, triage workers consider numerous trivial cases as suitable for diagnosis and treatment within the emergency system. They mostly refer to situations in which the patient has health insurance coverage but lives in a place that is poorly serviced by family doctors and outpatient clinics. Nurses and clerks perceive situations of this sort as abnormal, but they consider equally abnormal to make the patients pay for structural problems that exist independent of their will. This view evokes the social function that hospitals, including emergency services, have traditionally accomplished,[26] and is consistent with the findings of recent studies on Romanian psychiatrists' approach to patients confined to mental health institutions.[27]

SOCIAL WORTH

In determining the legitimacy of the case and the reasonableness of the visit, triage nurses and clerks rely on several considerations about the moral quality of patients, such as trustworthiness, responsible conduct, and seriousness. However, assessing the social stature of the patient is a preoccupation in its own right for healthcare workers. Worth[28] is inferred from patient's social characteristics, conformity to dominant values and norms, and conduct within the ED. It serves to set apart people morally entitled to receive care from the undeserving others.[29]

In attributing worth, triage workers consider the relation of patients with the society at large by assessing their contribution to the general welfare. Being or having the potential to become a productive member of the society represents one of the tenets of social valuation in the EDs. People employed in the formal economy, who pay taxes and contribute to the social security, are held in high esteem, irrespective of the nature of job and position in the social ladder, and so are students whose characteristics indicate likelihood of employment upon completing education. The unemployed, on the other side, are faced with strong negative valuation. Staff in both hospitals tends to portray them as free riders, persons who take advantage of various social benefits they are entitled to, including free access to the emergency service, without giving much in return to the society. Unemployment is predicated upon laziness, unwillingness to work, and disregard of social norms, and is commonly associated with a penchant for economic criminality. By the same token, patients who are engaged in long-term migration abroad are negatively valued because they do not contribute, at least in a direct manner, to the funding of the healthcare system, but make use of services available to them by virtue of citizenship.

The patient's level of education also informs triage workers' assumptions about social worth. The educated patients are considered to have a fair understanding of health, to adequately handle illness, to avoid unnecessary visits to the ED, to acknowledge the competence of healthcare practitioners, and to show deference to them. The uneducated, contrarily, are linked to potentially dangerous folk beliefs and practices pertaining to health, and to irresponsible conduct. According to the staff, they tend to overreact to minor problems and to defer going to the doctor for serious problems until their condition aggravates considerably. Since formal education matters for securing a job, people with very low levels of instructions are overly represented in the unemployed population, which compounds their problematic orientation toward health with the negative connotations of contributing little toward the society at large.

Patients who abide by the dominant social values tend to be considered more worthy than those who do not, all other things being equal. Nurses and clerks give particular attention to the patients' marriage, family, or parenthood status, which can be detected with relative ease during the admission interview. A patient whose visit to the ED is planned beforehand, takes place outside usual office hours, and is motivated by disturbing symptoms is expected to be accompanied by one or more family members. If the patient is brought in by ambulance, the absence is understandable; otherwise, it triggers suspicion, and triage workers expect some explanation, even if they seldom explicitly ask for it.

Nurses and clerks recognize without difficulty a close-knit family from the ways in which companions participate to the admission interview and act toward the sick. Displays of care and affection are read as indicators of a functional family, which represents an important asset in negotiating access.

Meeting filial piety obligations is generally expected from companions, particularly in case the patient is an elder. Therefore, the admission interview
includes various questions that aim to elicit, in an oblique way, information
about the amount and quality of care the patient receives from the family. If
there are suspicions that the elder has been neglected by children and this has
had an impact upon her health condition, companions are usually admonished. However, there is considerable interpersonal variation in the ascription
of worth to the neglected elder patient, which is related to the different definition of the situation: some members of the staff regard it as a problem for
which the patient is not to be held accountable, whereas others see it as the
outcome of a long-term dysfunctional life, to which the patient is believed to
have contributed along the years. In spite of these differences, the worth of
the elder is never presumed exclusively from the perceived family relations.

Minors are not usually handled by the triage. At County, a semi-independent
pediatrics emergency service operates on the premises of the ED but has a
separate entrance and different procedures of access. Most of the minor
patients are directed there. Exceptions are orthopedic cases, which are pro-
cessed at triage regardless of age. The ED at City does not have a pediatrics
room either. All patients below 18 years old, be they orthopedic cases or not,
are directed to another hospital or to the outpatient polyclinic within the hospital, depending on the severity of the situation and the time of presentation.
Therefore, data on the handling of minors are scarcer than of any other age
group and are only gathered at County. With this caveat, it is worth mentioning that, as compared to the elder, the social valuation of pre-adolescent
minors is almost never affected by family relationships or the perceived
worth of the parents. This holds true even when parents display strong disreputable characteristics or verbally confront staff. However, when the patient
is an adult and a child accompanies her, a transfer of worth is usually realized.
This indicates that, on the one side, triage workers highly value parenthood,
and, on the other side, young age confers a privileged status that overrides
any other social characteristic.

Marital status is not an issue of interest in the case of the young and the
elderly but becomes so in the case of the middle-aged patients. Also, it
does not apply uniformly across class lines: while lower-class patients are
frequently asked whether they are married or not, the issue is seldom raised
with middle- and upper-class patients. Being single or divorced is generally
seen as a failure in the normative life course that is potentially imputable to
personal flaws, but it does not constitute, in and of itself, a major determinant
of social worth. More often than not, marital status is used to incline the balance when characteristics relevant to the assessment of worth are difficult to
ascertain or contradictory. In the case of users faring low in terms of social

value, it serves to establish the relative position they occupy in the hierarchy of unworthiness.

Although marriage is expected for patients past a certain age, it is seen as an aberration for those whose overall worth is extremely low and for persons with severe mental problems. Finding out that some highly undervalued patient, such as a homeless, has a husband or a wife, a fiancé or a fiancée, or plans to get married soon, represents a noticeable event, which is usually shared with other members of the staff and occasionally becomes a topic of gossip throughout the department. It goes without saying that the astonishment is even greater when staff finds out that the patient is not only married but also has an affair.

The assessment of worth does not rely exclusively on social characteristics and the presumed relationship with the society at large, but also draws largely from the conduct of patients and companions at the ED. Patients who are calm, understanding, and polite, comply with instructions from the staff and do not go to great length in attempting to secure quicker access to consultations are positively valued. Those who, on the contrary, put on deceitful presentations of the case, display patronizing attitudes, challenge the authority or the competence of staff, and act or talk in an aggressive manner tend to be categorized as low in worth.

Triage workers are inclined to see a strong correlation between demeanor at the ED and social standing, as the following excerpt indicates:

AMBULANCE NURSE: Serious people, like this lady, who worked their entire life and paid their taxes, are the most civilized. The others, who need [emergency healthcare the] most, are the ones to act badly, to aggress us. (Field note, City)

Comforting as it is, such dichotomous view, opposing people who participate to the well-being of the society, abide by dominant rules, and act in a considerate way when looking for healthcare to those who fail to make a significant contribution to the general welfare and behave badly at the ED, is difficult to sustain in practice. The employed often claim faster access on the ground of their long-term contribution to the social security system. The highly educated are prone to rebuke fiercely if admonished, and occasionally mobilize the education level as an argument in the verbal confrontation. As for the unemployed, they frequently display conspicuous politeness in interactions with staff and avoid making faux pas. The tendency of staff members to project an unambiguous distinction between the deserving and the undeserving delineated in terms of worth is indicative of the typified representation of the clientele, a topic that will form the substance of the next chapter.

SITUATIONAL WORTH

Triage workers' general representation of worth equates individual merit with favored social characteristics, expected life course, and desirable conduct within the department. However, throughout fieldwork I have observed many instances in which nurses and clerks display unmitigated sympathy toward certain patients conspicuously failing to meet such expectations. These patients are the ones staff members laugh with and occasionally laugh at during amicable encounters. While the flexible boundary between these forms of laughter[30] makes it difficult to tell one from the other at times, humorous exchanges that indicate situational worth can be rather easily set apart from other encounters containing fun utterances, primarily because of their benevolent character. They take the form of teasing, badinage, and facetious remarks, but are never rude or scornful. The laughing at the patient is benign and imbued with a certain playfulness that evokes friendly feelings. This stands in stark contrast to the spiteful, contemptuous mockery staff sometimes uses to sanction inappropriate use of the service or objectionable conduct.

This suggests that triage workers operate with a situational version of worth, which values patients based on the opportunities they provide to the staff to get a temporary exit from the emotionally strenuous triage activities. I refer to it as "situational," because it typically emerges from the interaction, has a momentary character, and is largely subjective. The situational worth is largely independent from the presumed overall worth and temporarily suspends its negative valuation.

In general, two categories of patients are likely to achieve situational worth: the witty individuals, and the vulnerable regular users. I use the "witty" label to designate those patients who make triage workers laugh through interactional moves that may include self-derisive comments; puns; goofy remarks; allusions to famous movie quotes, songs, and other popular culture products. The witty also crack jokes, feign misunderstanding, comically exaggerate trivial conditions and downplay severe ones, deliberately use old-fashioned or provincial words instead of more current equivalents, and describe ordinary conditions through vivid, evocative metaphors. They are the ones to initiate humorous exchanges with nurses and clerks.

The "regulars" are patients whose frequent return to the ED gained them special status. In many cases, triage workers are well acquainted with their biography and know a great deal about their health condition and medical history, as well as lifestyle and habits. While regulars are generally despised because of the illegitimate use of the service, those in a vulnerable position due to advance age, social problems, and mental disorders tend to escape the negative evaluation. They become object of friendly teasing and gentle mockery during the admission interviews, to which they usually consent. However, as compared to the witty, their participation to comical exchanges tends to be reactive rather than proactive.

To illustrate situational worth, I will present two cases encountered at County. The first is that of a middle-aged male who got a finger smashed when his wife opened a door. The patient provides a jocular description of the accident, framing it as an intentional act of domestic violence that might call for retaliation:

PATIENT: She [the wife] must have had a grudge against me!

NURSE (laughing): How come? Give me your ID!

PATIENT: Just a moment. (Laughing:) If this proves serious, I go back home, and she comes in. (Field note, County)

The triage nurse reacts positively to the comical interpretation of the circumstances in which the finger got broken. She laughs and asks a question ("How come?") that prompts the interlocutor to maintain the same line. The patient does not respond to the question but makes another statement that triggers nurse's laughter.

The second case is that of "Mrs. Croak,"[31] an eighty-eight-year-old woman who has been admitted numerous times to the ED at County over the past decade for various health problems. When she arrives one evening accusing general malaise, nurse Andra greets her with a playful remark: "There has been 10 years since I've met you. Every time you show up here you say you're dying, but so far, you've never kept your word!" (Field note, County). The nurse does not ask the usual questions about health insurance, duration of the problem, and visits to the family doctor, nor does she criticize her for making an inopportune presentation, as it happens with other patients disclosing similar symptoms. Instead, she wants to find out whether the woman still chain-smokes cigarettes and has solved some of the family issues, and asks about these topics through mordant, yet unambiguously affectionate, questions. The patient replies through succinct utterances punctuated with laughter.

While both social and situational worth and relational, the former describes the presumed relation of the individual with the society at large, whereas the latter is confined to the interaction with ED staff. It draws to a lesser extent from the social characteristics of the individual and more from the practical benefits they bring to triage workers. Cases acquire situational worth if they manage to disrupt the routine of intense emotional labor[32] that characterizes triage work by injecting a note of familiarity to the encounter. Some patients ("the witty") manufacture situational worth by initiating humorous exchanges with staff members. For others ("the regulars"), making an appearance suffices to trigger the sympathy of triage nurses and clerks. The concept of "situational worth" provides a tentative explanation for the marks of friendliness emergency healthcare practitioners occasionally display[33] toward frequent users, a category of patients that is generally disliked.[34]

INCLUSION AND EXCLUSION

By virtue of reasonability, triage workers consider numerous trivial cases as suitable for diagnosis and treatment within the emergency system. This happens usually when the patient has health insurance coverage but lives in a place that is poorly serviced by primary healthcare and specialist care. Triage workers regard such visits as "abnormal," that is inconsistent with mission of the ED, but they consider equally abnormal to make the patients pay for structural problems that exist independent of their actions. This view evokes, to a certain extent, the social function that hospitals, including emergency services, have traditionally accomplished,[35] and is by and large consistent with the findings of recent studies on Romanian psychiatrists' approach to patients confined to mental health institutions.[36] Nevertheless, the logic informing the favorable treatment granted to the "legitimately illegitimate" patients does not seem to be originated in a charitable orientation to vulnerable individuals. On the contrary, reasonableness is rarely granted to the most economically disenfranchised patients, because triage workers tend to link poverty to alleged moral flaws. An exception from this regularity is found in the handling of the homeless, euphemistically referred to as "social cases,"[37] but in their case the charitable treatment is related to the extended familiarity nurses have with their biographies.

Reasonableness has not been recognized in the literature as a criterion for the non-clinical evaluation of patients, albeit several works address issues related to it. Roger Jeffery mentions in passing the staff's concern "with the ascription of responsibility and reasonableness"[38] in the case of patients regarded as a nuisance, but, in the wake of Parsons, his analysis focuses on the overall responsibility for the condition[39] and dismisses altogether the social context of the visit. Carine Vassy[40] identifies "an informal system of positive discrimination" devised by staff members in a French ED to respond to the cultural and economic barriers faced by vulnerable members of the society in accessing primary healthcare. More recently, Mara Buchbinder[41] describes the ED gatekeeping in a US hospital in terms of structural competence.

"Positive discrimination" is similar to reasonableness in the sense that both extend the entitlement to emergency healthcare to individuals whose condition falls outside the mission of the medical service. Thus, they counterbalance the assessment in terms of legitimacy in a way that is advantageous to the patient. Moreover, they incorporate considerations pertaining to the social characteristics of the individual and the practical obstacles they face in accessing primary care. However, the reasonableness criterion is concerned not as much with the vulnerability of the patient as it is with the personal responsibility for the situation. Triage workers attend to the immediate responsibility of the individual for the onset of the problem for which they seek assistance, as well as to her general responsibility for lacking practical alternatives, if this is the case. None of the exemption criteria recorded by Vassy (lack of familiarity with the functioning of the medical system, poverty, lack of enrolment with a family practitioner and lack of insurance) are taken into consideration in the assessment of reasonableness. Patients of Roma origin, many of whom face both cultural and economic barriers to accessing primary care, are systematically denied exemption from the legitimacy criterion, and so are most of the urban and rural poor.

Reasonableness also intersects only partially with the concept of structural competence[42] adopted by Buchbinder. Romanian triage nurses tend to avoid incorporating judgments about patients' presumed social, economic, and cultural vulnerability in their gatekeeping practice. While they attend to the structural problems in the organization of the healthcare system and use them to establish legitimate visits for illegitimate problems, this is not a trained ability, but a response embedded in and deriving from their membership of a healthcare organization. Moreover, reasonableness does not reflect a systematic, coherent, and explicit understanding of the wider social forces shaping inequality of access to quality healthcare. More often than not, triage agents turn a blind eye to most structural problems affecting the society and prefer to dismiss a priori patients' attempts to make sense of their unfortunate situation in a structural way. Equally important, structural competence goes beyond, but incorporates, cultural and ethnic explanations of inequality.[43] The triage actors show little, if any, interest in, and consideration for, cultural differences. Finally, structural competence emphasizes the need for "rendering structural mechanism of stigma and marginalization visible."[44] In their day-to-day work, triage nurses almost never talk, directly or indirectly, about stigma and marginalization. In the few instances the issue was brought forth, they typically blamed the stigmatized or marginalized for their situation.

Nevertheless, the practical indifference to structural issues unrelated to the organization of the healthcare does not mean obliviousness. During the interviews, nurses provided complex accounts of post-socialist transformations that reconfigured the social hierarchy and generated poverty and exclusion. The refuse to incorporate considerations of this sort into the non-clinical assessment of patients is most likely related to organizational concerns.

Extending the exemption from legitimacy to all patients making convincing claims of vulnerability would contradict the staff-devised mission of the ED, ineluctably affecting the already precarious balance between resources and demands. The structural sensitivity toward the drawbacks in the organization of medical care can be read not only as a form of catering to the needs of patients, but also as a tactic of everyday resistance against medical authorities whose reforms triage workers deeply resent.

To sum up, reasonableness appears to be the missing link between legitimacy and deservingness in the non-clinical evaluation of ED users in Romania, attenuating their exclusionary consequences and addressing some pitfalls in the organization and delivery of primary care. Thus, the assessment of reasonableness during the triage admission interviews illustrates the hitherto largely neglected "facilitative component of medical gatekeeping."[45] However, in Romanian EDs, reasonableness does not apply to the most vulnerable members of the society and is not consistent with the ideas of structural and cultural competence. The difficulty of getting adequate primary healthcare and the fear of being mistreated at the ED have already been acknowledged as major sources of stress, reliance on self-care, and avoidance of healthcare institutions among the impoverished pensioners in Romania.[46] Examining only at the inclusionary dimension of gatekeeping can divert attention from the pernicious consequences of the practice. Comparative cross-cultural studies are necessary to examine in a systematic way the interplay between structural conditions, cultural expectations, organizational concerns, and gatekeeping practices in healthcare settings.

NOTES

1. Roth, "Staff and Client Control Strategies in Urban Hospital Emergency Services," 846; Mannon, "Defining and Treating 'Problem Patients' in a Hospital Emergency Room," 1007; Vassy, "Categorisation and Micro-Rationing: Access to Care in a French ED," 623.

2. They do not use the concept of "legitimacy" per se, but frequently talk about "true emergencies" *(urgențe adevărate)*, "real emergencies" *(urgențe reale)* and "emergencies-[that-are-]emergencies" *(urgențe-[care-sunt-cu-adevărat-]urgențe)* to present the cases that are considered serious and appropriate enough for being handled at the ED. Discursively, they represent these cases in medical terms, indicating specific clinical parameters that have to be met. However, in practice they rarely attend to these parameters when conducting the assessment of the case. Even though I preferred the etic concept of "legitimacy" to the emic concept of "real emergency" for comparability purposes, this is just a matter of labelling a cognitive pattern that I have reconstructed based on participants' verbal accounts and practical actions. Therefore,

the theoretical construct relies primarily on the meanings given to the practice by participants themselves.

3. While some variation among triage workers exists in making sense of the temporal features of the presentation, the timing plays an important role in constructing background expectations about the legitimacy of the case and the moral character of the patient or companion. I have examined the use of temporal typification for the moral evaluation of patients in a different paper. See Marius Wamsiedel, "Temporal Typifications as an Organizational Resource: Experiential Knowledge and Patient Processing at the Emergency Department," *Time & Society* 31, no. 2: 157–76.

4. Mannon, "Defining and Treating 'Problem Patients' in a Hospital Emergency Room," 1007.

5. Niels Buus, "Categorizing 'Frequent Visitors' in the Psychiatric Emergency Room: A Semistructured Interview Study," *Archives of Psychiatric Nursing* 25, no. 2: 105.

6. Jo Hadfield et al., "Analysis of Accident and Emergency Doctors' Responses to Treating People Who Self-Harm," *Qualitative Health Research* 19, no. 6: 759.

7. Mannon, "Defining and Treating 'Problem Patients' in a Hospital Emergency Room," 1007; Roger Jeffery, "Normal Rubbish: Deviant Patients in Casualty Departments," *Sociology of Health & Illness* 1, no. 1: 92–94; Nicholas Dodier and Agnès Camus, "Openness and Specialisation: Dealing with Patients in a Hospital Emergency Service," *Sociology of Health & Illness* 20, no. 4: 429–30; Michael Nurok and Nicolas Henckes, "Between Professional Values and the Social Valuation of Patients: The Fluctuating Economy of Pre-Hospital Emergency Work.," *Social Science & Medicine* 68, no. 3: 506–09; Julius A. Roth, "Some Contingencies of the Moral Evaluation and Control of Clientele: The Case of the Hospital Emergency Service.," *American Journal of Sociology* 77, no. 5: 845.

8. Erving Goffman, *The Presentation of Self in Everyday Life* (Edinburgh: University of Edinburgh Social Science Research Center, 1956), 1.

9. Havi Carel and Ian James Kidd, "Epistemic Injustice in Healthcare: A Philosophial Analysis," *Medicine, Health Care and Philosophy* 17, no. 4: 529.

10. Talcott Parsons, "Illness and the Role of the Physician: A Sociological Perspective.," *The American Journal of Orthopsychiatry* 21, no. 3: 452–60; Talcott Parsons, *The Social System* (Glencoe, IL: Free Press, 1951).

11. Neil McKeganey, "On the Analysis of Medical Work: General Practitioners, Opiate Abusing Patients and Medical Sociology," *Sociology of Health & Illness* 11, no. 1: 35; Renee R. Anspach, "Notes on the Sociology of Medical Discourse: The Language of Case Presentation," *Journal of Health and Social Behavior* 29, no. 4: 368.

12. Anne Werner and Kirsti Malterud, "It Is Hard Work Behaving as a Credible Patient: Encounters between Women with Chronic Pain and Their Doctors," *Social Science & Medicine* 57, no. 8: 1409–19; Anne Werner, Lise Widding Isaksen, and Kirsti Malterud, "'I Am Not the Kind of Woman Who Complains of Everything': Illness Stories on Self and Shame in Women with Chronic Pain," *Social Science & Medicine* 59, no. 5: 1035–45; Francine Toye and Karen Barker, "'Could I Be Imagining This?'—the Dialectic Struggles of People with Persistent Unexplained Back

Pain," *Disability and Rehabilitation* 32, no. 21: 1722–32; Immy Holloway, Beatrice Sofaer-Bennett, and Jan Walker, "The Stigmatisation of People with Chronic Back Pain," *Disability and Rehabilitation* 29, no. 18: 1456–64; Anne Werner and Kirsti Malterud, "'The Pain Isn't as Disabling as It Used to Be': How Can the Patient Experience Empowerment Instead of Vulnerability in the Consultation?," *Scandinavian Journal of Public Health* 33, no. 66 suppl: 41–46.

13. Bezzina et al., "Primary Care Patients in the ED: Who Are They? A Review of the Definition of the 'Primary Care Patient' in the ED," 476.

14. While triage workers reflexively construct the legitimacy of the case by using the language of the "real"/"true"/"actual" emergency, and being able to frame it in clinical terms, they never explicitly articulate the concept of reasonableness. I have constructed this concept by making use of the constant comparative approach. More specifically, I have investigated the commonalities and differences of all the cases that, albeit violating the staff-devised expectations pertaining to the legitimacy of the claim for healthcare, have not stirred up strong negative reactions, be they verbal or practical, on the part of the staff.

15. Reasonableness and legitimacy are standalone criteria that inform the non-clinical evaluation of patients, and it is by no means unusual for a patient to meet or fail to meet them both. It is also possible for a presentation to be considered legitimate yet unreasonable. For instance, suicide attempts and inebriation are acute health problems that qualify for immediate medical assistance, but they are unreasonable because the patient is held accountable for the onset of the problem. I decided to single out one of the four logical possibilities (the illegitimate but reasonable presentation) for a couple of reasons: first, because this situation is more common than the opposite one in both departments in which I conducted fieldwork; and second, because it is the only one bearing practically consequences on the handling of the patient. For sure, suicidees and the intoxicated constitute a source of frustration for triage agents, but this does not impact the conditions of their admission in a significant way. Patients deemed reasonable, on the other hand, typically enjoy the treatment reserved to legitimate cases without meeting the legitimacy criteria.

16. "Normal Rubbish," 98.

17. Ibid., 99–101.

18. "Openness and Specialisation: Dealing with Patients in a Hospital Emergency Service," 426.

19. "L'Organisation Des Services d'urgences, Entre Le Social et Le Sanitaire [The Organization of Emergency Services, between Social and Sanitary]," *Mouvements* 32, no. 2: 70.

20. "Categorisation and Micro-Rationing: Access to Care in a French ED," 629.

21. Ibid., 628–30.

22. Helen B Marrow, "Deserving to a Point: Unauthorized Immigrants in San Francisco's Universal Access Healthcare Model.," *Social Science & Medicine* 74, no. 6: 846–54; Susann Huschke, "Performing Deservingness. Humanitarian Health Care Provision for Migrants in Germany," *Social Science & Medicine* 120, no. 11: 352–59.

23. While there is considerable disagreement among staff with regard to the placement of particular individuals into one of the two subtypes, the criterion itself is remarkably stable.

24. Nikesh Parekh and Tamsin Rose, "Health Inequalities of the Roma in Europe: A Literature Review," *Central European Journal of Public Health* 19, no. 3: 139–42.

25. It also serves to sanction those whose visit is imputed to personal decisions or character flaws. However, since most cases of unreasonable visit correspond to illegitimate claims for admission, there is no additional sanction for the perceived lack of reasonability. In the few instances of legitimate but unreasonable use, patients either got away without any sanction or were verbally reprimanded.

26. Agnès Camus and Nicolas Dodier, "L'admission Des Malades. Histoire et Pragmatique de l'accueil à l'hôpital [Patient Admission. History and Pragmatics of Hospital Admission]," *Annales. Histoire, Sciences Sociales [Annals. History, Social Sciences]* 52, no. 4: 739–40; Ruth E. Malone, "Whither the Almshouse? Overutilization and the Role of the Emergency Department," *Journal of Health Politics, Policy & Law* 23, no. 5: 814; Julie Sanders, "A Review of Health Professional Attitudes and Patient Perceptions on 'Inappropriate' Accident and Emergency Attendances. The Implications for Current Minor Injury Service Provision in England and Wales," *Journal of Advanced Nursing* 31, no. 5: 1098.

27. Jack R. Friedman, "The 'Social Case': Illness, Psychiatry, and Deinstitutionalization in Postsocialist Romania," *Medical Anthropology Quarterly* 23, no. 4: 375–96; Jack R. Friedman, "Thoughts on Inactivity and an Ethnography of "Nothing": Comparing Meanings of 'Inactivity' in Romanian and American Mental Health Care," *North American Dialogue* 15, no. 1: 6.

28. Staff members use the language of worth themselves. In Romanian, the same verb *(a merita)* represents the equivalent of the English verbs "to be worthy (of)," "to merit," and "to deserve." Triage workers commonly use it to convey both social worth and deservingness of treatment at the ED. The context provides unambiguous cues regarding the proper interpretation, but it is more common for nurses and clerks to refer only to individual "worth" rather than to moral entitlement of care.

29. Roth, "Some Contingencies of the Moral Evaluation and Control of Clientele: The Case of the Hospital Emergency Service.," 840–43.

30. As Phillip Glenn argues, *"laughing at* and *with* are alignments to which participants [to social encounters] orient; [. . .] these alignments are not fixed but changeable, sometimes equivocal, and subject to moment-by-moment negotiations." *Laughter in Interaction* (Cambridge: Cambridge University Press, 2003), 115.

31. Due to a speech disorder, the patient's utterances occasionally resemble the onomatopoeia for frogs. Hospital workers gave her the nickname Mrs. Croak (in Romanian, *Doamna Oac*) in reference to this impairment.

32. Arlie R. Hochschild, *The Managed Heart: Commercialization of Human Feeling*, 2nd ed., vol. 8 (Berkeley, CA: University of California Press, 2008).

33. Malone, "Whither the Almshouse?," 806; Mannon, "Defining and Treating 'Problem Patients' in a Hospital Emergency Room," 1011.

34. Peneff, *L'hôpital En Urgence: Étude Par Observation Participante [The Hospital in Emergency: A Study by Participant Observation]*, 91–93; Olsson and

Hansagi, "Repeated Use of the ED"; McArthur and Montgomery, "The Experience of Gatekeeping," 491; Hadfield et al., "Analysis of Accident and Emergency Doctors' Responses to Treating People Who Self-Harm," 760; Malone, "Heavy Users of Emergency Services," 470.

35. Camus and Dodier, "L'admission Des Malades. Histoire et Pragmatique de l'accueil à l'hôpital [Patient Admission. History and Pragmatics of Hospital Admission]," 739–40; Malone, "Whither the Almshouse?," 814.

36. Friedman, "The 'Social Case': Illness, Psychiatry, and Deinstitutionalization in Postsocialist Romania"; Friedman, "Thoughts on Inactivity and an Ethnography of "Noth," 6.

37. Wamsiedel, "Lay Values, Organizational Concerns, and the Handling of 'Social Cases' in Romanian EDs."

38. "Normal Rubbish," 98.

39. Ibid., 99–101.

40. "Categorisation and Micro-Rationing: Access to Care in a French ED," 629.

41. "Keeping out and Getting in: Reframing Emergency Department Gatekeeping as Structural Competence," *Sociology of Health & Illness* 39, no. 7: 1166–79.

42. Jonathan M. Metzl and Helena Hansen, "Structural Competency: Theorizing a New Medical Engagement with Stigma and Inequality," *Social Science & Medicine* 103, no. Supplement C: 126–33; Jonathan M. Metzl, JuLeigh Petty, and Oluwatunmise V. Olowojoba, "Using a Structural Competency Framework to Teach Structural Racism in Pre-Health Education," *Social Science & Medicine*; Mirko Pasquini, "Like Ticking Time Bombs. Improvising Structural Competency to 'Defuse' the Exploding of Violence against Emergency Care Workers in Italy," *Global Public Health*, 1–12.

43. Metzl and Hansen, "Structural Competency," 131.

44. Metzl and Hansen, 130.

45. Buchbinder, "Keeping out and Getting In," 1166.

46. Gerard A. Weber, "'Other Than a Thank-You, There's Nothing I Can Give': Managing Health and Illness among Working-Class Pensioners in Post-Socialist Moldavia, Romania," *Human Organization* 74, no. 2: 115–24.

Chapter 3

Patient Types

Like other street-level bureaucrats, triage nurses and clerks work under severe time constraints. The preliminary clinical evaluation and the moral evaluation that accompanies it are conducted in the space of a few minutes, during which time a certain amount of bureaucratic information needs to be collected as well. Therefore, triage workers do not have the opportunity to delve into the particularities of each case and collect as much information as they need in order to determine the patient's entitlement to and deservingness of emergency healthcare. Instead, they infer the presumed characteristics of patient based on the categories to which he or she belongs based on a master status. Therefore, typifying the clientele is a practical necessity.[1]

Staff-devised patient types are elaborate discursive constructions that situate the individuals in relation to the society at large and the ED, and they are the medium through which triage workers apply the abstract classification criteria discussed in the previous chapter to the patients they handle. The patient types bring together considerations about the patient's everyday life, lifestyle, family issues, preoccupation with health, work ethic, moral character, intelligence, and social stature, as well as demeanor in hospital settings, strategies of self-presentation, and interaction with healthcare workers. Each patient type is assigned a tentative configuration of legitimacy, reasonableness, and worth, which is the background against which nurses and clerks assess patients' performance during the triage admission process.

The sphere of staff's a priori assumptions about patients and cases is vast, but the most coherent and complex types are those involving "problem patients."[2] Triage workers apply this label to the ED users whose handling is problematic due to perceived illegitimacy, unreasonableness, low social worth, or any combination of them.[3] In this chapter, I will discuss the typification of the elderly, the Roma, the intoxicated, the mentally ill, the people who attempted suicide.[4] Another patient category (the international migrants) makes the object of equally elaborate discursive constructions on the part of triage staff. However, I will not discuss it here because I have not encountered enough cases to reach theoretical saturation of this category.[5]

THE ELDERLY

The material situation of the Romanian elderly deteriorated considerably after the country's passage to market economy. While the pension and various social benefits, including subsidized public transportation, provide them a safety net that is inaccessible to other "losers of socialism,"[6] many of the urban working-class retirees experience poverty and are unable to cover the formal and informal costs of healthcare services.[7] In addition to economic hardship, many elderly also face a lack in filial support due to children's migration abroad.

In spite of these difficulties, the elderly are generally held in high regard in the Romanian society. In many families, they are actively involved in raising grandchildren,[8] which allows parents to get full-time jobs while saving the costs of babysitting. No matter how convenient from a financial standpoint, such arrangements are not merely economically driven. They also reflect a moral order that considers the socialization of new members of the society as a family task that cannot be properly accomplished by a stranger. In this moral order, being a grandmother is "a much desired and highly prized identity,"[9] and a major source of personal fulfillment.

Information about patients' age and retirement status is collected during the admission interview and included in the clinical file of the patient and the electronic registry. Triage workers commonly consider as "elderly" the individuals who are past the retirement age (which is currently set at sixty-five years for males and sixty years for females), regardless of their status on the labor market. However, the category is not homogeneous; a distinction tends to be drawn between the elderly and the very elderly based on their different health conditions and expectations for recovery in case of illness. Triage nurses at County tentatively indicate the age of 80 as the threshold between the two categories, but the degree of interpersonal variation is considerable, and the patient's overall state of health also plays a role in it.

Advanced age is typified along conflicting lines: high social worth is opposed to low reasonableness of the visit in the case of the elderly, and to low legitimacy in the case of the very elderly. By and large, reaching an old age is perceived as an accomplishment in itself, which generates reactions of sympathy from staff. It is worth noting that only in relation to this category of patients, staff members use the language of fictive kinship ("grandma," "grandpa," or, if the triage worker is herself not very young, "mom," "dad") instead of formal honorifics, and this happens without regard to class and social background.[10] The social valuation is even higher if the patient shows signs of happy family life, is involved in rearing grandchildren, maintains an active lifestyle, and displays good spirits during the admission interview.

Being old and not receiving family support is regarded as an anomaly in the order of things. Therefore, the biographical context of these patients, albeit irrelevant from a clinical standpoint, is a matter of high interest for triage workers. The following excerpts indicate how paramedics bringing elderly patients to the ED make sense of their solitude and lack of family ties:

> PARAMEDIC 1: The poor lady is alone and has no one to take care of her. For an entire lifetime, she hasn't thought of getting like this. (Field note, City)

> PARAMEDIC 2: She has two children, but they are both in America. She lives now at [retirement home of the Jewish community], because she's a Jew. She pays a lot for it, but the conditions there are bad. They don't even have a doctor . . . (Field note, City)

Both admissions have taken place the same day at City hospital. In the first case, the paramedic presents the case of an eighty-nine-year-old woman brought in a state of unconsciousness. In an oblique way, he considers her responsible for having no family or close friend to support her at this stage of her life (the intonation of "poor" is ironical). In the second case, that of an eighty-six-year-old woman with a minor health problem, the presentation of case is favorable to the patient. She is confined to a retirement home that allegedly provides substandard service, and she has no relative to care for her. Nevertheless, she is not to be held accountable for the unfortunate situation. The indirect reference to wealth ("She pays a lot for it") and the mentioning of family status (children who live abroad) concur in suggesting that the patient has led what staff considers to be a decent life. The lack of family support is attributed to children's failure to meet filial piety obligations rather than to patient's own fault.

Patients of advanced age are included in the category of 'problem patients' based on organizational considerations. Nurses and clerks consider that the elderly are prone to make unnecessary visits to the ED for minor health concerns, and to show up at times that are inconvenient for the staff, particularly in the early morning, when the night shift ends and the day shift begins. They are also associated with a stubborn refusal to seek help from primary health providers, even if they are entitled to see family doctors[11] and have enough free time for doing so. When the underlying assumption of unreasonable use of the ED service is confirmed during the admission interview, triage workers tend to expose the elderly patients to protracted waiting:

An old lady from the countryside is brought in by her niece after feeling sick for many hours. Raluca, the triage nurse, informs the companion about the lengthy waiting. An ambulance nurse who happened to be in the triage room also gets involved in the discussion:

NURSE: I admit her, but I warn you that some folks here have been waiting since 10 a.m. [the discussion takes place in midafternoon]

AMBULANCE NURSE: [It would be] at least five hours of waiting . . .

NURSE: Five hours? Way longer than that . . . *(To the companion:)* [What can I do] if you don't go to the family doctor . . . Don't you have a family doctor in [your village]?

COMPANION: Well, nobody accepts us without an appointment.

NURSE: In this case, you have to wait. In the polyclinic, there are two [public] medical offices, five private offices, what can I do? Let grandma enter the next room to have an ECG. (Field note, County)

The nurse in the field note above avoids a confrontational stance and uses the language of fictive kinship ("grandma") but assigns the patient a blue code that places her to the bottom of the waiting list.

On rare occasions, the tension between elderly's worth and unreasonableness is solved by treating the patient as if their social valuation were low. For instance, when a woman with high blood pressure seemed confused by the invitation to go to a nearby healthcare facility, the triage nurse repeated the instruction by dividing words into syllables, as if speaking to a child: "Go to the *pol-ee-klin-ik*. Do you know the polyclinic? You go there, to the *pol-ee-klin-ik*" (Field note, County).

In the case of the very elderly, the concerns regarding the reasonableness of the visit are secondary to those related to legitimacy. The very elderly are typified as problematic due to the overall frail state of health, including numerous conditions that could explain the acute symptoms. The brevity of the ED encounters precludes a lengthy investigation that could discern the etiology of the problem. Moreover, because of the poor state of health, resources allocated to the very elderly are on average more numerous than would be to patients with similar complaints in other age groups.[12] Despite the problematic aspects of their case, triage workers rarely delay and never deny admission to the very elderly. Moreover, comments about the perceived illegitimacy of the visit are only expressed in the back region of the triage room, and the very elderly are commonly exempted from staff's moralizing discourse.

The typification of elderly patients in the Romanian EDs reveals that triage workers do not consider the advanced aged clientele to be homogeneous.

The two sub-types—the elderly and the very elderly—originate in different assumptions about the nature and practical consequences of the visit, which in turn generate dissimilar background expectancies. In both cases, there is a clash between social and organizational norms, that is between the valuation of the advanced age individuals and the challenges their presence poses to the efficiency of the ED.

Triage workers' more benevolent handling of the very elderly indicates that when the perceived social worth of the patient is high, organizational concerns, albeit important, are superseded by moral considerations. The elderly, on the other side, enjoy only partially the benefits of advanced age. Triage workers often use a combination of gentle admonition and protracted waiting to persuade them to choose alternative healthcare providers in the future.

A distinction exists between City and County regarding the perceived problematic character of the very elderly. While nurses at County are more concerned with the difficulties of handling this segment of the clientele, this issue rarely surfaces in the talk of clerks at City. This difference points out the different weight social and organizational concerns have for various categories of triage workers. Clerks, who are only superficially integrated in the organizational culture of the ED, appear to be less inclined to incorporate concerns of this sort into the assessment of the case. Nurses take organizational concerns into account but render this aspect of the classification practically invisible. This finding contradicts the supposition of increased "objectivity and rationality" brought by the professionalization of triage work.[13] In Romania, at least, the decision-making process continues to be heavily permeated by social values and concerns.

THE ROMA

A recent study on moral evaluation conducted in the United States recorded the adamant refusal of healthcare workers "to verbalize stigma about race."[14] In my research, the situation was strikingly different. Although some triage workers appeared to be more cautious and calculated in talking about Roma during the formal, type-recorded interviews than they were in informal verbal exchanges, most staff had some stories about Roma to share with me. Very often, innocuous questions triggered complex and passionate responses, as the following excerpts indicate:

INTERVIEWER: Are there any categories of patients that are more difficult to handle?

NURSE VERA: [. . .] Among all, of course the patients of Roma nationality[15] pretend to be seen before others and they become recalcitrant if not given attention. They probably have inferiority complexes or they may think that because they are Roma we do not pay attention to them, [and] they insult us almost all the time. (Interview, County)

INTERVIEWER: Are they [the Roma] different from the other patients?

CLERK CRINA: Well, they are more violent, more dirty, insolent, disrespectful . . . I mean, they know they have no [health] insurance, they do not belong—they have no reason to come to the ED, yet they still behave rudely. (Interview, City)

Patients of Roma origin are given the most unflattering representation in the accounts of triage workers at both hospitals. They are unambiguously portrayed in strong negative terms. Moreover, the Roma constitute the only segment of the clientele that fails to meet any of the three moral evaluation criteria, namely legitimacy of the case, reasonableness of the presentation, and social worth. The Roma are also regarded as a major contributor to the crisis of the emergency healthcare system. Some triage workers consider that Romani patients make up to half of all the presentations, whereas others consider the proportion to be much lower. Nevertheless, all of them agree that Roma are overrepresented in the clientele as compared to their share in the general population.[16] Based on my observations, on a regular day, Romani patients make around 5 to 10 percent of the total presentations in each hospital.[17]

The typification of Roma as illegitimate users of the emergency service relies on several generalizations that staff members believe to hold true—seeking emergency care for ordinary symptoms (e.g., headaches, coughing) or ongoing ailments (e.g., cardiac problems); arriving at the hospital at convenient times; returning frequently to the ED; being deceptive in presenting the case and interacting with the staff; and having a penchant for adopting confrontational stances during encounters with the healthcare practitioners.

Triage workers consider that the lack of medical insurance makes the Roma prone to use the ED as a substitute for primary care:

NURSE JENNY: Most of them are uninsured. And because they are uninsured, the only place they can go to is the ED, so they come here. [. . .] [Whispering:] They are swarming here[18] [laughs]. (Interview, County)

CLERK CRINA: They come for any kind of problem, not necessarily emergencies. That's because most of them are uninsured. If you ask them, they say they have insurance, but if you question them in detail, they start admitting they're uninsured. Because they have no family doctor, they come to the emergency [department] to get treated for free. (Interview, City)

The lack of medical insurance also serves as an argument for the unreasonableness of the visits made by the Roma. Triage nurses tend to attribute the uninsured status to moral flaws (such as laziness) and the disregard of dominant social norms:

> NURSE ANDRA: They never pay for the health insurance, and they think it's weird to ask them if they have a job, and they laugh at you, because they don't have the notion of "work." Only stupid people work. They have only rights but no obligations. (Interview, County)

The structural determinants of unemployment are never brought into discussion in the case of Roma, as it happens, for instance, with the homeless. In their case, nurses and clerks distinguish between people who are unable to abide by social expectations or indulge in living on the streets and people who are unable to bounce back after experiencing a serious misfortune, such as getting fired or losing the house as a result of a divorce or some poor financial choices.[19] While some degree of personal responsibility is attributed to each homeless, the judgment is attenuated by the consideration of the wider social transformations that created new forms of vulnerability. In discussing the situation of Roma, however, considerations of this sort are silenced. The poor economic integration of the Roma is attributed, without exception, to alleged moral or cultural shortcomings. In other works, triage workers consider that Romani people do not have jobs just because they do not want to work or do not know how to integrate in the workplace.

As the excerpt above suggests, triage workers regard Romani people as the paradigmatic free riders—people who take a lot from the society while giving little, if anything in return. The different welfare payments (e.g., guaranteed minimum income; pregnancy, postnatal, and childhood allowances; other social benefits) are seen as part of the problem, because they incentivize the Roma to stay unemployed. Moreover, some triage workers call into question the poverty of the Roma, being intrigued by the display of ethnic jewelry: "They only come here to display their gold. [. . .] I don't know how they make a living, but they have more money than we think" (Nurse Jenny, County).

The Romani culture constitutes another source of frustration for triage workers. Nurses at County often complain about the practice of coming in large numbers at the ED:

> NURSE JENNY: When a dame[20] faints, the entire clan[21] shows up. (Interview, County)

> NURSE ANDRA: When a țigan has a problem, the entire clan[22] comes here. Twenty people [come], and everybody cries, howls, roars, smashes the head against the wall, and lifts the skirt, and the circus is in. Just to impress us. From

seven- to eight-month-old babies to ninety-year-old men, they all come here to accompany the patient. (Interview, County)

Triage workers dislike the fact that companions agglomerate the waiting room, exert pressures on staff, and communicate between themselves in Romani, a language that none of the staff members understands. Some nurses suspect that companions take advantage of this situation by making derisive comments about healthcare workers in their face. Although nurses strongly dislike the tendency of Roma to come to the hospital in large groups, they acknowledge that this practice can play in their favor. On the one hand, this increases their bargaining power in relation to the triage worker. On the other hand, the nurses are more likely to admit the patient quicker in order to maintain the orderliness of the waiting room.

The low social worth attributed to Roma also comes from their alleged aggression. In chapter 6, I examine in detail the stereotype of Roma aggression and the ways in which it impacts the interaction between Romani patients and triage workers.

During admission interviews, the negative evaluation of Roma in terms of worth, legitimacy of the case, and reasonableness of the visit often translates into supercilious tone, treatment as non-persons, and derisive comments on the part of triage workers. For instance, one time an eighteen-year-old Roma female from the countryside came to the triage complaining about what she believed to be appendicitis. The female, who revealed to be married "without papers," out of school and without employment, was thoroughly questioned about her life, including questions unrelated to her medical condition, such as the whereabouts of her partner, the planned date of marriage, and the intention to give birth.

In the middle of the interview, the data-entry operator sitting next to the triage nurse commented excitedly: "A wedding? Just imagine her wearing a wedding dress!" The nurse laughed heartily, as if such an event would be completely unimaginable. The patient did not react in any way to their small talk. The interactional objectification of the Roma female goes one step further than the treatment as non-person, since, in Goffman's classical formulation, the "presence [of non-persons] in a region typically places some restrictions upon the behavior of those who are fully present."[23] In this case, the nurse and the clerk did not refrain from making demeaning comments about the patient in her presence. The "unimaginable" event came, most likely, from juxtaposing the dark skin complexion of the young female to the whiteness of the wedding dress and, at a symbolical level, the dirtiness and pollution associated with Roma in the collective imaginary to the purity of marriage. It is worth mentioning that such breach of line between front and back stages is relatively rare, and it only takes place with some patients show-ing disreputable characteristics.[24]

The same patient was also laughed at when she exposed some folk medi-cal beliefs. In presenting her symptoms, she mentioned having "appendicitis, especially when there are clouds on the sky." The nurse and the operator inside the triage room both laughed heartily and teased her: "so you only have appendicitis only it's cloudy? Are you alright when it's sunny?" The patient explained that the pain was ongoing, but it was stronger on cloudy days, "because when it's cloudy it presses down there, you know." The nurse pretended that the story made complete sense. However, after the encounter ended, she recounted the story to several other staff members who happened to pass through the triage, mimicking the patient and repeating her idiom of distress.

THE INTOXICATED

Inebriated individuals represent a minority of cases, but they trigger strong reactions on the part of nurses and clerks. They stand out through the tempo-ral pattern of presentations to the service and the erratic behavior within the department. Their visits are more frequent in late evening than other periods of the day, in weekend than weekdays, and in holidays than usual working days. The predictability of the timing of arrival stands in sharp contrast to the unpredictability of their demeanor during the admission interview and throughout the stay in the hospital. The inebriated can be motionless or agi-tated, upbeat or dreary, compliant with staff or defiant of their instructions, solicitous to please everyone or recklessly inconsiderate of others. They can act decently or be violent to the point that staff members need to physically restrain them. Moreover, they are susceptible of abrupt mood swings and sudden changes in behavior. This diversity notwithstanding, triage workers unequivocally portray the inebriated in strong negative terms, associating them with recalcitrance, verbal and physical aggressiveness, and various sorts of trouble.

Patients with alcohol intoxication constitute a sui generis category of cli-entele because the legitimacy of their admission is taken for granted. Alcohol intoxication is a condition eligible for urgent medical care, and there is no need for triage workers to use non-clinical criteria to validate the claim for admission since signs of inebriation are easily recognizable. Furthermore, it is extremely uncommon for a would-be patient to feign inebriation in order to secure access,[25] which renders the credibility of the accounts provided during the admission interviews a matter of little controversy.

The inebriated do not constitute a homogeneous category of emergency service users. In spite of regarding alcohol intoxication as an intrinsically reprehensible state, triage nurses and clerks operate a neat distinction between two types of patients making an appearance to the ED by reason of inebriation, namely the "drunkards"[26] and the "occasionally drunk." The distinction, albeit objectivized through reference to an impersonal, empirically measurable criterion (the frequency of heavy drinking episodes), is largely built upon conjectures about the patient's moral character and the timing of arrival.

Drunkards

A distinguishing feature of patients labeled as "drunkards" is the inability to exert self-control. It is worth noticing that staff members prefer using the colloquial term to describe the category instead of talking about alcoholism, even if, similarly to alcoholics, "drunkards" are depicted as alcohol abusers who are exposed to important health risks. Framing the problem in medical terms would, however, entertain the idea of diminished responsibility for the condition. Such an extenuating circumstance is never granted to "drunkards," who are invariably considered culpable for drinking too much and too often. Since staff members rarely inquire about the life conditions of persons included in this type, few biographical conditions can be mobilized to offset the imputation of defective will.

Remarkably, triage workers refer to the patients whose chronic conditions (e.g., cirrhosis of the liver) could be attributed to a history of heavy drinking but whose appearance to the ED is unrelated to an episode of intoxication as actual or former "alcoholics" rather than "drunkards." Furthermore, in their case staff members are eager to find out about personal circumstances and structural factors that might have played a role in the addiction. If such information exists, the patient tends to escape moral blame and to be perceived as a victim of an unfortunate situation, very much like it happens with the social case who has maintained an ordinary lifestyle before experiencing downfall. The following field note excerpt illustrates one nurse's gradual moving away from an accusatory stance during the admission interview of a person suspected of cirrhosis as more information about the peculiar life situation of the patient becomes available:

> A sixty-year-old male with abdominal and leg swelling is brought in by a friend. The companion informs Nina that the patient started having this health problem about four months earlier, and that he went to the family doctor, who redirected him to the ED.

NURSE: Nobody has seen him in four months? It's swollen, so it's probably cirrhosis. He couldn't eat much food during this period. How about drinking?

COMPANION: Yes, he's been drinking.

NURSE [in an accusing tone]: Why?

COMPANION [in a defensive tone]: He didn't want to eat that much, but he wanted alcohol. They brought him to the bed.

NURSE: Who was bringing him [alcohol]?

COMPANION: It was a neighbor of him.

NURSE [concerned, in a benevolent tone]: But doesn't he have a family, a wife?

COMPANION: He has a wife and a son, but they are [abroad]. But, you know, he's not a . . . [hesitation], he's an engineer. (Field note, County)

Were the same patient to come to the ED a few months earlier, during an acute episode of alcohol intoxication, the triage nurse would have most likely shown no interest in the reasons for drinking and the person's family situation and would have missed the opportunity to find out his occupation. The plausibility of this scenario derives from the master rule of keeping interviews with "drunkards" as brief as possible, by avoiding questions that are unrelated to the procedures of admission. It is difficult to say precisely why such a rule exists, but it is very likely to be related to the assessment in terms of reasonableness.

Since inebriated patients are willy-nilly accepted as legitimate users of the service, triage workers can only express frustration toward their presence in the department by obstinately refusing to admit that their visits are reasonable. From an organizational standpoint, the inebriated are problematic because, as compared to the average non-intoxicated patient, they demand more attention from staff, occupy beds for a longer period, and act erratically, in many cases posing a threat to the well-being of others and disturbing the regular flow of activities. Their handling frequently involves dirty work.[27] Moreover, the severely inebriated are unable to provide accurate information about medical history, current medication, and drug allergies. To nurses and clerks, all these challenges could have been easily avoided if the patient were willing to exert self-control. To maintain such a stance, they have to discard any information that might indicate that the patient has diminished responsibility (e.g., addiction) or is affected by unfortunate circumstances.

Occasionally, staff members articulate in an oblique way the tension between the obligation to admit inebriated patients and the perceived unreasonableness of their visit to the ED:

An ambulance doctor brings an admission file and tells triage nurses: "We send him to the surveillance [room], because he is drunk as a fiddler."[28] The nurse in charge with the admission process makes a gesture of contempt. Then, the two nurses talk about the patient:

NURSE 1: Who is he?

NURSE 2: One [who is] so drunk that he doesn't even know his name.

NURSE 1: And we admit him to the emergency [department] if he is drunk?

NURSE 2: Maria [another nurse] says that he left from here in the morning. He's been drinking and now he needs lodging [again]. (Field note, County)

In this casual conversation, one nurse addresses the patient's entitlement to emergency care, but the question is rhetorical. Both participants to the encounter know well the protocols of admission, but at the same time they consider the visit unjustified. The other nurse adds supplementary information that reinforces the placement of the patient into the "drunkard" type (the use of the service one night earlier) and frames the visit as unrelated in any way to the purpose of the service, that of providing timely care to the critically ill ("in need of lodging").

In general, "drunkards" fare very low in staff's ranking of worth due to their lifestyle, but also because of the social class to which most of them belong. The vast majority of persons included in this emic category come from working-class backgrounds and, while this may be due to the higher incidence of alcohol intoxication among working-class individuals, it may also reflect the staff's tendency to assign middle-class inebriated patients into the more favorable "occasionally drunk" type, regardless of the severity of intoxication and the history of heavy drinking.

Unlike other patients, "drunkards" tend to be negatively valued if they come to the hospital accompanied by relatives. While family status constitutes an important proxy for one's perceived merit, the interpretation given by staff is different in their case. Particularly if relatives appear to be decent members of society, the environment is discounted as a source of strain that could explain the engagement in heavy drinking. The negative evaluation of the patient does not extend to companions. On the contrary, staff members tend to be considerate toward companions and to display compassion for the trouble the serial drunk procures them.

That being said, a certain degree of variation in the social valuation of "drunkards" does exist. It derives primarily from patients' conduct at the ED. All other things equal, those who create little disturbance, cooperate with staff, and do not require extensive attention are valued higher than those creating trouble. This is related, undoubtedly, to organizational issues, but is also consistent with the widespread belief among hospital workers that the true character of someone is revealed in the state of drunkenness, when one loses the capacity to self-censor.

Occasionally Drunk

Triage workers construct the "occasionally drunk" sub-type to designate the patients whose episode of intoxication is singular, fortuitous, and not severe. In practice, nevertheless, it applies preponderantly to individuals who fail to meet the profile of a "drunkard" (that is, lower-class, middle-aged male, either unemployed or holding a menial job, and often unable to establish or maintain a satisfactory family life), even if there is knowledge about previous admissions to the ED for alcohol-related problems.

As compared to "drunkards," the "occasionally drunk" are exempted from immediate responsibility for inebriation. The intoxication is presumed to be the outcome of a miscalculation, of not knowing how much is too much when it comes to drinking, rather than the consequence of poor self-control abilities. Furthermore, the representation of drinking as accidental also exon-erates the patient from the negative effects of intoxication. The staff usually maintains a benevolent stance toward the "occasionally drunk," tolerating improper behavior as long as it is not extremely aggressive.

The worth is derived primarily from the social characteristics of the patient, and the profile and demeanor of companions. In most cases, the "occasionally drunk" fare well above the average, and this is largely due to circular reason-ing: possessing valued social characteristics (young age, middle-class back-ground, normal family life) increases the patient's chances to be considered as "occasional drunk," and type membership in turn discounts unfavorable elements in the self-presentation, such as improper behavior. This further reinforces staff's conviction that the patient is worthy.

Users included in this type enjoy some privileges derived from the positive non-clinical evaluation: favorable information about them is readily circu-lated among staff; they are treated as if they were sober; and staff members refrain from turning them into the target of jokes and ridicule, as it commonly happens with patients labeled as "drunkards." The following vignette, which describes interactions taking place in the surveillance room at County, illus-trates the typical handling of the "occasionally drunk":

A twenty-three-year-old male is introduced to Dr. Pais by Nina, the triage nurse. She cheerfully tells that the patient was brought by two friends and his first words as he entered the department were: "Nurse, excuse me, I'm roaring-drunk." Nina adds that "he is not the type" [of drunkard]. The patient enters the surveillance room in good spirits, supported by one of his friends, and cracks some jokes. The doctor smiles and, after the patient is put in one of the beds, sighs.

Soon after being placed in a bed, the young man starts talking about his situation: "I've drunk like a vagrant."[29] In a motherly tone, the nurse aide replies: "Do you think we don't know what a vagrant looks like?" She then asks him about the circumstances of inebriation. The patient recounts that he just broke up with his girlfriend. He went to have a drink with friends and got a little bit over the edge, ending up at the hospital. The lady, who is in her late fifties, connects the event to a personal experience: "I am a boy's mother and I know what it's like. My son also got into depression [at the end of a romantic relationship]. He was in the third year at the post-secondary medical school and he [suddenly] lost interest in anything. He got beyond it and now he works as a nurse in this hospital. I told him: How come, my dear, all this just for the sake of a stinky girl?"[30]

An orderly who happens to be in the surveillance room goes to his bed. The two, who are about the same age, engage in some badinage about drinking.

The only member of the staff showing little sympathy toward the patient is the surveillance nurse. She asks him several questions about the health condition in an inimical voice and demands him to only use formal language since the hospital is a public institution. The patient complies but does so on a jocular tone. (Field note, County)

It is worth remarking that some members of the staff refuse to grant privileges of any sort to the "occasionally drunk." The nurse in the surveillance room treats the patient condescendingly and refuses to establish a personal connection with him despite the visible sympathy displayed by the doctor, the triage nurse, the nurse aide, and the orderly. Throughout his two-hour stay in the room, she remains aloof. Her reaction is by no means extraordinary. Although most ED workers consider useful to draw a clear line between the habitual and the casual heavy drinker, and to treat the two types in opposite fashion, there are some who refuse to show any sympathy to the inebriated.

THE MENTALLY ILL

Neither of the two EDs provides psychiatric service. Persons with known or suspected mental illnesses are given the recommendation to consult a psychiatrist. However, because many patients equate mental illness with insanity and the psychiatric establishment with the mad house, an institution whose alleged purpose is confining of the individual rather than curing the illness, obstinately refusing to see a psychiatrist is very common.[31] Clinical interactions of this sort are prone to contention, patients doing their best to frame the case as non-mental and medical practitioners attempting to overcome their resistance in order to impose their diagnostic.

There are some notable differences between City and County regarding the handling of the mentally ill, which are due to the local organization of medical care and the different triage arrangements. Firstly, in the administrative unit where County Hospital operates, there is only one psychiatric hospital. Patients who, after examination, appear to have no acute somatic problem but a mental one, are strongly encouraged to accept transfer to one of the three facilities of the local psychiatric hospital. If they agree, the staff arranges their transportation by medical ambulance. In the municipality where City is located, there are several institutions providing psychiatric service and numerous independent practitioners. Patients are also given the recommendation to consult a psychiatrist, but doctors do not insist on this, and no transfer service is available except for the most serious cases. Secondly, triage nurses at County, who are experienced and well acquainted with ED doctors' handling of mental cases, are prone to tentatively categorize a patient's condition as panic attack, anxiety, or depression. However, they make clear that this is only a possibility, and the doctor is the one to clearly establish the nature of the case. The tentative diagnostic is practically relevant because it introduces a horizon of expectation for the patient and their family. Triage clerks at City, who lack nursing qualification and are not aware of the way in which doctors react toward cases of this sort, generally refrain from making any comments on the possible diagnostic even when they anticipate the lack of somatic problems. Therefore, the typification of the mentally ill is more elaborate at County than at City.

These differences show that the non-clinical evaluation of patients cannot be divorced from the structures in which it is accomplished. The local organization of healthcare and the degree of professionalization of triage work are two of the factors that impact the unfolding of triage encounters. Two sub-types of "mentally ill" emerged from the data, the so-called "NVDists" and the "severely mentally ill."

NVDists

NVD stands for "neuro-vegetative dystonia." Nurses at County use the derivative "NVDists"[32] to refer to patients with mild mental health issues, such as anxiety and panic attacks. The emic concept emphasizes the lack of somatic problems:

> INTERVIEWER: Are there any other categories of patients that stand out? So far, we have talked about patients of Roma ethnicity [and] about social cases. [. . .]
>
> NURSE NINA: The imaginary illnesses.[33]

NURSE VERA: There are the NVDists.

INTERVIEWER: What does "NVDist" mean?

NURSE VERA: NVDist, with neuro-vegetative dystonia, people [. . .] with panic attacks, with imaginary illnesses. They have the sensation of imminent death and have to come to the emergency [department].

NURSE NINA: Like that lady from P. who dreamt—

NURSE VERA:—so she dreamt that a bull was chasing her, [and] she got so scared that she called the ambulance, and she came here wearing a nightgown. [It happened] last year. Wearing a nightgown and a bath wrap on top of it [. . .]

NURSE NINA: Can you imagine, as she'd been waiting for the ambulance, she couldn't find time to get dressed.

NURSE VERA: So, she came here with panic attack. NVD. (Interview, County)

Nurses often use medical jargon. Even in casual conversations, they prefer to talk about "dysuria" instead of "difficult urination," "epistaxis" instead of "nosebleed," "colic" instead of "intense pain," and so forth. Mastering the language of medicine is undoubtedly related to asserting an occupational identity focused on the scientific assessment of cases encountered in practice, but it also serves other purposes. Cases that cannot be easily discussed in lay terms because they are considered taboo, such as gynecological and urological problems, are usually framed in medical terms. This also confers protection to the patient by avoiding the potential stigma immanent in a lay interpretation of the situation. Another use of the medical jargon is to restrict patient's access to information,[34] particularly when the information is discreditable or unfavorable. Thus, the "NVD" label can be applied to patients without triggering any reaction from them, which is rarely the case when nurses talk openly about "anxiety" or "mental problems."

The NVDist is, by definition, an illegitimate case, because psychiatric care falls outside the mission and capacity of the ED. Reasonableness is generally granted if the patients meet two conditions: first, there is no record of a previous visit to the department for a similar problem; and second, they cooperate with staff by accepting the referral to psychiatric care. Since NVD is regarded as a minor form of mental illness, it is assumed not to hinder the patients' judgment. Thus, the patients are not held immediately responsible for the mental problem if they have not been diagnosed by a healthcare specialist, but they become so if they have refused a psychiatric examination or have not accepted the treatment. Similarly, even if the patients are under psychiatric treatment, they are held accountable if attempting to bypass the specialist by coming to the ED instead. Patients who refuse to cooperate with staff and insist to be considered as a somatic rather than mental case are more severely assessed because they also challenge the professional competence of the ED doctors.

The worth of the NVDists largely varies. Triage workers refrain from making assumptions about merit since the typification is primarily related to a medical condition rather than to a social characteristic, as in the case of other categories of problem patients. Worth is generally contingent upon the person's demeanor in interaction with healthcare practitioners. Those who agree with the diagnostic and comply with the doctor's instructions tend to trigger favorable reactions from staff, whereas those fiercely opposing the medical categorization and rejecting the recommendations are less valued.

Severely Mentally Ill

As compared to the NVDists, the severely mentally ill are not considered capable of assuming decisions. Therefore, even though the organizational trouble due to their presence is considerably higher than in the case of patients with anxiety-related problems, they tend to trigger a certain sympathy from hospital workers.

The severely mentally ill are considered to be illegitimate cases unless they have an acute somatic illness. For example, patients confined to psychiatric institutions are brought to the ED if they have acute problems that cannot be properly dealt with in the psychiatric facility. The legitimate cases represent, however, only a small share of the total presentations made by the severely mentally ill.

In terms of reasonableness, the severely mentally ill constitute a peculiar category. Since reasonableness is predicated upon full capacity of rationing, it does not properly apply to patients whose decision-making capacity is impaired by disease. Staff members still consider the visits of the mentally ill as avoidable, but they are less inclined to sanction in any way the patients for making them. Thus, the visits are perceived to be objectively unreasonable, but their unreasonable character is practically inconsequential. It goes without saying, the patients with acute somatic illness, particularly if referred to by a specialist, are deemed to be objectively reasonable.

The worth of patients with serious mental illness is also a matter of secondary interest for staff members. Like reasonableness, worth is premised on full rationing ability. Since this premise does not hold true, the patients' relationship with the society at large, the family, and the hospital workers they encounter cannot be used to infer social value. In general, the severely mentally ill are regarded as amoral, in the sense that their wrongdoings are discounted as irrelevant. Even bad temper or violent acts seldom trigger staff's wrath, which is not the case with other patients with diminished responsibility, such as substance abusers.

Instead of making assumptions about actual worth, members of the ED tend to operate with what I would call, for lack of a better term, "virtual worth." This refers to the potential merit of the patient were they not incapacitated by the illness. Thus, some social characteristics (age, social class of parents and siblings, personal attributes and skills) are used as proxies for determining the possible locus of the patient in the society if they were mentally healthy. For example, a young male patient at County was held in high esteem by the staff despite his verbal violence and stubborn defiance of hospital rules. The nurse in the Surveillance room told me that his deceased father had worked as a doctor in the same hospital, and the patient lived in an affluent neighborhood. His mental problem was congenital and had gradually worsened over time. For staff members, it appeared reasonable to think about the privileged position the person would have occupied in the society in more fortunate health circumstances. They translated virtual worth into actual social status, which entitled the patient to some privileges, such as respectful handling, more attention, and better care as compared to other patients in a similar condition.

In other cases, worth is inferred from personal accomplishments before the onset of the illness. An elder woman, whose demand of excessive attention and indefatigable insistence to recount a hard to believe family plot to assassinate her made staff uncomfortable. However, their attitude turned to sympathy after the patient revealed to had worked as a nurse in another department of County hospital. Her claim was deemed plausible because she mentioned the names of fellow colleagues and talked about hospital spaces that were inaccessible to outsiders.

SUICIDEES

Triage workers do not usually frame the suicide attempt as a mental problem, unless there is evidence that the patient has previously been diagnosed with a psychiatric condition. This implies that the suicidee is held wholly responsible for their act, and hence does not escape assessment in terms of reasonableness of visit and social worth. However, the suicidee type is not homogenous. Based on purported intention of the act and severity of self-inflicted harm, staff members distinguish between two distinct sub-types of failed suicides: the "staged suicide attempt" and the "real suicide attempt." Triage workers tend to consider both as legitimate cases for emergency care because the health problem is acute, has occurred shortly before the presentation, and requires in-depth examination to precisely determine the actual degree of self-injury.

Staged Suicide Attempt

Nurses and clerks consider that most failed suicide attempts fall in this sub-type, which is easily recognizable because the bodily harm is inconsistent with the stated intention of killing oneself: either the injuries are superficial, or the substance ingested is insufficient to put life in danger. The staged suicide is also commonly referred to by triage workers as "blackmail suicide" because it is believed to occur most frequently in couples facing romantic difficulties and be motivated primarily by the patient's desire to elicit a strong emotional response from their significant other.

Staff members regard patients making instrumental use of the suicide attempt as attention seekers or "drama queens," and oftentimes tease them during the admission interview:

> A middle-aged Romani woman attempted suicide by ingesting "about twenty" pills. The woman was brought by the ambulance in a conscious state. She invoked a domestic dispute as reason for her failed suicidal attempt and confessed to have had also ingested alcohol before taking the medicines.
>
> An orderly who assisted to the admission interview jokingly admonished her: "Other people can't afford to buy medicines and you have too many!" On a similar tone, the triage nurse asked the patient:
>
> NURSE: Did you try to kill yourself?
>
> PATIENT: Yes.
>
> NURSE: Next time, just jump in front of a train. By taking pills, you will never die. [The patient laughs.] (Field note, County)

This encounter reveals two assumptions underlying the "staged suicide" sub-type: the unserious nature of the act and the patient's unmitigated responsibility for it. Both hospital workers interacting with the patient frame the problem as trivial: the orderly regards it as a foolish consumption of medicines, whereas the nurse sees it as a failure in the performance of a mundane activity that invites for a change in modus operandi. Remarkably, both staff use jocular definitions of the situation, which do not allow for a literal interpretation. The patient's laughter indicates a correct reception of the message, but also suggests an indirect admission of the unserious character of the suicide attempt. The laughter buttresses the staff's representation of the act as a staged, rather than genuine, attempt.

The circumstances that have triggered the ingestion of medicines (an argument with the partner) and the quantity of pills taken fit the expectation of emotional blackmail. The patient took enough pills to make the partner worry for her condition and feel guilty, but not as many as to really put her own life in danger. Moreover, she revealed the ingestion of medicines soon after it took place, so that she could be rushed to the hospital to receive assistance immediately. To staff members, all these elements concur to suggest a calculated, responsible decision rather than an outburst of genuine despair. The melodramatic undertone of the entire story made staff dismiss the existence of suicidal tendencies in the patient. She was regarded as unlikely to escalate the self-harm to the point where it would pose a real threat to her life, and as such she was denied a suicidal career. It was this realization that prompted the orderly to crack jokes about the situation and the nurse to suggest a more efficient approach of suicide in future attempts.[35]

The presentation is regarded as unreasonable because it would have been avoided were it not for the patient's desire to get attention or to find a favorable exit from a domestic problem. The staff's hostility toward the patient usually mounts if she has ingested substances. In this case, nurses and nurse-aides have to perform gastric lavage, an extremely unpleasant and time-consuming procedure, and the patient's stay in the department is longer.

Patients believed to make instrumental use of suicide attempts tend to be associated with low worth, which is largely due to their social characteristics. Most situations of this sort encountered during fieldwork involved lower class patients with limited formal education. However, the assumption of low worth also acts as a self-fulfilling prophecy. In encounters with suicide attempters ranking high in the social hierarchy, triage workers are more inclined to take their statements at face value and to subsequently include them in the "real suicide" type, even if the self-harm is insufficient to cause voluntary death. This tendency, in turn, increases the proportion of persons holding low positions in the social ladder among the "staged suicide" attempters, further reinforcing staff's initial considerations pertaining to worth.

Real Suicide Attempt

This sub-type accommodates cases of failed suicide that serve no instrumental purpose. Triage workers attribute it to patients whom they believe to be deeply committed to end their life due to the inability to cope with personal troubles. Inclusion in the "real suicide attempt" type is more likely if the patient's degree of self-harm is considerable; the suicidal deed is accompanied by other destructive or self-destructive acts, such as arson or mutilation; there is at least one experience of successful suicide in the patient's family; the proximate cause for suicide is serious; and the person has highly valued social characteristics. While any one of these conditions is sufficient for staff to presume genuine suicidal intentions, patients satisfying only one of them are generally considered to just test the waters. Staff members still consider such cases as "real attempts," however, because they see suicide as a progressive accomplishment rather than a singular event. In this understanding, those testing the waters are motivated to put an end to their life, but they lack either courage or skills (or sometimes both) to successfully carry out the suicidal act. Some of them are expected to learn from the current failure and to repeat the act at some point in the future, with a higher likelihood of success.

Some of the inclusion criteria for the "real suicide attempt" sub-type are easily amenable to discovery, whereas others are more difficult to establish precisely. Nevertheless, even though there is no clear-cut demarcation line between what constitutes "considerable" and "minor" self-harm, or "serious" and "unserious" proximate cause, triage workers have little difficulty in practically assessing most cases. Since ingestion of medicines appears to be the method of choice for people attempting suicide in both hospitals, the degree of self-harm is commonly estimated based on the type and quantity of drugs used. Nurses at County appreciate that an overdose of up to 20 or 25 pills of over-the-counter medicines indicates minor self-harm, and it is particularly so if the patient takes a cocktail of different drugs. They increase the magnitude of self-injury if the quantity is higher and/or the ingested medicines are stronger.

As for the motives that have triggered the suicide attempt, triage workers tend to separate domestic and work problems from disruptive life events, such as loss of job, divorce, and death of a cherished one. The former are represented as "unserious" causes for self-inflicting death, and persons experiencing them are considered prone to make suicidal gestures in order to gain bargaining power and secure favorable exit from a difficult situation. Disruptive life events, on the other side, constitute "serious" proximal causes of attempting suicide. While not justifying the act, they make it intelligible.

The legitimacy of such cases does not represent a topic of controversy among staff. However, the reasonableness of the visit is surrounded by ambiguity. Triage workers hold the patient responsible for the suicide attempt, but also take into consideration the circumstances that contributed to its production (e.g., propensity to engage in self-injury, if similar events have taken place in the family; experience of serious personal trouble; evident inability to cope with life problems, etc.) These circumstances do not provide exemption from blame, but they do mitigate responsibility in a manner that resembles the categorization of social cases. Moreover, the assessment of reasonableness is less salient for the non-clinical evaluation of "real" suicidees than it is in general. Usually, triage workers do not bring the issue of reasonableness to the fore but maintain a meaningful silence around it.

"Real" suicidees tend to be the object of intense scrutiny about worth. During the admission interview, triage workers ask numerous questions about the life of the patient, addressing issues like family status, occupation, lifestyle, and habits. Although the information thus gathered is sufficient to infer worth, staff generally refrains from making any comments on the social valuation of individuals during and after the interview. Even in general accounts of the clientele, they do not provide a clear moral profile of the "real suicidees," mentioning only their remarkable heterogeneity in terms of social characteristics and demeanor.

PATIENT TYPIFICATION AND MORAL EVALUATION

The two components of typifications are *types* as constructs and *the act of typifying* as the interpretive process through which individuals are clustered into types. Types are collectively produced, complex, internally consistent, homogenous, and relatively stable, whereas the act of typifying is necessarily subjective and based on oversimplification. Therefore, it is susceptible of interpersonal variation in use and its outcomes are prone to negotiation, as the next chapter will amply illustrate. Both components play an important role in the non-clinical evaluation: types provide triage agents with the general orientation toward various categories of patients and make their decisions morally and procedurally accountable, whereas the act of typifying practically accomplishes the assessment by assigning patients to pre-defined types.

Types consist of remarkably elaborate narratives that incorporate considerations pertaining to patients' state of health, health knowledge and behavior, personal life, social life, and demeanor in medical settings. For instance, with regard to health condition, the "elderly" type presupposes the existence of concurrent illnesses of various etiologies that require laborious examination and prolonged clinical observation; the "Roma" type includes the assumption of trivial acute or chronic health problems for which timely assistance in unnecessary; and the "social case" type takes for granted the existence of communicable diseases, such as tuberculosis and sexually transmitted infections, which conveys a sense of risk to workers handling them.[36]

The various constitutive elements of a type are not isolated from each other, but interconnected, creating a whole that is more than the sum of its parts. For instance, the "Roma" type presents a straightforward representation of a "problem" patient through a combination of elements indicating illegitimacy of the visit, unreasonableness, and abysmally low worth. The type contains assumptions about the current state of health, and about the general context in which the health problems originate. The context amalgamates folk beliefs pertaining to health with unhealthy habits and lifestyle choices, including smoking, heavy drinking, having unbalanced diets, avoiding regular check-ups, and neglecting doctors' recommendations and treatment schemes. According to the type, Roma depart from the ideal of health-consciousness the same way they depart from dominant social norms: by obstinately refusing to embrace the values of the majority society, or, to use a phrase of wide circulation in both EDs, by "refusing integration." In concrete terms, this means engaging in practices like early marriage and early childbearing; having disproportionately large families; taking part to lucrative economic activities that are illicit, immoral or both; contributing little, if anything, toward the social security system; disregarding the institutions of the state and the bureaucratic agents; and having a penchant for recalcitrance and violent behavior.

Typifying allows triage workers to restrict the virtually unlimited ways of being and acting of patients to a narrow range of possibilities, each of them calling for a specific course of action. Therefore, the correctness of the approximation (i.e., the congruence between the characteristics of the type and empirically verifiable facts) matters less than its practical relevance. For example, the "Roma" type discussed earlier posits a remarkably homogenous community when, in fact, the Roma population is remarkably diverse in terms of history, culture, and socio-economic status. There are traditional and assimilated communities, compact settlements and dispersed groups, and the relation with the ethnic majority population ranges from perfect cohabitation to open conflict.[37] Even in the two EDs where I conducted fieldwork, the Roma patients were remarkably diverse socially, economically, and culturally, but this did not impact in any way the unity, internal consistency, and stability of the "Roma" type.[38] In chapter 6, I explain the mechanisms that lead to the reproduction of the stereotypical representation of Roma despite ample empirical evidence discounting it.

Although types are complex constructs, triage workers typify patients based on a limited number of characteristics. This simplification is inherent to the typification process, which, by definition, involves the reduction of complex phenomena to a small set of recurrent features.[39] As a consequence, triage workers do not need to attend to all the elements pertaining to the "biographical situation"[40] of the individual, but only to those that are momentarily meaningful.

NOTES

1. The typification work applies not only to patients but also to cases. I have discussed in a separate paper how nurses and clerks use the temporal features of presentations to the ED (e.g., the time of the day when the people show up at the hospital) to infer the severity of the health problem and the social worth of the patient. Wamsiedel, "Temporal Typifications as an Organizational Resource: Experiential Knowledge and Patient Processing at the ED."

2. Literally *pacienții problemă*, or, more frequently, "the patients who give us trouble" (*pacienții care ne fac probleme*).

3. This understanding is by and large consistent with that of earlier studies on the moral evaluation of patients. Hospital workers designate as problem patients those people whose case characteristics do not match the values of the organization (Mannon, "Defining and Treating 'Problem Patients' in a Hospital Emergency Room," 1007) and the expectations of physicians (Roth, "Some Contingencies of the Moral Evaluation and Control of Clientele: The Case of the Hospital Emergency Service," 848), whose disruptive behavior increases staff workload (Judith Lorber, "Good Patients and Problem Patients: Conformity and Deviance in a General Hospital," *Journal of Health and Social Behavior* 16, no. 2: 213–25), or whose conduct rejects practitioners' therapeutic aspirations (David May and Michael P. Kelly, "Chancers, Pests and Poor Wee Souls: Problems of Legitimation in Psychiatric Nursing," *Sociology of Health & Illness* 4, no. 3: 292).

4. Another category of patients that is typified by nurses and clerks are the homeless people or "social cases" (*cazurile sociale*), as they are euphemistically referred to at the ED. I have examined their typification in a different publication. Wamsiedel, "Lay Values, Organizational Concerns, and the Handling of 'Social Cases' in Romanian EDs."

5. Romania has experienced in the past two decades a massive migration of population to more affluent Western European countries, with about 2.7 million Romanian citizens living abroad in 2013–2014. While some of them have severed ties with the country of origin, the majority continue to be anchored in the Romanian society and return to their hometown periodically, to attend special family occasions and major religious holidays, and spend summer holidays. However, the experience of migration is not easily apparent unless the patient discloses it, directly or indirectly, during the admission interview. The representation of migrant patients is fraught with controversy. Nurses and clerks lament their alleged tendency to abuse the system in order to get free treatment during the visits back home, for problems that do not qualify as medical emergencies. At the same time, they are regarded as free riders as they do not make any direct financial contribution to the healthcare system. On the other hand, their relative prosperity is positively valued, except for the cases in which it is conspicuously displayed. Some staff members call the migrants' morality into question on the grounds that many are relinquishing family responsibilities (especially breaching the norm of filial piety).

6. Jonathan Stillo, "'We Are the Losers of Socialism!': Tuberculosis, the Limits of Bio-Citizenship and the Future of Care in Romania," *Anthropological Journal of European Cultures* 24, no. 1: 132–40.

7. Weber, "Other Than a Thank-You, There's Nothing I Can Give."

8. Jack R. Friedman, "Ambivalent and Manichean: Moral Disorder Among Romania's Downwardly Mobile," *The Annual Review of the George Barițiu History Institute, Series Humanistica* 6, no. 1: 150.

9. Borbála Kovács, "Nannies and Informality in Romanian Local Childcare Markets," in *The Informal Post-Socialist Economy: Embedded Practices and Livelihoods*, ed. Jeremy Morris and Abel Polese (London and New York: Routledge, 2013), 68.

10. The language of fictive kinship is often, but not always, used in the interaction with elder Romani patients.

11. Since unemployment was exceptional in urban socialist Romania, most urban elderly had contributed to the social security. As a consequence, they receive a pension and health insurance coverage.

12. Vassy, "L'Organisation Des Services d'urgences, Entre Le Social et Le Sanitaire [The Organization of Emergency Services, between Social and Sanitary]," 72.

13. Lara-Millán, "Public Emergency Room Overcrowding in the Era of Mass Imprisonment," 871.

14. Lara-Millán, 877.

15. The nurse uses "nationality" instead of "ethnicity." Although the official category "cohabiting nationalities" (*naționalități conlocuitoare*) existed throughout the socialist period, Roma were not formally recognized as one. After 1989, the ethnic minorities, including Roma, are formally categorized as "national minorities."

16. According to the 2011 Census data, Roma account for slightly more than 1 percent of the population in the municipality where City hospital is located, and around 5 percent in the municipality where County is located.

17. This estimation is based on the hetero-identification of patients, as the admission process does not involve the collection of ethnic data. I discuss in chapter 6 the hetero-identification criteria and practices.

18. *Năvălesc aici.*

19. Wamsiedel, "Lay Values, Organizational Concerns, and the Handling of 'Social Cases' in Romanian EDs."

20. *Țață.* The term describing Roma females here was originally used in the rural areas to designate aunts. The initial meaning was lost, and now it is commonly used as a pejorative term for females with vile behavior.

21. *Toată șatra.*

22. Idem.

23. *The Presentation of Self in Everyday Life*, 96.

24. During encounters, unaccompanied women tend to be exposed more often than accompanied women to ridicule and sarcasm, whereas this happens only seldom with males. Also, Roma females bearing the marks of belonging to a traditional community (e.g., dressed in long dresses with flower motives, wearing the headscarf and showing the traditional hairstyle; communicating in Romani language; or having a very strong accent) are more exposed to the negative handling as compared to their counterparts who do not display any immediately visible cultural marker of ethnicity.

25. I have neither assisted to nor heard of such an event taking place in the two EDs in which I conducted fieldwork.

26. *Bețivii.*

27. Jean Peneff made the important point that although dirty work is in itself detestable, staff members' attitude toward it depends largely on the moral evaluation of the situation in which it occurs. Thus, vomiting is seen as tolerable if it is the result of some gastric illness, but strongly abhorrent if it is the outcome of acute alcohol intoxication. Peneff *L'hôpital En Urgence: Étude Par Observation Participante [The Hospital in Emergency: A Study by Participant Observation]*, 63–64.

28. *Beat criță.*

29. *Am băut ca un boschetar.*

30. *Pentru o putoare de fată.*

31. The anthropological research conducted by Jack R. Friedman in psychiatric institutions in Romania suggests that this representation is not preposterous. Psychiatric establishments are primarily oriented toward the management of symptoms through heavy medication, and this tendency is more pronounced if the patient is either poor or has experienced downward mobility in post-socialism. Psychiatrists seldom contemplate recovery as a clinical goal and rarely attend to the extra-somatic elements of cases in their practice. This contrasts with the dominant approach in nowadays American psychiatry. See "Thoughts on Inactivity and an Ethnography of "Noth," 5. "The Challenges Facing Mental Health Reform in Romania," *Eurohealth* 12, no. 3: 37. "The 'Social Case': Illness, Psychiatry, and Deinstitutionalization in Postsocialist Romania," 380–81.

32. *Deneviștii.*

33. *Bolile închipuite.*

34. Gail Henderson and Myron Cohen, *The Chinese Hospital: A Socialist Work Unit* (New Haven: Yale University Press, 1984), 114.

35. In the novel *Almost Transparent Blue*, Ryu Murakami includes a very similar handling of a patient whose suicide attempt is suspected to be fraudulent:

"A suicide, is it? Well, since you're not dead it's just attempted suicide, but the fact is, you didn't do things right. Even cutting your wrist, well, human beings are pretty well put together, so as to keep on living. You'd have to press your wrist hard against a wall or something and pull up the skin to get the vein to stand out and then slash it. But if you were serious about it, if you really and truly want to die, you'd cut here, look here, under the ear, with a razor, and then even if an ambulance brought you to me right away there'd be no saving you."

That was what the doctor who fixed Yoshiyama's wrist had said.

Ryu Murakami, *Almost Transparent Blue*, trans. Nancy Andrew (Tokyo; New York: Kodansha USA, 2003), 104.

36. Wamsiedel, "Lay Values, Organizational Concerns, and the Handling of 'Social Cases' in Romanian EDs."

37. Dena Ringold, Mitchell Alexander Orenstein, and Erika Wilkens, *Roma in an Expanding Europe: Breaking the Poverty Cycle* (Washington, DC: World Bank Publications, 2005), 88–122; Gábor Fleck and Cosima Rughiniș, *Come Closer: Inclusion and Exclusion of Roma in Present Day Romanian Society* (Bucharest, Romania: Human Dynamics, 2008), 35–62; Zoltan D. Barany, "Living on the Edge: The East European Roma in Postcommunist Politics and Societies," *Slavic Review* 53, no. 2: 324–25.

38. The tendency to homogenize Roma in spite of obvious cultural and economic differences is common in the dominant academic and public discourse in Europe,

from the society at large. See Vera Messing, "Methodological Puzzles of Surveying Roma/Gypsy Populations," *Ethnicities* 14, no. 6: 811–29.

39. John C. McKinney, "Typification, Typologies, and Sociological Theory," *Social Forces* 48, no. 1: 3.

40. Alfred Schütz, "Common-Sense and Scientific Interpretation of Human Action," *Philosophy and Phenomenological Research* 14, no. 1: 1–38.

Chapter 4

Credibility Work and the Assessment of Legitimacy

Nearly every person entering the ED gets subjected to an initial assessment based on the staff's momentarily impressions. However, this assessment is merely provisional; its validation depends largely upon the patient's performance during the encounter. Classification schemes and patient types represent the a priori component of the non-clinical evaluation, which delineates triage workers' horizon of expectation regarding the patient and influences their approach of the admission interview. Thus, in the case of negatively evaluated patients, triage workers question more vigorously the trustworthiness of the person and the credibility of their accounts, in an attempt to confirm the first impression. However, patients have considerable leeway in overturning the unfavorable categorization during the interaction by manufacturing worth, legitimacy, and credibility. In this and the next chapter, I examine the moral boundary work jointly performed by patients, companions, and staff. This chapter unravels the credibility work and the assessment of legitimacy, whereas the next one looks at the interactional negotiation of reasonableness and worth.

"They say one thing here, and another thing there. Not all of them are honest," Nurse Lucia tells me in the backstage of the triage booth at County. Her complaint about patients who drastically change their statements, including the description of symptoms, after getting admitted, is by no means singular. Nurse Tatiana at County describes the rectification of statements in remarkably similar terms: "There is a high discrepancy between what patients say here, what they say during the consultation, and what they say at the lab. And one doesn't even know which version to believe." Clerk Crina at City mentions her concern with patients' honesty when communicating their insurance status, a piece of information for which no documentary evidence could be produced at the time of fieldwork:[1] "They say they're insured but I don't think they are. I think they lie, many times I caught them lying." The "deceiving patient" is a recurrent theme in the atrocity stories[2] nurses and clerks at both hospitals recount. Time and time again, I would hear about patients departing from the initial presentation of the case by invoking completely different symptoms, providing different accounts of the onset of illness, and changing parts of their medical history. The repertoire of deceptive moves in these stories goes beyond the rectification of statements to also include exaggerations, omissions, and fake displays of intense suffering.

For sure, the popularity of the "deceiving patient" atrocity story among triage workers is partly related to the boundary-work through which they define their occupations and develop a collective identity.[3] The narrative highlights the complexity of nurses' and clerks' work and the contentious environment in which it takes place.[4] But, beyond its rhetorical purposes, the story points out important features of the social order of the ED that shape the interaction between staff and clients and impact on the moral evaluation process. Nurses and clerks have good organizational reasons to stand guard against deception. On the one side, patients have incentives to put on dishonest self- and case-presentations. By successfully manipulating statements, ordinary users gain fast-track admission to medical examination, the individuals in vulnerable situations secure the healthcare assistance they could not get elsewhere,[5] the homeless benefit of temporary shelter,[6] and the abusive or negligent parents escape moral and legal responsibility for their actions.[7] On the other side, the features of the triage encounter create a fertile ground for dishonest performances. The brevity of the admission interview and the limited supply of information available to triage workers make it difficult for them to prove deceit. Even when they manage to do so, the fraudulent patient has little to lose from committing the "capital social sin" of "defining oneself in terms of status while lacking the qualities the incumbent of that status is supposed to possess"[8] since the patient identity is, in most cases, short-lived and inconsequential for the self-conception of the individual.

While the staff's concern about patients' actual or potential dishonest performances is undeniable, it only tells part of the story of credibility work at the ED. As I became more familiar with the field and the social worlds of nurses and clerks, I realized that the triage workers held more nuanced views on patients' rectification of statements. The shock of entering a bureaucratic setting with which they are unacquainted, the emotional distress of the illness, the use of idioms of distress, the poor health literacy, and the inability to properly verbalize their symptoms are some other explanations for patients' self-contradictions and out-of-ordinary conduct. Moreover, determining patients' credibility as reporters of symptoms is not always directed toward a moral assessment. Instead, it is often a subtle interactional process through which nurses and clerks decide on a tentative and provisional diagnosis and place the patient into a priority category.

The clinical and bureaucratic functions of the credibility work stem from the particular context of the ED. The culture of biomedicine encourages decision-making based on objective, factual evidence at the expense of patients' accounts and interactional performance.[9] While symptoms, appearance, and demeanor are useful in making initial sense of the nature and severity of a health problem,[10] purportedly objective signs of biological functioning (e.g., vital signs, laboratory results, MRI scans, and X-rays) tend to be given precedence over patients' complaints in medical diagnosis.[11] However, the development of sophisticated medical technology has not suppressed the clinical relevance of patient-reported symptoms. On the contrary, many healthcare practitioners still privilege symptoms over objective clinical information in their decision-making.[12] This holds particularly true for emergency triage work, where the availability of factual information is limited, the responsibility for mistakes is high, and the initial assessment of cases needs to be done rapidly.[13] Under such conditions, patients' appearance, demeanor, and reported symptoms become salient resources for tentatively determining the nature and severity of cases. Nevertheless, these elements cannot be taken at face value. Because symptoms describe a deeply subjective experience, they stand as a poor proxy for disease severity. The most compelling example is that of pain. Although the self-assessment of pain is part of the formal procedures for patient classification, nurses and clerks avoid it in their day-to-day practice due to its incommensurability: "for me pain is in a way, for the patient in another way, for you in still another way. Everybody perceives pain differently" (Nurse Jenny, County).[14] Another complication comes from the existence of psychosomatic illnesses, a category of problems that fall outside triage workers' understanding of a medical emergency. Thus, judging patients' credibility as reporters of symptoms and performers of distress is a practical necessity: through it, nurses and clerks make sense of cases and decide on their handling.

This chapter examines the credibility work jointly performed by triage workers and patients. The staff's "organized skepticism"[15] surrounding what patients say and do turn credibility work into a salient aspect of the moral evaluation process. Therefore, I begin by unveiling three strategies through which ordinary patients achieve credibility during the triage assessment: embodying distress, limiting the voice of the lifeworld, and conveying narrative frankness. Patients belonging to groups typified by triage workers as dishonest and those presenting invisible symptoms face the additional task of establishing themselves as trustworthy interlocutors. In the second part of the chapter, I examine the relation between trustworthiness and credibility, showing the importance of mobilizing worth claims to overcome triage workers' heightened suspicion. I conclude the chapter with an overview of the contribution of credibility work to the moral evaluation in terms of legitimacy and reasonableness and a discussion of the differences between the two settings.

CREDIBILITY WORK

Embodying Distress

The assessment of patient credibility is shaped by triage workers' typified representation of medical emergencies.[16] To nurses and clerks, a "genuine" emergency is a condition that produces a fair amount of pain and bodily discomfort. Patients are expected not only to have an illness, but also to be taken into possession by it to the point where their social functioning becomes temporarily impaired. Thus, looking weak, dizzy, disoriented, out of place, and livid are consistent with the representation of an emergency, whereas showing even tiny signs of vigor, coherence in actions and talk, and interest in what is going on around are not. As Clerk Aspazia at City put it, "Sick people are quiet. The others, who are agitated, 'I'm dying here,' are the ones who want to jump the queue." However, distinguishing between authentic and fabricated embodiments of distress is not always as simple as this quote suggests.

In some cases, appearance alone suffices to lend credence to patients' illness claims. Triage workers acknowledge that symptoms and signs can be misleading and recount situations in which a patient reporting ordinary symptoms had, in fact, a life-threatening condition, such as pulmonary embolism. To deal with clinical uncertainty, they occasionally rely in the initial assessment of the case on the "sixth sense," a practical knowledge acquired through experience.[17] The sixth sense allows them to spot red flags in presentations that may otherwise be unexceptional:

> NURSE ANDRA: You look at the patient and see that something is not as it should be, there is something you don't like, but you can't tell what it is. It can be his complexion, it can be the way he is looking, maybe how he breathes or keeps his mouth open, something that is not how it should be, and here comes the sixth sense, and you find out later on whether he was in a really bad condition or not. But it's always good to take this into consideration. (Interview, County)

As the excerpt above suggests, deviations from "normal" appearance tend to be equated with potentially severe conditions, particularly if they are small, relatively uncommon, and difficult to stage. Patients' elaborate and conspicuous projections of distress, on the other hand, are usually met with reluctance. Some physical and verbal acts almost always elicit suspicion. Rolling the eyes, keeping the eyes closed for seconds, making lengthy interruptions while speaking, taking deep breaths, sighing, moaning, grimacing, and suddenly contorting body during the admission interview are typically read as indicators of an exaggeration. The concurrent use of various acts of this sort during the presentation of the case in the absence of any obvious somatic problem that would justify them reinforces the suspicion.

Although triage workers rarely confront patients regarding their bodily acts, they often talk in the back region of the triage room about people "acting" pain or distress. Sometimes, as the following field note shows, the refuse to take the patient's performance at face value is obliquely but unambiguously communicated to other members of the ED:

> Twenty-nine-year-old woman accompanied by a friend. The companion asks whether the woman can have a sit because she "is falling down." The patient keeps looking down and covers the face with hands. She tells she started feeling "badly dizzy" while driving the car a little earlier. She pulled over, called a friend, and they rushed to the hospital together. She responds the clerk's questions selectively, in a faint voice, sometimes mumbling. When asked whether she had lost consciousness, she replies, "Almost."
>
> Later, while the patient is in the waiting room, the security agent asks clerk Doina if it is possible to speed up the admission because the patient looks bad. The clerk calls the Minor Emergencies room and presents the case to a nurse: "I've got a twenty-nine-year-old little girl, dizzy, fainted, is there any free bed? . . . Okay, I tell her to wait." (Field note, City)

By referring to the patient as a "twenty-nine-year-old little girl," the clerk calls into question her maturity and advances a tentative explanation for her visit. To further emphasize the perceived illegitimacy of the patient's claim to admission, the clerk uses in the informal presentation of the case the lay words "dizzy" and "fainted" instead of their medical correspondents ("vertigo" and "syncope," respectively). Triage workers at both EDs reserve medical vocabulary to cases regarded as properly fit into the mission of the service.

The admission interview represents a pivotal moment for assessing the credibility of patients' embodiment of distress. However, triage workers also attend to their appearance and demeanor before and after the interview.[18] This allows them to spot inconsistencies between the presentation of the case and the patient's conduct in the waiting room. For instance, Nurse Andra at County told me about a male who went down from the car without any difficulty, kissed his girlfriend, and only started hobbling as he entered the ED. In other cases, the claim of being in distress is invalidated by patients' preoccupation with, or involvement in, mundane activities such as talking, joking, initiating phone calls, going out for smoking, or watching videos running on the TV in the waiting room. In many a case, the incongruence between patient conduct and staff's understanding of an emergency is found in less conspicuous actions:

> An ambulance nurse brings a woman, and after reporting the symptoms, she comments:
>
> AMBULANCE NURSE: She's in intense pain. She lay down on a chair.
>
> NURSE JENNY: Don't tell me, I've seen many like her.
>
> [...] Later, after the ambulance nurse is gone, Jenny points to the patient and tells me: "The lady brought by the ambulance is in such great pain that she wanders around with the purse in her hand." (Field note, County)

The ironic remark of the ambulance nurse and the triage nurse's response unravel a shared understanding of typical emergencies, derived from practical experience. Seasoned nurses see in the apparently innocuous act of sitting down a red flag for deception because it includes an element of calculation that is inconsistent with the reported symptom. The preoccupation with finding a seat to lay down violates staff's assumption that excruciating pain deprives the sufferer of strength, composure, and coherence in actions. The patient's subsequent actions (walking around and taking care of her belongings) only buttress the initial evaluation.

The assessment of embodied distress is gendered. Gender norms impact both patients' presentation of the case and its interpretation by triage workers. Men are expected to exhibit composure and equanimity when dealing with pain, whereas women are exempted from the moral obligation to exert strict self-control. These expectations are consistent with the traditional social construction of manliness in terms of toughness and self-discipline, and of femininity in terms of fragility and vulnerability.[19] These norms and values, although never articulated in talk, inform the joint production of non-clinical evaluation. For example, male patients making an appearance after suffering accidents tend to downplay and laugh off the severity of injuries:

> NURSE: What happened to you?
>
> PATIENT: A knock to the head.
>
> NURSE: What did you bump against?
>
> PATIENT: I didn't bump against anything; something fell on my head. A piece of wood . . . I wanted to see what was inside *(laughing)*. Inside the wood, I mean. Inside the head, I knew it was nothing *(laughing)*. [After a few seconds:] I did not want to come, but they [the coworkers] swooped on me. (Field note, County)

The patient in the field note above has blood all over his head, but he refers to his problem in a detached, casual way. Then, he cracks a joke and lets the triage nurse know that his coworkers pressured him to go to the hospital for investigation. At a later moment during the admission interview, he mentions that "blood spilled as from a faucet," but his words sound devoid of any emotional participation.

The range of acceptable behavior for males in distress goes from acting as if nothing out of ordinary took place, as in the excerpt above, to putting on a performance that conveys concern without explicitly articulating it (see infra). Although male patients can verbalize the severity of symptoms in unambiguous terms, sufferance cannot be performed through bodily gestures without transgressing dominant gender norms. In my fieldwork, I have encountered very few situations of non-Roma men conspicuously displaying pain during the admission interview. Without exception, nurses and clerks have appreciated their performance to be genuine and refrained from conducting any explicit credibility check.[20]

Female patients encounter peculiar obstacles in passing as genuine sufferers. Triage workers often interpret their condition through the lens of secondary gain. By projecting distress, female patients can look for, and receive, attention, affection, and care from significant others and friends, as the clerk in the following field note suggests:

A young woman approaches the triage looking disoriented, weak, and unable to walk without being supported by two men, one on each side. The clerk [Aspazia] anticipates the diagnostic and shares with me the presumed reason for the presentation: "Calcium drop. When you want to impress a man, that's what you do." (Field note, City)

At the same time, triage workers seem to regard females as more inclined than males to engage in emotion-expressive behavior. Although none of the participants verbalized this stereotype, it emerged from their patterned response to female patients' verbal and non-verbal manifestations of distress, as the excerpts above indicate.

In embodying distress, the patient's appearance and demeanor matter. Nevertheless, the space for negotiation is drastically limited by the tacit nature of the assessment and triage workers' understanding of the typical bodily manifestations of a "genuine emergency." Thus, conspicuous displays of distress tend to undermine patients' attempts to pass as credibly ill. Patients have more opportunities to actively engage in credibility work in the verbal exchanges with triage workers.

LIMITING THE VOICE OF THE LIFEWORLD

The second dimension of the credibility work performed at the ED focuses on the narrative construction of the case by the patient. As mentioned earlier, triage workers regard the acute illness as an experience that depletes sufferers of energy and temporarily impairs their social functioning. Therefore, a tacit underlying assumption informing the initial assessment at the triage is that patients become absorbed by their illness and show little concern for anything else. This assumption translates into the expectation that during the admission interview patients are largely reactive, suppress or limit considerably the talk about issues without direct clinical significance, and lack the means to defend themselves if challenged.[21]

These expectations become obvious when they are blatantly transgressed, as in the following case recalled by a clerk at City:

> CLERK ZINA: There was something. I was trying to get more information about the identity of the patient. She said she had a sore throat and couldn't talk. She was accompanied by someone. I didn't understand well the street name, and I asked her "tell me again the street so that I put it into the database." And at that point she became verbally aggressive, she began shouting, and then I told her, "it means your throat is not that sore if you can shout and don't want to repeat. I feel sorry for not knowing where you live." (Interview, City)

While this case is extreme, triage workers maintain a skeptical stance toward patients who introduce during the admission interview "the voice of the life-world"[22] by talking about personal life, meanings given to illness, pressing concerns, or other things without direct clinical relevance. Patients talking parsimoniously, describing symptoms without any adornment, avoiding ingratiation maneuvers altogether, and reducing eye contact with the triage agent are more likely to pass as credibly ill as compared to those who actively engage in persuading efforts. The austere presentation of the case indicates that the concern of the patient lies outside the encounter itself. At the same time, the voluntary surrender to the will of hospital workers conveys a message of extreme vulnerability, which usually triggers a favorable reaction on their part.

Embodying distress and limiting the voice of the lifeworld stem from the same understanding of "genuine emergencies" as conditions that temporarily deplete the patient of energy, focus, and creativity. However, they differ with regards to the space allowed for individual maneuver because verbal conduct is subjected to looser surveillance than appearance and demeanor. Thus, patients have the chance to tactfully introduce the voice of the lifeworld into the conversation and, by doing so, assert worth or repair possible flaws. Successful attempts to manufacture worth take place reactively and are decoupled from any explicit demand for favorable treatment. For example, when an elderly female patient is asked about the time when her hand got swollen, she replies: "Right now, as I was walking my grandson, I observed [it]" (Field note, City). By mentioning her earlier activity, she lets the clerk know that she has a family and is actively involved in rearing her grandson. Thus, she presents herself as a devoted grandmother and a contributor to the family's well-being and, in a broader sense, to the society. The medically irrelevant utterance is introduced reactively into the conversation and does not trigger any opposition from the triage worker.

Another female patient, with breathing difficulties, takes advantage of a break in the admission interview to add, "In the morning, I was even able to sing, because I had a rehearsal with the children" (Field note, County). The statement is somewhat ambiguous: it does not make clear in what capacity she had the rehearsal, who were the children, and for what they were rehearsing. Nonetheless, this piece of information suffices to pass the idea that the woman is involved in the community and provides some service to local children. The voice of the lifeworld is introduced smoothly into the conversation and framed as a contextual information with potential clinical relevance.

Triage workers rarely confront patients who limit the voice of the lifeworld. When they do so, they tend to use the confrontation instrumentally, as a credibility check. If the patient does not retort, or does so in a weak way, this reinforces the belief of dealing with genuine physical distress. Patients who vocally defend their cause and volunteer unrequested information, on the other hand, tend to have the claims of being credibly ill invalidated. The following excerpt comes from an admission interview taking place at County. The source of contention is the interpretation of the medical problems faced by the patient, a seventy-year-old female. She and her family connect the presumed high blood pressure, dizziness, and headache with the previous experience of stroke, whereas the triage nurse suggests that the problem is most likely psychosomatic and, therefore, a poor candidate for emergency service. Her tentative assessment seems to incorporate knowledge about the patient's medical history, which includes several hospitalizations in a psychiatric facility, and her general appearance and demeanor, which are judged against typical manifestations of stroke:

NURSE: WHAT HAPPENED TO YOU, MA'AM? What happened to you? [To me: "I asked her to come here[23] because I want to see how she walks." The lady walks slowly to the triage desk, supported by her companions. The nurse comments: "She doesn't lose her balance."]

PATIENT: I have high blood pressure.

NURSE: How do you know you have high blood pressure?

PATIENT: I've checked it with a monitor.

NURSE: The monitor may not be working well.

PATIENT: And I feel sick.

NURSE: In what ways do you feel sick?

[Four lines omitted]

PATIENT: I'm dizzy, and my head is bursting, and here it's heating up, and my brain is reeling.

[Five lines omitted.]

PATIENT: I've climbed the walls.

NURSE: How can you climb the walls? If I try to climb the walls, I fall down. I cannot get up the walls like that, I simply cannot. (Audio-recorded interaction, County)

This excerpt shows that, albeit analytically distinct, the two dimensions of credibility work discussed so far are often interwoven in the initial assessment of the case. The acts of sitting down and walking steadily are inconsistent with the expected demeanor of a patient in severe distress. By giving clear and coherent answers, describing the symptoms in vivid terms, and taking a proactive stance once during the conversation, the patient further distances herself from staff's ideal-typical representation of a "genuine emergency." This becomes evident when the nurse takes her idiom of distress literally. Later, she proposes redirecting the lady to a psychiatric facility, which she and her family firmly refuse.

CONVEYING NARRATIVE FRANKNESS

Many presentations fail to meet the criteria for inclusion in the emic category "genuine emergency" for various reasons: the problem is either chronic or has been ongoing for more than twenty-four hours; the pain or distress is at a bearable level; or symptoms are trivial, such as coughing or strep throat. The family doctor could have handled such cases. Although misuse of the emergency service is fiercely rebuked, not all inappropriate presentations are deemed morally unjustified. As discussed in chapter 2, nurses and clerks know that the current organization of primary care fails many bona fide users because scheduling appointments is fraught with difficulties, and the diagnosis pathway is long, tedious, and often expensive:

NURSE ANDRA: So, you call the family doctor, let him know that you have a problem, and he schedules an appointment for next week. You go there that day, and he orders some analysis or an X-ray or refers you to a specialist. You go there and schedule another appointment for the next week or even the next month [. . .] Next month, you get the analyses done, and with the medical letter, you go back to the family doctor who sets yet another appointment. This means that for a medical problem, you have to wait for at least a couple of months to get a prescription. (Interview, County)

As a rule, patients who are not immediately responsible for their condition and cannot access primary care for reasons beyond themselves (e.g., because family doctors are either unavailable or fully booked) escape disciplining actions altogether. The exemption from blame is typically not granted to patients who willingly bypass the family doctor to cut costs and time or get better service. Lack of insurance coverage is particularly rejected as a valid ground for presentation because it is equated with disreputable personal characteristics, such as laziness.

While triage workers attend to the circumstances of the presentation, they are aware that patients have strong incentives to engage in dishonest performances. To uncover false claims, they routinely subject patients to credibility checks during the admission interview:

CLERK CRINA: They say they have insurance, but I don't believe they have insurance, I think they lie, I've found them lying very often.

RESEARCHER: How?

CLERK CRINA: Well, I was asking: do you have a family doctor? Yes. What's the name of your family doctor? They threw up a name. Oh, I said, I know that one, let me give them a call. No, no, don't call, I didn't go there because I'm uninsured, I don't work, whatever. Yes, and sometimes when you ask them about the doctors, where is their office, especially those from outside [City], they start saying oh, we have no insurance, we have no family doctor, we have no job, but at the beginning, when you were writing their file, they said they had insurance, they had an occupation. (Interview, City)

Credibility is achieved when the triage agent has no means to prove, or strong reasons to suspect, deceit. Since objective proofs to substantiate the claims regarding the duration of the illness or the attempts to visit a family doctor are difficult, if not impossible, to produce, credibility work revolves around "narrative frankness," the ability to provide an account that is coherent, consistent, and compatible with staff's expectations of responsible use of the service.

The following extracts present two presentations taking place at County on the same day and handled by the same triage nurse. In the first case, the patient (Daniel) is an elder male accompanied by his niece:

PATIENT: For two days, I've felt chest pain. Yesterday it got worse.

NURSE: Yesterday? How about the family doctor?

PATIENT: The family doctor is not available.

NURSE: What's her name?

PATIENT: Dr. [name].

NURSE: And isn't her office open?

COMPANION: She has left to attend a symposium, that's what her nurse told me. She will only be back after 6 [p.m.]. (Field note, County)

The second case is that of Ruxandra, a thirty-year-old single mother:

PATIENT: Good afternoon! I feel leg pain, and I'd like to be seen by someone at the orthopedics. [Description of the onset of pain]

NURSE: Why didn't you go to the family doctor? He could have given you a referral letter for the polyclinic.

PATIENT: I thought it's better to come here.

NURSE: Excuse me?

PATIENT: I thought it's fine, it's no problem, but now the pain got unbearable. And there's no one at the doctor's office now.

NURSE: [Are you] employed?

PATIENT: No, I get alimony.

NURSE: So, you had plenty of time to see the doctor.

PATIENT: When you have a child, you have no time for anything else. Especially if you're alone.

NURSE: Sure. (Field note, County)

In terms of content, the presentations are similar—the health problems occurred several days earlier but became distressing over the previous twenty-four hours and consulting the family doctor was practically impossible for reasons independent of the patients. However, the nurse only accepts the first presentation as credible. In their day-to-day practice, triage workers are more inclined to accept the symptom claimed by Ruxandra ("leg pain") as a valid reason for presentation. "Chest pain," the symptom that brought Daniel to the ED, triggers suspicion because it can indicate a variety of anxiety-related problems that fall outside the professional jurisdiction of emergency medicine, and, at the same time, is frequently contrived by individuals who want to gain speedy access to examination by a physician. Therefore, an assessment based solely on the stated symptom would have cast doubt over Daniel's credibility rather than Ruxandra's.

The explanation for the different outcomes is to be found in the narrative frankness of the two accounts. The nurse subjects both patients to questions about the reasons for bypassing the primary care physician and uses credibility checks to establish the plausibility of patients' accounts. In Daniel's case, she questions him about the doctor's name and the reasons for his unavailability, whereas with Ruxandra, she asks about her employment status. Daniel and his niece provide straightforward and simple answers spontaneously, which makes their story believable in the absence of factual evidence that could discredit it. Ruxandra, on the other hand, explains the practical impossibility of attending the family doctor only after the nurse reacts to her initial response ("I thought it's better to come here") with disapproval. The rectification of statements raises a red flag about the honesty of the account. This triggers another question from the triage nurse. Because the patient's stated preference for the emergency service is consistent with the idea of making an appearance by reason of convenience, she asks about work status to test the veracity of this possibility. Ruxandra's unemployment fuels the suspicion and damages the credibility of her version of the events.

The two cases indicate that in the assessment of credibility, it matters not only what patients say, but also how the relevant information emerges during the interaction. Narrative frankness is achieved when patients volunteer information, present the situation in a simple, straightforward manner, and do not recede from the initial statements. Conversely, the reactive disclosure of information, the use of ambiguous words, and the rectification of statements erode credibility even though the information is, in itself, plausible.

TRUSTWORTHINESS AND CREDIBILITY

There are two categories of patients typified as prone to engage in deceitful conduct, namely the Roma and the social cases: "[The Roma] feign, they feign a lot, they act a lot—fabricated pains, imaginary illnesses, affections they actually don't have, and so on" (Interview Nurse Vera, County). Also, there are some health complaints that nurses and clerks meet with suspicion, including the invisible, potentially factitious, symptoms. In these cases, the credibility assessment is interwoven with and influenced by the assessment of the patient's trustworthiness, and the interactional framing of the health concern by the patient is of peculiar importance. The following excerpt presents the admission interview of Daria, a middle-aged Roma woman who tries to convince the triage nurse at County that she experiences a skin problem for which there is no direct physical evidence:

PATIENT: My hand got swollen.

NURSE: It got swollen like this, by itself? Traumatized, hit?

PATIENT: No. I have a rash.

NURSE: What?

PATIENT: I have a rash and my fingers get numb.

[The nurse examines her hand]

NURSE: But there's nothing there. Did you wash with something, did you use chlorine?

PATIENT: No, because I have a [washing] machine.

NURSE: Ok, I thought you might have used something.

PATIENT: I have a bad rash.

NURSE: Where? Because I see nothing there.

PATIENT: It hurts.

NURSE: It hurts, or it itches?

PATIENT: It hurts really badly.

NURSE: IT EITHER HURTS OR ITCHES on that place?

PATIENT: It itches, and it also hurts really badly, madam.

NURSE: You will take a seat and wait. (Audio-recorded conversation, County)

While in the cases of Daniel and Ruxandra the nurse uses credibility checks to infer reasonableness, in this interaction her main concern lies in establishing the legitimacy of the claim for emergency care. The encounter takes only fifty-nine seconds, an unusually short time for situations of disputed credibility. It consists of a rapid succession of relatively short utterances from both participants. The turn-taking proceeds smoothly, with little overlap and a brief pause during which the triage nurse inspects visually and tactilely the hand of the patient.

Ethnicity surfaces in the conversation in a roundabout way, through thinly veiled assumptions about the patient and her condition. As it is often the case in interaction with members of stigmatized groups, the occurrence of the problem is a matter of particular interest because it conveys information not only about the nature and the gravity of the condition but also about the person's degree of fit into a pre-defined type. The framing of the initial question is, hence, not innocuous. While non-Roma patients with similar problems are asked in a neutral way about the origin of the problem (e.g., "How come?"/"How did it happen?"), in Daria's case the triage nurse advances potential explanations that are consistent with the assumptions of negligence ("traumatized") and violence ("hit") inherent to the staff-devised "Roma" type. The patient invokes the existence of another symptom (the skin rash), which reinforces the initial presentation of the health problem as unconnected to personal actions and shifts the flow of the conversation.

Despite her initial reaction of surprise, the triage nurse appears to accept the swollen hand as something that just happened and exempt Daria from responsibility for the situation. Although she contemplates the exposure to harmful chemicals as a way of making sense of what caused the skin problems, this has nothing to do with assigning the patient to a blameworthy category since triage agents consider events of this sort as fortuitous. The expectation of doing laundry by hand is not necessarily related to the ethnicity of the patient. However, Daria takes advantage of the question to provide supplementary information that further sets her apart from Roma's stereotypical representation as poor, traditional, and uncivilized. The possession of a washing machine buttresses the claim of having had no direct contact with chlorine detergent, but it also subtly introduces an element of respectability into the conversation. Remarkably, this is the only departure from transactional talk in the entire admission interview.

By departing from the "Roma" type, Daria establishes herself as a trustworthy interlocutor and shifts the nurse's attention from the moral profile of the patient to the medically relevant concern. This is not enough to elicit belief but creates the conditions of possibility for engaging in credibility work during the case presentation. Daria's coherent story, communicated through laconic utterances in an assertive yet polite way, can be considered as a successful presentation of the case in this respect: the nurse does not challenge her account despite repeating the lack of any visual or tactile evidence for the skin rash, does not employ any further credibility checks, and treats the problem as if it were real.

The success of the interaction is largely due to Daria's skillful avoidance of the voice of the lifeworld. By keeping the story simple and focusing on the distressing symptoms, she conveys a sense of genuine preoccupation with the health problem. As shown earlier, patients who use excessive casual talk, dramatize symptoms, and introduce the problem in vivid detail often trigger suspicion. As compared to them, Daria begins by stating symptoms matter of factually ("My hand got swollen"; "I have a rash"), and only as the interview progresses, she passes from objective to subjective, talking about the experience of feeling ill. Even though there is a gradual increase in complexity, it is communicated succinctly ("bad rash," "it hurts really badly").

During triage encounters, patients with invisible symptoms face the practical difficulty of bringing forth issues of personal concern and stressing the salience of the problem without challenging the format of the admission interview and, thus, defying the authority of the triage agent. Volunteering unrequested information risks compromising the power balance between interactants if it is not performed competently. Daria, however, manages to impose her agenda tactfully twice: first, she turns the focus of examination from the origin of the skin rash which makes the object of the previous exchanges to the experience of distress; and second, her penultimate response focuses on the intensity of pain instead of the type of symptom, which interests the nurse. In the first case, she takes advantage of the end of a sequence of talk (and the only instance in which the nurse does not use the turn-taking to ask another question) to tell what she regards as important. In the second case, she insinuates the reference to the intensity of pain in answering a question, but it does so by prolonging her words in a way that makes clear the salience of the issue. The nurse resists this attempt to change the topic by turning back to the previous question. This time, she speaks in a higher pitch and frames the question as close-ended ("It either hurts or itches?"); these changes indicate the refusal to accept the surplus information and the desire to maintain the leading position in the interaction. Daria's final reply eliminates the ambiguity of her previous utterance by making explicit that she experiences both pain and itching, reiterates the magnitude of the symptoms, and repairs the transgression of the power structure by using the honorific "Madam," for the first and only time in the encounter, to conclude the statement. In doing so, she reaches an equilibrium between compliance and assertiveness, making her point clear despite the nurse's indirect objection and avoiding being reprimanded.

Credibility is achieved when the triage agent has no means to prove, or strong reasons to suspect, deceit. There is no clear indication in the interaction itself whether Daria succeeds in passing the credibility test, but the unfolding of the interview reveals the sudden passage from a sequence of talk in which the nurse confronts the patient to one dominated by ambiguity. This corresponds to a shift from confrontational to bureaucratic format, which suggests that the patient's interactional efforts paid off.[24]

Daria's case provides various insights into the collaborative accomplishment of credibility in triage interactions. Trustworthiness represents a precondition of credibility.[25] Patients belonging to categories to which triage agents attribute the assumption of dishonesty (such as Roma and social cases) need to establish themselves as trustworthy first, an intermediary step that does not apply to other social groups. The most efficient way to manufacture trustworthiness is to provide elements that do not fit into the ideal type of the stigmatized category. In Daria's case, the separation maneuvers consist in dismissing negligence and violence as potential explanations for the swollen hand; suggesting a decent lifestyle through the reference to owning a washing machine; and alternating assertiveness with compliance in talk, a strategy that in the Romanian hospitals where I conducted fieldwork is characteristic to middle-class patients. In general, Roma patients refer to living ordinary lives, having jobs, attending educational programs or encouraging their children to do so; the elderly insist on being active despite retirement; the homeless emphasize a misfortune that altered their life course; the mildly inebriated emphasize the accidental nature of their intoxication, and the urban poor stress out their commitment to the norms of decency.

Patients who are unable to pass as trustworthy have low chances to persuade nurses that what they say is correct, and this is particularly so when they claim to experience severe distress. However, the existence of visible bodily signs of illness compensates for the purported faulty character of the individual, which explains why cases triage agents regard as legitimate are handled accordingly irrespective of patient's social worth. A strategy that works for persons typified of untrustworthy who attempt to establish credibility is to provide medical documents that buttress their accounts. For instance, prior validation of the claim to illness by a physician alleviates nurses' and clerks' suspicion even if the two events are temporarily separated, or the conditions are not identical. Similarly, bringing a bag containing the current medication and showing it to the triage workers during the interview dispels doubt much more efficiently than merely mentioning drug names in the case of persons considered unreliable by reason of little formal education or reduced mental capacity.

So far, I have examined the credibility work in the two settings without mentioning the differences that exist between them. The peculiar triage arrangements at City and the clerks' lack of or incomplete nursing training make them adopt a more defensive approach to the initial assessment of patients. This happens even though the general orientation to patients and the reluctance to take their statements and performance of distress at face value are by no means different from those of nurses at County. Clerk Zina summarizes the logic underlying the defensive approach:

CLERK ZINA: Some [patients] learned that trick and they come here telling "I've got chest pain." [. . .] And then, to rule out the worst-case scenario,[26] you let her in to a room where she occupies a bed unnecessarily. And there are cases in which, for any chest pain, you let your colleagues from the ED room know [about the case] and ask them to do an ECG to rule out the worst thing, a heart attack.[27] (Interview, City)

Clerks at City are also less inclined than their counterparts at County to engage in vigorous confrontations with patients to determine the veracity or plausibility of their claims. After some admission interviews, they shared with me, either directly or through knowing smiles and nods, their disbelief in patients' accounts. However, as the first-come-first-served admission principle renders the credibility assessment less practically relevant, clerks are more inclined to let suspicious presentations go.

CREDIBILITY WORK AND MORAL EVALUATION

As the cases discussed in this chapter suggests, the assessment of credibility is deeply connected to moral evaluation. Nurses and clerks use patients' appearance, actions, and interactional demeanor to infer the nature and severity of the medical condition and spot urgent, potentially life-threatening cases. At the same time, they often use credibility checks to find inconsistencies in patients' self- and case-presentations, which would disprove their explicit or implicit claims to get fast-track access to the ED. Credibility work is, thus, instrumental to policing the borders of proper use of the emergency service. As street-level bureaucrats whose formal gatekeeping role has been restricted by current policies, nurses and clerks at both EDs engage in credibility work to exert discretion in the handling of patients. The partial recognition of the sixth sense as a legitimate resource in the initial assessment of cases facilitates this arrangement as it renders the informal considerations procedurally accountable.

The analysis of credibility work reveals patients' active contribution to the initial assessment. While triage workers' criteria for making sense of cases are relatively fixed, the practical categorization of patients is an ongoing process that is largely influenced by their interactional prowess. Patients who embody distress by aligning their appearance and demeanor to triage workers' understanding of a "genuine emergency" have more chances to pass as legitimate users than those who exaggerate their distress.[28] Patients with trivial symptoms whose orientation to what constitutes an emergency coincides with that of the staff have more chances to get admitted without sanctions. However, as compared to the UK hospital studied by Alexandra Hillman, the acceptance of illegitimate patients is further conditioned by the ability to justify the inability to get the needed services elsewhere.[29] Finally, patients who tactfully introduce into the flow of the interaction favorable information about themselves are less likely to be challenged during the encounter or sanctioned thereafter. These findings indicate that interactional prowess is a salient resource for patients, and a hitherto insufficiently examined contributor to the moral evaluation process.

The next chapter extends the analysis of patients' active role in negotiating access to the ED by examining their strategies of manufacturing responsibility and worth during the triage admission interview.

NOTES

1. The national insurance card would be implemented only in 2015. At the time of fieldwork, nurses and clerks had to rely on patients' statements to enter the insurance status, a required piece of information, into the hospital's electronic system.

2. "Atrocity stories" are interactional devices through which members of a social group account for and make sense of their (often negative and dramatic) experiences with others. Robert Dingwall, "'Atrocity Stories' and Professional Relationships," *Sociology of Work and Occupations* 4, no. 4: 371–96. Nurses rely on atrocity stories to set themselves apart from the other occupational groups they work with (Davina Allen, "Narrating Nursing Jurisdiction: 'Atrocity Stories' and 'Boundary-Work,'" *Symbolic Interaction* 24, no. 1: 75–103; Matthew J. Cousineau, "Accomplishing Profession through Self-Mockery," *Symbolic Interaction* 39, no. 2: 213–28.) and to morally classify patients (Julius A. Roth, "Some Contingencies of the Moral Evaluation and Control of Clientele: The Case of the Hospital Emergency Service," *American Journal of Sociology* 77, no. 5: 839–56; Sarah Li and Anne Arber, "The Construction of Troubled and Credible Patients: A Study of Emotion Talk in Palliative Care Settings," *Qualitative Health Research* 16, no. 1: 27–46).

3. In this respect, the "deceiving patient" is a sub-category of the broad "problem patient" category discussed in the previous chapter.

4. As mentioned in the introductory chapter, the perceived enmity of medical authorities, patients, and the media is the backdrop against which nurses and clerks conduct their day-to-day work.

5. Nicholas Dodier and Agnès Camus, "Openness and Specialisation: Dealing with Patients in a Hospital Emergency Service," *Sociology of Health & Illness* 20, no. 4: 424.

6. Roger Jeffery, "Normal Rubbish: Deviant Patients in Casualty Departments," *Sociology of Health & Illness* 1, no. 1: 79.

7. James M. Mannon, "Defining and Treating 'Problem Patients' in a Hospital Emergency Room," *Medical Care* 14, no. 12: 1008.

8. Erving Goffman, "On Cooling the Mark Out: Some Aspects of Adaptation to Failure," in *The Goffman Reader*, ed. Charles Lemert and Anne Branaman (Oxford: Blackwell, 1997), 5.

9. Gordon, "Tenacious Assumptions in Western Medicine," 25.

10. Womack, *The Anthropology of Health and Healing*, 1972.

11. Winkelman, *Culture and Health: Applying Medical Anthropology*, 42.

12. Dodier, "Clinical Practice and Procedures in Occupational Medicine: A Study of the Framing of Individuals," 65.

13. Lori. A. Roscoe, Eric M. Eisenberg, and Colin Forde, "The Role of Patients' Stories in Emergency Medicine Triage," *Health Communication* 31, no. 9: 1.

14. The situation is similar in the Norwegian emergency service documented by Lars E.F. Johannessen "The Commensuration of Pain: How Nurses Transform Subjective Experience into Objective Numbers," *Social Science & Medicine* 233: 38–46, where nurses use their assessment of pain at the expense of patients' self-assessment, regarding the latter as less reliable.

15. David Hughes, "When Nurse Knows Best: Some Aspects of Nurse/Doctor Interaction in a Casualty Department.," *Sociology of Health and Illness* 10, no. 1: 13.

16. L. Sbaih, "Initial Assessment: Gaining Impressions and 'Normal Cases,'" *Accident and Emergency Nursing* 6, no. 2: 70–74.

17. The "sixth sense" has a semi-formal status. The National Protocol of Triage acknowledges it as a legitimate resource for assessing patients' condition. See Romanian Ministry of Health, "Ordinul Nr. 48/2009 Privind Aprobarea Protocolului Naţional de Triaj Al Pacienţilor Din Structurile Pentru Primirea Urgenţelor [Order 48/2009 Regarding the Approval of the National Protocol for the Triage of Patients in Emergency Units]" (2009). However, the Protocol restricts the use of experiential knowledge to upgrading the priority level of a patient whose condition may be more severe than the symptom and vitals suggest. Nurses at County appropriated and re-signified the concept, using it preponderantly to distinguish "genuine" emergencies from cases for which the immediate allocation of resources is deemed unnecessary. The ambiguous status of the "sixth sense" allows them to account for the differential handling of patients with apparently similar health problems.

18. Bernie Edwards and David Sines, "Passing the Audition—the Appraisal of Client Credibility and Assessment by Nurses at Triage," *Journal of Clinical Nursing* 17, no. 18: 2445–46.

19. Although Romania has become relatively equalitarian with regards to employment over the past century, this change did not translate into a radical transformation of the traditional gender regime. See Mălina Voicu and Paula Andreea Tufiş, "Trends in Gender Beliefs in Romania: 1993–2008," *Current Sociology* 60, no. 1: 61–80; Susan Gal and Gail Kligman, *The Politics of Gender After Socialism: A Comparative-Historical Essay* (Princeton, NJ: Princeton University Press, 2000); Alice Iancu et al., "Women's Social Exclusion and Feminisms: Living in Parallel Worlds? The Romanian Case," in *Gendering Post-Socialist Transition: Studies of Changing Gender Perspectives*, ed. Krasimira Daskalova et al. (Münster: LIT Verlag, 2012), 183–216. The representation of female patients as fragile, vulnerable, emotional, and unable or unwilling to exert self-control echoes traditional gender expectations and contributes in subtle ways to the inequity of access to emergency care.

20. The situation is different in the case of Roma males, whose expressive displays of pain tend to be met with skepticism and disapproval.

21. These expectations do not hold true for patients having or suspected to have medical conditions that impact their behavior, such as severe hypoglycemia, alcohol withdrawal, or stroke.

22. Elliot George Mishler, *The Discourse of Medicine: Dialectics of Medical Interviews* (Norwood, NJ: Ablex Publishing Corporation, 1984).

23. The patient is on a seat in the waiting room at the beginning of the interaction.

24. The examination did not end at the triage counter. Daria's presentation took place at a time when only one nurse was on shift at triage. Therefore, after filling in the registration forms, the nurse invited her to the adjacent room to perform the anamnesis and check vital signs, which is the standard procedure of admission. I have not attended that episode, but the nurse talked to me about it afterward. During the examination, she found out that a doctor had prescribed Daria a specific painkiller after another similar crisis. This piece of information changed completely the nurse's definition of the situation and assessment of credibility and legitimacy because the drug was very strong and was usually administered to patients in atrocious pain, including the terminally ill. After the admission interview, she told me that the initially suspected a minor skin problem, but then she considered the problem to be much more severe.

25. Under ordinary circumstances, the client's trustworthiness represents a precondition for the credibility of her account, yet it does not necessarily imply it. Nurses and clerks have serious reasons to adopt a cautious line: some patients try to work the system by presenting the case in very somber terms; others are overly concerned about very minor problems; still others lack the ability to properly verbalize what they experience.

26. *Ca să excluzi ce e mai rău.*

27. A few moments later, during the interview, Clerk Zina shares with me the case of a young female patient with seemingly trivial chest pain who had in fact a heart attack and almost lost her life due to the incorrect initial assessment. To her, and to other clerks at City, it is preferable to refer all potentially suspicious cases to the ED staff and perturb the functioning of the service rather than to put one single patient's life into jeopardy.

28. Johannessen, "The Commensuration of Pain: How Nurses Transform Subjective Experience into Objective Numbers."

29. It is unclear whether the more confrontational format of the assessment of reasonableness in Romanian EDs is a byproduct of the analytical framework or an actual occurrence.

Chapter 5

Manufacturing Responsibility and Worth

This chapter completes the discussion of the joint accomplishment of moral evaluation by examining how triage workers and patients negotiate reasonableness and worth during the admission interview. Nurses and clerks lead the assessment of patients' credibility as reporters of symptoms, and the subtle cues on which they rely often go undetected by ED users. Therefore, patients' self- and case-presentation strategies are less focused on the production of credibility than they are on asserting moral character. However, the patients' agency is constrained by the organization of the admission interview and the asymmetry of power between the interactants. Therefore, I begin this chapter by discussing the two interactional formats (bureaucratic and confrontational) that structure the verbal exchanges between patients and triage workers, showing how triage arrangements impact upon the structure and content of admission interviews. Then, I delve into the patients' moral boundary work by exploring their attempts to manufacture responsible use of the service and social worth.

INTERACTIONAL FORMATS

Unlike everyday conversations, interactions in institutional settings have a more rigid organization, being parceled out into sequences related to the tasks to be accomplished through the encounter.[1] Service sector interactions, albeit less structured than ceremonies and rituals, impose constraints on participants' dramaturgical maneuvers because of their orientation toward achieving specific goals.[2] It is therefore necessary to examine the social organization of triage encounters before proceeding to the analysis of patients' active role in manufacturing reasonableness and worth.

In a comparative study of pediatrician-patient encounters in Scotland and the United States, Philip M. Strong identified two models of interactional order, which he called the "bureaucratic format" and the "charity format."[3] The bureaucratic format, which "was standard in the NHS [British] consultations and common in the American consultations,"[4] posited an idealized representation of the patient's mother as "good [. . .], loving, honest, reliable, intelligent and caring, whatever she had actually done"[5] and affirmed this image during the interaction by discounting any evidence to the contrary. Encounters in the bureaucratic format were governed by the etiquette rules of concurrently saving one's face and protecting the other's face[6] and, as such, they tended to be amiable and polite. In the charity format, on the other hand, "the principle was reversed: the initial rule here being that every mother was now stupid, lazy, incompetent and unloving, unless she could prove otherwise."[7] Doctors scrupulously examined the mother for any potential fault and were eager to confront her on any purported wrongdoing. The charity format represented an anomaly in Strong's dataset, being used by only one American doctor. However, anecdotal and incidental evidence suggested that this format used to be widespread in the past with very poor patients and was still present in interactions with stigmatized ones,[8] which conferred this format theoretical meaningfulness.

The social organization of the interactions to which I have assisted during fieldwork resembles to a considerable extent the two formats advanced by Strong, but there are also a few notable differences. First, the format of the outpatient pediatric consultations examined by Strong depended upon the doctor's attitude toward the clientele. Doctors harboring favorable feelings toward users engaged in verbal exchanges with them that affirmed such a representation and protected the face of the interlocutor, whereas the doctor typifying clients as unworthy subjected them to "character work,"[9] a minute scrutiny of their moral profile aiming to unravel discreditable information. Although the two formats occurred in different social contexts,[10] the lack of internal variation based on the characteristics of the person suggests that the format of the encounter predates the encounter and influences its unfolding without being influenced by it. This situation differs significantly from what I have seen at the Romanian EDs where I have collected data. Despite some triage agents appearing to be more inclined than others to take belligerent stances toward patients, all nurses at County and clerks at City alternate in their day-to-day work the bureaucratic and the confrontational interactional frames. Moreover, what the patient says and does during the admission interview can make the triage worker switch the format of the conversation from bureaucratic to confrontational, and vice-versa. Therefore, my data agree with Paul Ten Have's[11] observation that while formats are predefined, the formatting process is fluid and co-constructed, even if inadvertently, by the participants.

Second, Strong argues that the typification of clients as good or bad, caring or negligent, hardworking or lazy shapes the format of the interaction. My findings support the idea that membership of a devalued category, be it based on moral or organizational criteria, increases the likelihood of facing contentious triage encounters. However, this tells only part of the story. In deciding how to approach patients, triage nurses and clerks attend not only to the moral profile of the patient, but also the circumstances of their presentation (symptoms, immediate responsibility for the health problem, and handling of the situation prior to making an appearance to the ED), and their conduct within the hospital and during the interview. For instance, Roma patients tend to attract intense "character work" in ordinary circumstances, but they escape moral profiling altogether if their health condition appears to be severe enough to grant them immediate access to medical care. High-status patients lacking any apparent disreputable characteristic, on the other hand, can be subjected to a confrontational encounter if the triage agent considers that the health problem does not meet the exigencies of a "real emergency," or the patient could have received adequate care from a different therapeutic agency. Ignoring such aspects leads to an oversimplified and misleading account of what is at stake and what is going on in the non-clinical evaluation of clientele.

This difference from Strong's model probably originates in the peculiarities of the institutional context in which I conducted the research. Unlike doctors, triage agents exert a gate-keeping role in the organization, making decisions on the admission and conditions of admission of would-be patients. They also assume the role of safeguarding the mission of the ED, by attempting to discourage inopportune visits and prevent the return of persons with trivial health concerns. The ED also includes a higher variety of situations as compared to outpatient pediatric consultations, which increases manifold the variables triage agents must take into consideration in handling patients.

With these caveats in mind, I will introduce a modified version of the two interactional formats developed by Philip M. Strong, which is consistent with the empirical data that I have gathered in the Romanian hospitals.

BUREAUCRATIC FORMAT

The bureaucratic format describes encounters that are oriented toward fulfilling the manifest functions of the interview admission: assessing the condition of the patient, assigning it to a priority class, and filling in various registration forms. The admission interview taking place in this format is brief and rigorously organized,[12] with the sequences of talk following closely the template of the patient file. As a rule, it takes around two minutes, which is the recommended maximum time for the initial assessment according to the guidelines in use.[13] The following excerpt provides a typical admission interview taking place in the bureaucratic format:

[The patient approaches the triage counter and hands the nurse his ID card.]

PATIENT: I want a referral to the orthopedics.

NURSE: What happened to you?

PATIENT: I fell down from a ladder.

NURSE: Where are you hurt?

PATIENT: My leg.

NURSE: Only the leg?

PATIENT: Yes.

NURSE: Nowhere else?

PATIENT: No.

NURSE: The left leg or the right one?

PATIENT: The left one.

NURSE: Is there any wound on the leg as well?

PATIENT: There is no wound, but there's (inaudible) and it starts bruising.

NURSE: [Are you] Employed? Retired?

PATIENT: Employed.

NURSE: Here's your ID. Have a seat, and we'll find an orderly to go with you to the orthopedics. (Audio-recorded conversation, County)

The bureaucratic format has a relatively standardized structure. It contains four sequences of talk dedicated to a topic of interest for the triage worker (the nature of the problem, the severity of the problem or extent of the injury, additional medically relevant information, and personal information about the patient) and a concluding part through which the triage worker gives instructions to the patient about what is going to happen next. The excerpt above contains each of the five sequences.[14] The nurse begins by asking the neutral question "what happened to you,"[15] which prompts the patient to talk about the nature and origin of the health concern. Four of the following five turns focus on determining the severity of the problem, with one turn collecting additional information (the affected leg). The question about employment status is often used as a proxy for health insurance status, because all formally employed people and pensioners are covered.[16] The final line marks the end of the admission interview and gives the patient information about what is going to happen next.

The ordering of the talk sequences tends to be relatively stable, except for the one pertaining to the social characteristics of the patient. Usually, the nurse or clerk asks for the ID card either after the conclusion of the first sequence of talk, the one related to the nature of the case, or after establishing that the case is severe enough to qualify as an emergency. Some patients, as in the excerpt above, pass their identification document to the nurse or clerk before or shortly after beginning the interview. In this case, personal information that cannot be retrieved from the ID, such as insurance status, is asked toward the end of the conversation.

Encounters taking place in the bureaucratic format are dominated by transactional talk,[17] and tend to be relatively austere, distant, and impersonal. All transactions are not the same, however, and occasionally nurses and clerks display overt sympathy toward patients and attempt to boost their morale during interaction.[18] While the bureaucratic format does not exclude amicableness, it does not require it either. This represents a clear distinction from the type described by Strong, in which doctors engaged in friendly interactions with their clients and actively pursued "cosmetic face-work."[19] It is consistent, however, with the "indifference" of healthcare practitioner toward patients during the socialist time,[20] which suggests a possible cultural explanation for the deviation from the original model.

CONFRONTATIONAL FORMAT

I refer to the second interactional format encountered in the Romanian EDs as "confrontational" rather than "charity" for accuracy reasons. Strong's term carries the underlying assumption that this format applies exclusively to persons negatively typified by healthcare actors based on some social characteristics, such as poverty. As I mentioned earlier, at City and County this peculiar organization of the interaction applies to patients belonging to stigmatized categories under ordinary circumstances, but it is also common with patients lacking obvious discreditable characteristics if the triage agent suspects foul play under the guise of insincere statements and incorrect use of the service. Each interview admission under this format contains a sequence of controversy, for the resolution of which the triage agent confronts the patient. For these reasons, I consider "confrontational format" to be a more appropriate label for the interactional order that deviates from the tenets of strictly bureaucratic encounters.

The confrontational format is oriented toward accomplishing the latent functions of the admission interview: identifying presentations that do not meet the perceived mission of the emergency service and sanctioning users making these presentations, socializing patients with regards to the pathway to healthcare, and affirming the dominant values and social norms by challenging patients considered to be morally undeserving of care.[21] Therefore, the overwhelming majority of interactions dealing with the non-clinical evaluation of patients occur in this format.

Despite the clear analytical separation between them, the two formats share some structural and expressive characteristics. All confrontational encounters necessarily include the five sequences of the bureaucratic format, because they are practically relevant for medical and administrative purposes. In addition, they also contain one or more sequences of talk concerning controversial aspects of the case or disreputable characteristics of the patient. The structural resemblance facilitates the shift from one template to the other during an interview, and it is by no means exceptional for a conversation to begin in the bureaucratic format only to slip into the confrontational one as soon as the patient makes a conversational faux pas and reveals some discreditable information, or for a confrontational encounter to turn into a bureaucratic one after participants conclude the controversial sequence by reaching surface agreement.

The confrontational format does not have a predefined style of communication. Encounters in which the triage agents check the patient to make sure that the characteristics of the case conform to their organizational concerns and who receive satisfactory answers tend to adopt the impersonal style of the bureaucratic format. In situations of this sort, the only difference between the two models lies in the structure of the interaction. Encounters in which nurses and clerks spot elements that do not match their expectation often take more personal expressive forms, ranging from insinuations to overt admonishment. There are also situations in which triage agents find typical situations of incorrect use of the service. Some of them end up as "status degradation ceremonies,"[22] through which undesirable conduct and the presumed motives leading to it are openly exposed to an audience constituted by staff members and persons in the waiting room. On such exemplary occasions, triage workers not only expose the violations of organizational values and norms, but also strip away patients' sense of dignity through contemptuous remarks, mimicking, ironical reiteration of grammatically incorrect statements, embarrassing comments, accusations of various sorts, allusions to possible insanity, and other similar rhetorical maneuvers.

The protean nature of the confrontational format makes it impossible to identify a paradigmatic example. Nonetheless, since this is the format of choice for conducting the non-clinical assessment of patients, I present in this chapter numerous examples of confrontational encounters, ranging from impersonal and morally neutral questioning to status degradation ceremonies.

DIFFERENCES BETWEEN COUNTY AND CITY

I have shown in the previous chapters that triage workers in both hospitals hold very similar views about the mission of the emergency service and the criteria for assessing patients' degree of conformation to it. With few exceptions, they also typify users along the same lines. Given these resemblances, it makes sense to expect that nurses at County and clerks at City organize the admission interviews the same way.

Indeed, the bureaucratic and confrontational formats are common in both settings. However, an important difference occurs when it comes to the prevalence of each format. Since this did not constitute an issue of interest for me at the moment of conducting fieldwork, I have focused my field notes on encounters with potential relevance for the non-clinical evaluation of patients, that is to say encounters taking place in the confrontational format. Consequently, I have ignored many encounters whose exclusive concern was with the manifest function of triage assessment, so that I do not have any evidence on the statistical distribution of the two interactional formats at each hospital. Based on my recollections, I roughly approximate that controversial encounters make about three quarters of the interactions at County and only about one third of the interactions at City. While these figures might not be perfectly accurate, it is beyond doubt that the bureaucratic format prevails at City and is more scarcely used at County.

A potential explanation for this disparity might be looked for in the different situations encountered at the two EDs. To put it otherwise, the preference for bureaucratic format at City could be due to fewer presentations violating clerks' expectations about responsible use of the service and to fewer patients exhibiting disreputable traits. This is manifestly not the case, however, since the profile of the clientele and the reasons for presentations are remarkably similar in both EDs.

The difference lies in triage agents' approach of undesirable patients and cases rather than in the uneven distribution of such situations: while nurses at County are adamant in challenging any single transgression of organizational norms, clerks at City only selectively do so. I have encountered numerous interactions organized in the bureaucratic format at the end of which clerks talked to me at length about what was wrong with the patient or the case. In some cases, they frankly ventured their frustration:

CLERK ASPAZIA: The last comer kicks up a fuss,[23] but he's been like that [i.e., sick] since Saturday, and today is Monday. (Field note, City)

Even when they challenge patients, clerks at City tend to adopt less harsh stances toward patients as compared to their counterparts at County. For instance, triage clerks mention the family doctor to convey the idea that the visit is inappropriate, but rarely pursue any investigation of the reasons for bypassing the primary sector provider. Despite talking about patients as unreliable, they usually avoid testing the credibility during the admission interview. Clerks refrain from overtly accusing the patient of making inopportune visits as well, except for the rare occasions when the patient adopts a quarrelsome line from the very beginning.

The avoidance of harsh contention is a local norm of utmost importance for understanding the practical accomplishment of non-clinical evaluation. In the final chapter of the book, I will discuss a possible explanation for the reluctance of clerks at City to vigorously confront patients who do not meet their expectations. For the purpose of this chapter, it suffices to note the existence of this difference. In the following sections, I examine the interactional negotiation of responsible use and social worth. Since the non-clinical evaluation appears mostly in the confrontational format, the relevant examples that I have chosen come predominantly from this type of interaction.

DOING RESPONSIBLE USE

Triage nurses and clerks attend to the legitimacy of the case and the reasonableness of the visit and have some background expectations regarding the patients considered as problematic. As mentioned in chapter 3, they assume that "drunkards" make legitimate but unreasonable visits, while the "occasionally drunk" fare high in terms of both legitimacy and reasonableness; the Roma and the migrants fail to meet both criteria; and the very elderly are inclined to make illegitimate presentations to the ED. Albeit analytically distinct, the two criteria are to a certain extent complementary: legitimacy refers to the staff-devised mission of providing care to "real emergencies" only, whereas reasonableness comprises a set of acceptable exceptions from this rule. The two issues are often inseparable in patients' presentation of case.[24] For these reasons, I treat them here as part of the same preoccupation with what Alexandra Hillman called "morally responsible service use."[25] The constant comparison of patients' interactional maneuvers reveals two strategies for manufacturing responsible use of the ED: accepting the staff-devised mission of the emergency service and averting responsibility for the health problem.

ACCEPTING THE MISSION OF THE ED

Patients whose case presentation displays an understanding of the pathway in case of illness that is consistent with the staff-devised mission of the emergency service are more likely than the others to pass as responsible users. This is even more so if legitimacy and reasonableness are constructed by the patient without any prompt from the triage agent, as in the excerpt below:

> PATIENT: I fell down and I talked to the [family] doctor, but he is on leave, and he told me there was nothing he could do [to help me], and it hurts me so much here and here [the patient points with her hands to the area around the abdomen and the ribs], I can hardly stand it. (Field note, City)

In this case, the patient claims to experience unbearable pain following a fall, a condition that, if accepted as credible, suffices to grant the patient admission without any reprimand. The patient also adds that it was not her intention to come to the ED but trying to reach the family doctor had proven impossible due to circumstances independent of herself. She gives more details about her efforts to see the general practitioner, and his reaction over the phone. Through this brief statement, the patient manages to convince the clerk that the case meets the criteria of legitimacy and reasonableness.

Another typical way of asserting responsible use is to make explicit the reluctance to come to the ED, and the pressure from concerned family members, coworkers, or friends:

> PATIENT: I didn't want to come, but I couldn't stand the pain. My daughter kept telling me "Go, father, go." (Field note, City)

This very brief, unprompted statement contains in a nutshell the strategies many patients use to make a case for admission. The patient, a Roma male who was sixty-one years old and experiencing backache and chest pain, conveys a sense of urgency both directly, through what he says ("I couldn't stand the pain") and indirectly, through the repeated plea of his daughter to make an appearance to the ED. At the same time, his initial reluctance to come is consistent with staff's expectation that the emergency service should only be used for acute problems that have an urgency. In this case, the unbearable pain justified the decision to bypass the general practitioners and come to the hospital. Moreover, he also engages in the strategy of manufacturing worth, which will be discussed later in this chapter, by mentioning the family status and the strong affective ties with his daughter. Notwithstanding these considerations, his presentation would have most likely triggered suspicion at County because the claim of excruciating pain is inconsistent with the disposition to volunteer information and because the patient belongs to a group typified as unreliable. However, the clerk admits him without switching to a confrontational format and further questioning the patient.

Some people, most of them particularly companions of very elderly patients, allude to the mission of the service while providing an explanation for failing to meet the legitimacy and/or reasonableness criteria. This renders the triage workers' moralizing discourse unnecessary, since companions already know and openly acknowledge that the presentation to the ED is problematic. Moreover, the vulnerability and social worth of the very elderly preclude to a certain extent the moralizing discourse. The following excerpt illustrates such an approach:

> COMPANION: Good afternoon. We came here with Grandpa. He's not a great emergency; he has some foot wounds.
>
> CLERK: Does he have diabetes?
>
> COMPANION: We don't know that.
>
> CLERK: How did he get them [the wounds]?
>
> COMPANION: I don't know; he got them over time. He didn't tell us anything, and now we didn't even go to the family doctor. So, we bought him N. [an ointment].
>
> CLERK: What can N. do for such craters?
>
> COMPANION: Maybe you order for us some tests.
>
> CLERK: I send you to the surgery [room]; they will order the tests for you. (Field note, City)

The companion, a middle-aged male, begins by saying that the case does not constitute "a great emergency." The statement minimizes the severity of the condition and implicitly conveys the idea that the ED is designed for dealing with severe health problems. However, the patient is in a precarious situation, with deep wounds visible on his left foot. The companion also brings forth the issue of not going to the family doctor, which suggests some familiarity with triage workers' orientation to cases. By disclosing this piece of unfavorable information, the companion presents himself as an honest, mature, and responsible person. After the admission interview ends, he lets the clerk know that he rushed to the hospital as soon as he found out the problem. This makes the decision to not seek care at the family doctor's office less reproachable.

Failing to recognize the mission of the emergency service during the interview usually triggers moralizing discourses. The attempts to justify the presentation by reference to some sort of personal vulnerability, especially poverty, are only rarely successful, as the two excerpts below indicate:

PATIENT: I come from [a different county]. I have spine problem. It hurts me so much that in the morning I could barely get up from bed. I would like to get an X-ray.

NURSE: X-rays are done when the doctor asks for them, not when the patient does. Don't you have a family doctor?

PATIENT: I do, but I live in [village in a nearby county].

NURSE: What does it mean that you live in [village]? Isn't there any family doctor?

PATIENT: There is, but if I go there, it costs me to do it, to go back. I would rather pay for it here.

NURSE: Well, you should not have come here to begin with. I will register you, but you should know that you will have to wait until afternoon.

PATIENT: We wait. (Field note, County)

NURSE: What happened?

PATIENT: I have tonsillitis. For two weeks, I've kept taking antibiotics, and it's still not over yet.

NURSE: What is the emergency here?

PATIENT: Well, I'm uninsured, and instead of paying 50 lei,[26] I decided to come here.

NURSE: That's not an emergency.

PATIENT: If I go to the polyclinic, is there anyone [there] to see me?

NURSE: Yes, but you have to pay for it. But go there, and if it doesn't work, come back here. I feel sorry, but you're not an emergency. (Field note, County)

Both cases concern patients who fail the legitimacy test. In the first one, the mentioning of unbearable pain is counterbalanced by the request to get an X-ray, which indicates that the acute episode of illness is over when the admission interview takes place. In the second one, the patient reveals the existence of an on-going problem and does not give any indication of a recent change that would warrant the visit to the ED.[27] In situations of this sort, triage workers consider that the patient should be seen either by the family doctor or by a general practitioner at the polyclinic.

The patients explain their visit by invoking the indirect cost of transporta-tion (in the first case) and the direct cost of consultation as the person has no health insurance (in the second one). Their honesty does not pay off. Triage workers tend to consider the patients' dire economic straits as an inacceptable reason for bypassing the primary sector practitioners because they assume poverty to be imputable to the individual rather than to structural conditions or unfortunate life circumstances. Therefore, the patients are sanctioned by prolonged waiting and conditional admission, respectively.

As mentioned in chapter 1, socializing patients about the role of the emer-gency service and the eligibility conditions is a major preoccupation for triage workers. Patients whose presentation of the case adheres to or is consistent with the staff-devised mission of the service are more likely to pass the moral evaluation than those who ignore it.

AVERTING RESPONSIBILITY

Parsons's sick role model posits the conditional exemption of the sick from responsibility for the onset of the illness. This holds only partially true in the triage assessment of patients. If a person has a chronic illness that might be attributable to lifestyle choices, like smoking and drinking, triage workers tend not to take this into consideration. What they are more concerned with is the individual accountability for the acute symptoms that brought the patient to the hospital. Thus, triage workers operate with a conception of immediate, rather than general, responsibility for the health conditions.

The degree of personal responsibility matters for the assessment of rea-sonableness and worth, but it is a matter of secondary importance for staff. Nurses and clerks often omit to address it when questioning patients, except when the patient belongs to groups for which the background expectancy of carelessness exists, such as the Roma, or when the circumstances of the case are unclear. Averting responsibility is more important for patients, who often use it to repair a presentational faux pas or to introduce some favorable infor-mation after a confrontational sequence:

NURSE: What happened?

PATIENT: Something fell on my leg, an iron bar.

NURSE: When did it happen?

PATIENT: Yesterday.

NURSE: Is it bleeding?

PATIENT: Yes, it's bleeding, and I have a hangnail.

NURSE: And why didn't you come here yesterday?

PATIENT: I thought it's not something serious.

NURSE: Don't you know that normally and legally you should have gone to the polyclinic today?

PATIENT: It happened last night.

NURSE: It doesn't matter, it was an emergency at that moment. [Filling in the patient file:] You were saying that something had fallen on your leg.

PATIENT: Yes, during the storm last night, there was a wind blast, and an iron bar fell on my small toe. (Field note, County)

The admission interview follows a bureaucratic format, punctuated by a short passage to the confrontational format, during which the triage nurse challenges the patient for coming to the ED too late. In terms of moral evaluation, the nurse enquires about the nature of the health problem, the temporal features of the case, and the extent of the injury, which serve to determine the legitimacy of the presentation. The confrontational sequence revolves around the reasonableness of the visit to the ED. The nurse makes it clear that "normally and legally" the patient should have gone to the primary care instead of coming to the hospital given that the problem was not urgent.[28] The patient does not retort, but when the conversation switches back to the bureaucratic format, as the nurse if filling in the electronic record, he takes advantage of the end of questioning to provide some additional information. He uses his turn to explain the circumstances in which his leg got hurt. He frames the situation as an accident, a situation that could have been neither anticipated nor prevented. By framing the problem as the outcome of a fortuitous event and mentioning the bad weather conditions at the time of the injury, he constructs the context in which his previous statements are to be interpreted and adds the missing parts of the puzzle. The patient's story appears now more coherent and intelligible, substantiating his decision not to look for healthcare shortly after the accident has taken place.

In the case of Roma and lower-class non-Roma, the staff's assumption of negligence is often verbalized during the admission interview. The assessment of personal responsibility is a matter of particularly high interest when the patient is a child. Usually, the patients exculpate themselves by framing the situation as accidental, as it happens in the following encounter involving a young Roma mother:

NURSE: Why didn't you take care of him?

PARENT: I was in a minibus, someone almost bumped into us, and he fell down and got injured.

The nurse begins the admission interview by adopting a confrontational stance and accusing the mother of being negligent. The woman does not appear to take offense. Instead of confronting the triage nurse, she calmly explains the circumstances that led to the child's injury (a sudden break of the minibus to avoid an accident).

Other parents accused on negligence react with hostility, as the non-Roma lower-class young parent in the fragment below, who arrives at the ED after his one-year-old daughter has fallen while holding a spoon in her mouth and got some injuries. The male openly defies the authority of the nurse by rejecting her moralizing comments:

PARENT: How long should we still wait here?

NURSE: I have no idea. An orderly has to come and pick her up. It can be thirty minutes, sixty minutes, maybe an hour and a half, I don't know.

PARENT: And I stay here 'til morning with a one-year-old baby in my arms?

NURSE: I have informed the doctor, he knows about it. An orderly should come, [but] now all of them are busy.

PARENT: When will he come? At 3 [a.m.]?

NURSE: It's not my fault that you don't know how to take care of a child. Next time, don't give spoons to a one-year-old.

PARENT: What a great advice! Thank you! I guess you'll write me an invoice for this great advice!

NURSE: You should be thankful that I don't call the Child Protection [Agency] to fine you for being irresponsible parents.

PARENT: But please, go on! Make the phone call. Please!

NURSE: Look, here is the phone number! [The nurse points to a poster on the wall on which it is written the phone number of the governmental agency in charge of child protection.]

PARENT: Go on, please! [He walks back to the waiting room] (Field note, County)

This discussion takes place a few minutes after the end of the admission interview. The man attempts to gain quicker admission to the consultation room by pointing out that the patient is an infant. The nurse counteracts by insisting on the unreasonableness of the request for immediate admission due to parental negligence. Although the patient replies to this accusation with haughty contempt, setting up another sequence of contentious talk, he does not reiterate the initial request, and resumes his seat in the waiting room at the end of the exchange.

This case shows that, albeit seldom and selectively used during triage encounters, the immediate responsibility for the health problem can have considerable impact upon the non-clinical evaluation of patients, potentially warranting delayed admission to consultation by a physician. Failing to avert responsibility impacts not only the assessment in terms of reasonableness, but also the evaluation of worth. While patients escaping negative typification can redress the situation through a successful self-presentation, Roma and low-class urban adults have fewer chances to persuade triage agents that the negligence was uncharacteristic to them.

MANUFACTURING WORTH

The assessment of legitimacy and reasonableness stems primarily from organizational concerns. The evaluation in terms of worth has other sources and serves different purposes; it originates in the socially dominant norms and values,[29] and strives to achieve a moral apportioning of resources.[30] As Yeheskel Hasenfeld has observed, the moral evaluation of users is omnipresent in organizations of various sorts, not only medical, and it impacts the distribution of services: "when a client is viewed as morally deficient she becomes 'undeserving' and is subject to a moral test before gaining access to organizational resources."[31]

In the Romanian EDs where I conducted fieldwork, triage workers attend to social worth, which they infer from the social characteristics of the individual and their performance during the admission interview, but they do so in a rather subtle way. The only questions pertaining to worth that nurses and clerks always ask are related to the occupational status of the user, which they use as a proxy for the insurance status, a mandatory field in the registration forms. This simplifies the collection of data because the legislation on health insurance is complicated, and many people are confused about their actual status. When the patient is unemployed, they or their companions often feel the need to explain the situation. For instance, the companion of a middle-aged female patient tells the triage nurse that she "doesn't have work, is out of work because she lives in the countryside" (Field note, County). As nurses know that the unemployment is high in the relatively underdeveloped rural regions, the information shields the patient from the potential imputation of laziness or poor work ethics.

The person's occupation can have a high impact on the moral evaluation. When an ambulance crew and a team of police officers bring a middle-aged female at the County ED, they reveal that the patient attempted suicide and tried to set her apartment afire. They also mention that the woman works as a teacher at a prestigious and highly competitive local high-school. The triage workers arrange the transportation to the psychiatric hospital, and in handling the case they refrain from passing any moral judgments.

Wearing a military of police uniform grants the patient a privileged position in the moral world of the ED. The social valuation often offsets the low legitimacy or reasonableness of the case, as the following field note extract illustrates. The participants to the exchange are three gendarmes (two males, one of them the patient; and one female). The admision is handled by the registration clerk as the triage nurse is away.

COMPANION: Dear lady, can we leave our colleague here, because we are during working hours?

CLERK: Let him if he can sit. What [is] his problem?

COMPANION: He hit a threshold with the leg, and it was bloody . . . a nail of his little toe.

CLERK: So, it's a canker sore!

COMPANION: A canker sore, if you say so!

Diana fills the admission registry while the gendarmes are talking on the hallway about the advantages of calling an ambulance instead of coming directly to the emergency ward. Meanwhile, Nurse Nina comes back to the triage office and immediately starts talking to them:

NURSE: When did it happen, today?

COMPANION: It's since yesterday.

NURSE: Oh, so it's not work-related.

COMPANION: No, it happened yesterday.

NURSE: Ouch! You'll see how fun it can be. A couple of days ago, I removed the nail from the small finger. But I did it at home, by myself.

PATIENT: Give me the file and I leave! [The patient laughs.] (Field note, County)

The favorable treatment given to the patient translates into exempting him from reprimands for the tardive presentation to the ED, the lack of moralizing discourse, and the use of a friendly tone, punctuated with jokes ("See how fun it can be"), a kind of conduct that is often reserved to nurses' friends and acquaintances.[32] The patient reciprocates, by jokingly asking to be allowed to go leave the hospital premises.

During the admission interview, patients and companions often volunteer information that, albeit clinically irrelevant, support their self-presentation as morally worthy and deserving of care. Since the evaluation of worth relies on norms and values that are not peculiar to the organization, there is a high degree of agreement between triage workers and users on what constitutes a morally fit individual. This makes patients more apt to manufacture worth than to assert responsible use of the service during triage encounters. An example comes from the admission of a teenager at County:

NURSE: What happened to him?

COMPANION: A small fight.[33]

PATIENT [TO COMPANION]: Beaten up.[34]

NURSE: Where did it happen?

COMPANION: It happened on the train; I don't know exactly where it was. They entered his train compartment. He was going back from school.

NURSE: Here is the ID card. You have to wait. Is he bleeding?

COMPANION: He bled.

NURSE: Is he still bleeding?

COMPANION: Now he is not. (Field note, County)

The patient delegates the task of presenting the case to the friend who accompanies him to the ED, a teenager himself. The companion uses a diminutive to minimize the incident. As the 'small fight' is an ambiguous information, which can be interpreted in different ways, the patient intervenes and makes it clear that he was the victim of the aggression. The companion uses the nurse's question about the location to develop the circumstances of the incident. Without any prompt, he mobilizes favorable information about the patient (he is a high-school student who needs to commute every day by train) and mentions his lack of responsibility for the event ("They entered his train compartment"). The nurse reacts favorable to the presentation of the case. She does not challenge the version of events, does not ask for further information, does not engage in moralizing discourse and, what is more significant, does not handle the case as an aggression.

The information about the person's social status and roles is instrumental to the worth assessment, but it is also important how the information emerges during the flow of the conversation. When the patient or the companion fail to exert tact, and claim favorable treatment based on their status, this usually backfires. An example comes from County, where an elderly companion complains about his son's long waiting time:

COMPANION: This man [pointing toward his son] serves the country. He is nothing less than a colonel[35] and waits in line here, among all these folks.

NURSE: I understand you, but there's nothing I can do. (Field note, County)

Although triage workers hold people in the military in high esteem, the companion's request of preferential treatment based on social status is rejected politely, yet firmly. The patient is left in the waiting room until the doctor on duty calls his name. More often than not, patients and companions allude to their status while describing the case or responding to the triage workers' question but do so tactfully and without conveying any sense of entitlement to speedy access.

THE ACTIVE ROLE OF PATIENTS IN
THE MORAL EVALUATION

The interactional strategies discussed in this chapter reveal that patients play an active role in the moral evaluation process. Although the power balance inclines in the favor of triage workers, who decide the format and content of the interaction, patients have more or less subtle ways to put on favorable self- and case-presentation and, hence, to actively negotiate access and conditions of access to emergency healthcare. When nurses and clerks adopt the confrontational format, the admission interview becomes a tense, unpleasant experience for many patients and companions. However, the confrontational format allows users to engage in more elaborate maneuvers to convey responsible use and social worth. As a consequence, it benefits patients belonging to marginalized groups, who have the chance to dismantle triage agents' initial assumptions.

The typifying work creates specific expectations for patients belonging to "problematic" categories, which often surface into the conversation. Nevertheless, these expectations do not automatically lead to a negative assessment in terms of legitimacy, reasonableness, and worth. My data fully support Alexandra Hillman's recent observation that "a patient's status is [. . .] fluid and continually in the making."[36] Patients' performance during the triage encounter does not change the staff-devised criteria for non-clinical evaluation or the types into which users with certain social and medical characteristics are routinely placed, but very often impacts their practical application. I develop this argument in the next chapter, which focuses on the ED experience of Romani patients.

NOTES

1. Paul Ten Have, "On the Interactive Constitution of Medical Encounters," *Revue Française de Linguistique Appliquée [French Journal of Applied Linguistics]* 11, no. 2: 86.

2. John Heritage, "Conversation Analysis and Institutional Talk," in *Handbook of Language and Social Interaction*, ed. Kristine L. Fitch and Robert E. Sanders (Manwah, NJ: Lawrence Erlbaum, 2004), 106–07.

3. Philip M. Strong, "Two Types of Ceremonial Order," in *Sociology and Medicine: Selected Essays by P.M. Strong*, ed. Anne Murcott (Aldershot: Ashgate, 2006), 57–81; Philip M. Strong, "The Rivals: An Essay on the Sociological Trades," in *Sociology and Medicine: Selected Essays by P.M. Strong*, ed. Anne Murcott (Aldershot: Ashgate, 2006), 119–36; Philip M. Strong, "Minor Courtesies and Macro Structures," in *Sociology and Medicine: Selected Essays by P.M. Strong*, ed. Anne Murcott (Aldershot: Ashgate, 2006), 37–56.

4. Strong, "Sociology and Medicine," 2006, 126.

5. Ibid., 70.

6. Erving Goffman, "On Face-Work: An Analysis of Ritual Elements in Social Interaction," in *Interaction Ritual: Essays in Face-to-Face Behavior* (New York: Anchor Books, 1967), 14.

7. Strong, "Sociology and Medicine," 2006, 52.

8. Ibid., 127.

9. Ibid., 71.

10. The asymmetry in social status and power between participants was more pronounced in the charity format, given that users were recruited from the most dispossessed and stigmatized members of the society.

11. "Formatting the Consultation: Communication Formats and Constituted Identities," in *Artikelen van de Tweede Sociolinguïstische Conferentie*, ed. Erica Huls and Jetske Klatter-Folmer (Delft: Eburon, 1995), 245–68.

12. David Hughes, "Paper and People: The Work of the Casualty Reception Clerk," *Sociology of Health & Illness* 11, no. 4: 388.

13. Hadrian Borcea, *Triajul În Structurile Pentru Primirea Urgenţelor [The Triage in Emergency Receiving Structures]* (Unpublished document, 2007), 12.

14. Although it is not exceptional for the patients to initiate the talk, more often than that it is the nurse or the clerk who begins the conversations.

15. In the case of negatively typified patients, especially Roma, the initial question is framed in a way that conveys the expectation of personal responsibility for the health problem (e.g., "What did you do?"). Although the difference is barely noticeable, it indicates a completely different approach. Almost every conversation that begins with the indirect imputation of responsibility takes place is a confrontational, rather than bureaucratic, format.

16. If the person does not fall into any of the social categories that are automatically covered by the national health insurance, there is an additional question about the insurance status, which can be individually purchased.

17. In discourse analysis, "transactional talk" refers to conversation directed toward attending the goal of the exchange. It contrasts with "relational talk," which "creates and maintains the interpersonal relations between participants, enhances discourse flow, and secures a positive outcome of the interaction." J. César Félix-Brasdefer, *The Language of Service Encounters* (Cambridge: Cambridge University Press, 2015), 8.

18. This treatment is reserved for patients who pass successfully the non-clinical evaluation and who show either discomfort with being in the hospital or excessive concern about the health condition. Children and young adults are most likely to receive such a treatment.

19. "Sociology and Medicine," 2006, 52.

20. Michele Rivkin-Fish, "Bribes, Gifts and Unofficial Payments: Rethinking Corruption in Post-Soviet Russian Health Care," in *Corruption. Anthropological Perspectives*, ed. Dieter Haller and Cris Shore (London and Ann Arbor, MI: Pluto Press, 2005), 49.

21. As Goffman ("On Face-Work: An Analysis of Ritual Elements in Social Interaction," 42.) pointed out, "it seems to be a characteristic of many social relationships that each of the members guarantees to support a given face for the other members in given situations." Why is this not the case with many of the triage admission encounters? What makes nurses and clerks willing to destroy the face of some would-be patients?

A possible answer is to be found in the mission of the triage service. The defensive practice of saving one's face and the protective practice of maintaining the other's face are necessary for the continuation of a social relationship (Goffman, *The Presentation of Self in Everyday Life*, 7). Encounters taking place in the confrontational format create a "state of ritual disequilibrium and disgrace" (Goffman, "On Face-Work: An Analysis of Ritual Elements in Social Interaction," 25) that cannot be ignored by the offended participants. A common face-work response to situations of ritual profanation of the self lies in the avoidance of such events (Goffman, 15–19). Since this response is consistent with nurses' and clerks' goal of preventing the return of illegitimate cases, the use of confrontation and ritual defacement can be seen as an instrumental behavior on the part of triage agents.

Such interpretation assumes that hospital workers constitute the unmoved mover of the interactional vandalism that is peculiar to the confrontational format. However, it can also be argued that patients set in motion the "aggressive interchange" (Goffman, 25) by introducing, wittingly or unintentionally, through verbal communication, appearance or manners, an element of deception into the conversation. The patient suspected of failing to meet one or more of the criteria on which the non-clinical evaluation is performed (legitimacy, reasonableness, and social worth) commits an indirect offense toward the face of the triage worker. Even though the manipulation of communicational content may be introduced in a polite and respectful way, it violates the assumption of honesty informing the interaction ritual. In this reading of the events, the confrontational format is reactive, and constitutes a form of expressive behavior.

The two interpretations, albeit analytically distinct, are not mutually exclusive. Since the expressive and instrumental behaviors are not always separate in practice

(Erving Goffman, "Community Conduct in an Island Community" (University of Chicago, 1953), 58), it is possible that the two uses of confrontation coexist. The matter requires further research, but a tentative hypothesis is that the instrumental use occurs in those confrontations that are relatively standardized, whereas the expressive use occurs in the most heated and creative encounters dominated by hostility. In the instrumental variant of confrontation, triage agents defend the face of the organization they represent, without having any emotional involvement in the situation. In the expressive one, they are defending their own face and therefore are more genuinely preoccupied with the outcome.

22. Harold Garfinkel, "Conditions of Successful Degradation Ceremonies," *American Journal of Sociology* 61, no. 5: 420–24.

23. *Face gât.*

24. For sure, patients are only partially aware of staff's moral evaluation criteria and conjectures. Their moral boundary work is conducted mainly to account for their presence there and project a favorable image of the self.

25. "Why Must I Wait?" 496.

26. Roughly US$15 at the time when the conversation took place.

27. In the case of patients with symptoms going on for a longer time, nurses and clerks often ask what is different today as compared to a few days earlier. The question is important for assessing the legitimacy of the case. An acute exacerbation of pre-existing symptoms is consistent with the mission of the service and warrants the visit to the ED. The failure to indicate a rapid and severe worsening of symptoms makes triage workers believe that the case is sub-threshold for admission ("not an emergency" or "not a real emergency").

28. The problem occurred within the past twenty-four hours, which triage workers regard as the temporal threshold between a "real" emergency and a non-emergency. Even if the problem happened earlier, there is no legal requirement to seek care at the policlinic. On the contrary, as indicated in Chapter 1, the current legislation allows people to use the ED for medically non-urgent problems. The triage nurse's most likely reasoning is that if the patient could wait for many hours, the problem was not severe enough to warrant a visit to the hospital.

29. Glaser and Strauss, "The Social Loss of Dying Patients."

30. Vassy, "Categorisation and Micro-Rationing: Access to Care in a French ED."

31. Yeheskel Hasenfeld, "Organizational Forms as Moral Practices: The Case of Welfare Departments," *Social Service Review* 74, no. 3: 332.

32. The comment that the health condition is not work-related is procedurally relevant. Were the case to occur during the gendarme's work time, the incident should have been treated as a labor accident, which required some additional bureaucratic steps.

33. *O bătăiţă.*

34. *Bătăiţă luată.*

35. *E ditamai colonelul.*

36. "Why Must I Wait?" 495.

Chapter 6

Producing Exclusion, Reproducing Racism

So far, I have argued that moral evaluation is the social process through which triage workers make sense of patients and cases and decide how to allocate the scarce available resources in a manner they consider fair. Moral evaluation is meant to keep the emergency service afloat rather than to exclude, and nurses and clerks adamantly reject the possibility of sanctioning people for who they are or where they come from. "We treat everybody the same" is their mantra, and several arguments are mobilized to support this claim. First, every patient with a life-threatening condition or multiple injuries gets admitted posthaste, irrespective of age, gender, ethnicity, socio-economic status, or place of living. Second, no one is denied access to the healthcare they need. Even patients with chronic conditions, in need of a second opinion, or wanting to get a prescription renewed end up being seen by a doctor. Third, the conditions of access (particularly the length of waiting) are determined based on the perceived severity of the case, which is the formal principle of admission. In other words, nurses and clerks acknowledge that the access to emergency care is unequal, but staunchly deny that it is also inequitable.

The previous chapters have shown that despite the professed objectivity and impartiality, the triage assessment occurs at the intersection between formal principles and informal practices, scientific knowledge and lay considerations, clinical concerns and moral beliefs.[1] The moral evaluation that informs the clinical assessment and shapes patients' triage experience often leads to the reenactment and reproduction of social dominance in healthcare settings, and this is nowhere as clear as in the case of the Romani patients. It is for this reason that this chapter examines the interconnectedness between the interaction order and the social order by zooming in on the production of social exclusion along ethnic lines and the reproduction of racism at the ED.

As discussed in chapter 3, triage workers typify Roma as being fundamentally different from the other patients and deeply problematic for the emergency service and the people staffing it. The background assumptions about Roma include cheating the system by coming to the ED for problems that fall within the competence of the family doctor, lacking health insurance due to unemployment, and being unruly and aggressive. Such assumptions are not without consequences; they shape triage nurses' and clerks' orientation to Romani patients, contributing to their differential treatment. Nevertheless, the triage admission interview provides the Roma with an opportunity to defy these assumptions and struggle with staff to claim entitlement to and deservingness of emergency healthcare. This negotiation process occasionally yields the desired outcomes but leaves the Roma type intact.

I begin this chapter by examining a master trait that triage workers attribute to Romani patients, namely aggressiveness. I will show that the stereotype of the physically aggressive Roma does not originate in personal or vicarious encounters with Roma perpetrated violence, but it is an import from the society at large. The triage encounters reproduce it through three inter-connected social mechanisms: encouraging stereotype-consistent behaviors, ethnicizing violence, and conventionalizing Roma aggression through storytelling.

THE "AGGRESSIVE ROMA" STEREOTYPE

The staff's discourse on Roma falls within a spectrum ranging from explicit racism to color-blindedness, the stated belief that patients' ethnicity is, and should be, irrelevant. The interview quotes below illustrate the two end points of this continuum:

> NURSE ANDRA: *Țiganii*[2] are aggressive by nature, because they have complexes, they feel marginalized, because they are used to having rights but no responsibilities. (Interview, County)

> NURSE LUCIA: From my point of view, they [the Roma] are not different as patients. [. . .] Some of them are actually very respectful, you know? They are respectful, wait patiently . . . Others are more recalcitrant, because that's how they are. Some, but not all of them. One cannot generalize. (Interview, County)

Albeit short, these excerpts show striking differences. Nurse Andra's statement contains many ingredients of classical racism: the belief in biological essentialism ("aggressive *by nature*"), with the corollary of ethnic homogeneity (conveyed by the repeated use of the generic "*they*"); the denial of a racial order that prevents the Roma from achieving their potential ("they *feel* marginalized"); and the explanation of ethnic disparities through alleged psychological or social flaws (having complexes and adopting a free-rider approach to the social contract). The fallacy of regarding an innate propensity as the outcome of social actions suggests that the nurse is more interested in othering the Roma than in producing a coherent folk theory of their presumed "aggression." The second account appears more calculated. Nurse Lucia depicts Romani patients as heterogeneous and explicitly warns against the peril of making ethnic generalizations. In this context, the comment "that's how they are" does not imply biological or cultural essentialism; instead, it suggests that diversity within the ethnic group is inevitable.

Equally telling is the use of ethnonyms. Nurse Andra prefers the exonym "Țigan," whereas Nurse Lucia, like most other triage workers, utilizes the endonym "Roma." The two terms made the object of an important culture war in the Romanian society around and after the country's accession to the European Union, in 2007. Roma scholars and activists and their allies have staunchly opposed the exonym *țigan*, regarding it as pejorative, inherently offensive, and intimately tied to a history of exclusion and oppression.[3] At the same time, many non-Roma have objected to the use of the endonym, arguing that it sounds too close to that of the majority ethnic group, and the conflation of Romani people with Romanians could compromise the country's image.[4] In the end, the term "Roma" imposed itself as the official name of the ethnic group despite some high-level political attempts to replace it.[5] It is against this background that Nurse Andra's use of the name *țigan* acquires a conspicuous reactionary character. Instead of merely describing a population group, it makes an unambiguous statement against political correctness and Roma's self-determination efforts.

These differences notwithstanding, the two stances are similar in their emphasis of "aggression" as a Roma trait. For sure, Nurse Lucia uses the qualifier "some" to limit her claim and makes it explicit that in her view not all the Roma are "recalcitrant." However, it is remarkable that out of the virtually infinite pool of dichotomies (e.g., friendly-unfriendly, educated-uneducated, talkative-quiet, humorous-unamusing, etc.), she chooses precisely the binary opposition respectful-recalcitrant[6] to describe the within-group diversity of Roma patients. Later during the interview, when asked about the meaning of "recalcitrance," Nurse Lucia indicates that this has to do with forms of aggression serious enough to warrant the intervention of the law enforcement: "There have been incidents, all sorts of incidents. The police and the security agents intervene when they [the Roma] become aggressive."

Roma's "aggression" emerged as a salient category during the interviews with triage workers at both hospitals. The category encompasses physical violence, verbal aggression, and unruly behavior. Some triage workers made their point clear, whereas others talked about the Roma's alleged propensity toward aggression in an elusive manner, relying on innuendos and unfinished sentences:

INTERVIEWER: Are they [the Roma patients] different from the other patients here? Is there any difference?

CLERK CRINA: . . . Well, they are more violent, more dirty, insolent, and disrespectful. They know they have no [medical] insurance, they don't belong . . . they have no reason to come to the ED, and they still act badly. (Interview, City)

INTERVIEWER: In your view, what makes the Roma different from the non-Roma at the ED?

NURSE VERA: In terms of attitude?

INTERVIEWER: In terms of attitude.

NURSE VERA: Generally speaking, some of them are more recalcitrant. From the very beginning. Before, there used to be respect for the physician, respect for us. Now, all that is gone. Because of the negative media reporting on us. And the Roma even more.

NURSE NINA: Not only the Roma, there are also Romanians who—

NURSE VERA:—there are Romanians too, indeed, but generally the Roma are the [more recalcitrant] ones . . . (Interview, County Hospital)

NURSE FLORICA: [After telling me that being insulted and threatened by Roma patients is common] Some colleagues of mine got their face cut by the Romani ethnicity [*sic*], and I don't know whether any measures have been taken [against them].

INTERVIEWER: Are the majority of Roma like that or only some of them?

NURSE FLORICA: Well, no, not the majority, but three quarters [*sic*] of them become very aggressive, many of them are drunkards and cannot control themselves, and they become aggressive with the staff because you have seen it yourself: we don't have enough beds, we don't have enough personnel to admit them as soon as they arrive. We ask them to wait, and they become really recalcitrant. (Interview, City)

The belief in Roma aggression is so pervasive and strong that it serves as the benchmark against which other patients' behavior is judged: "You can meet well-educated, well-dressed people who are more verbally aggressive than a Roma" (Interview Clerk Zina, City).

In many staff narratives, "aggressiveness" is presented as the culmination of a constellation of negative characteristics Romani patients allegedly possess, including poor hygiene, unhealthy lifestyles, disrespect for the orderliness of the ED and the work of nurses and clerks, lack of health insurance, and belonging to, or having connections with, the underworld.[7] This constructs a representation of Roma as the abject other of the nation,[8] morally undeserving of care. Moreover, the Roma are also considered to make inopportune visits to the ED, because in most cases their health concerns could have been addressed within the primary care system.

In triage workers' narratives, it was the Romani masculinity that was equated with the propensity toward violence and unruly behavior. Without exception, the nurses and clerks used the masculine third person plural pronoun to refer to the "aggressive" Roma, and most examples of aggression allegedly perpetrated by Romani patients and companions involved males. This is consistent with the socially dominant gender stereotypes surrounding the Roma community.

THE APPARENT PARADOX OF ROMA "AGGRESSION"

The staff's general perception is that Roma patients' aggression, ranging from physical violence to interactional insubordination and defiant conduct, is pervasive and routine. However, when asked to provide some examples based on their experience, many nurses and clerks had a hard time recalling any incident of such sort. Some explained that while it never happened to them, fellow staff members had fallen victim to Roma patients' aggression:

INTERVIEWER: Did you have any incident yourself?

NURSE ANDRA: Yeeeah. Many times. I didn't have that many [incidents] because they know me, I've been working in the emergency [department] for twenty years, and I have a way of swearing at them on one hand and smiling at them on the other hand that somehow, we reach a common ground. And I quiet them down. But some of my co-workers got beaten. Some of the doctors got beaten [as well].

INTERVIEWER: Could you tell me one such incident?

NURSE LUCIA: It never happened on my shift. But I have colleagues against whom they have been aggressive. (Interview, County)

Other participants recounted incidents of verbal abuse. The case described by Clerk Crina is paradigmatic for the nature of the reported aggression and the retrospective framing of the situation:

INTERVIEWER: What do you mean by saying that they are more violent? Did you have any incident?

CLERK CRINA: Well, it happened to me at the beginning [of my employment here], last year. I was in the night shift and a solid citizen of Romani ethnicity came with his minor wife, and I was doing an ambulance, I was doing—I was registering an ambulance, and he told me that he takes the [computer] monitor and wraps it around my neck. I was like "what?" He was thinking that the ambulance took too long [to register]. And when there's an ambulance, you have to get lots of information: the ambulance license plate number, the diagnostic, the names of the person, the driver, and the nurse, and to him that was taking too long. (Interview, City)

In this report, not only the threat itself is upsetting, but also the conditions in which it occurred and the social worth of the perpetrator. The trigger of the aggressive act (the delay in registering the Romani patient) is interpreted as unjustified, as the clerk was busy with filling the bureaucratic paperwork for the admission of the patient brought by the ambulance. By indicating the companion's body constitution ("a solid citizen") and the patient's age and marital status ("minor wife"), the clerk provides the context in which she wants the incident to be understood—one of imminent danger, involving people who do not abide by dominant social norms. The early marriage alludes to cultural backwardness and patriarchal oppression.[9] During the interview, the clerk added that she was tempted to call 112 (the emergency telephone number) to ask for police support. She was dissuaded by the security guard[10] who observed the incident. Later, he told her that the man proffering the threat was a member of the underworld.

None of the participants could indicate a specific example of physical violence perpetrated by Roma at the ED. They provided generic examples (e.g., "some of the doctors got beaten"; "some colleagues of mine got their face cut by Roma") or discussed the violence as potential rather than actual, as in the following account:

CLERK ZINA: We also had cases, one from C's clan, who was very aggressive from all points of view. You could say nothing, do nothing, and he would still get mad. So, he was very aggressive, and nobody dared say anything, nobody dared do anything. And then he could snap and beat you, give you a slap, I don't know, out of the blue. But we are lucky cause he got arrested, he seems to be under house arrest now. (Interview, City)

During fieldwork, I have observed only two cases of non-verbal violence involving Romani people, both taking place at County hospital. The first case was that of a male in his fifties who was about to be transferred to a psychiatric hospital because the ED did not provide emergency mental health services. As he was waiting for the ambulance to come, he asked to go out for a cigarette. When nurses refused to honor his request, the man became visibly angry. The hospital security guards arrived and surrounded him. He tried to escape by exerting force, but was immediately put on the ground, facedown. A quarrel ensued, during which the patient threatened to return to set the hospital afire. Later, he calmed down and was taken by the ambulance crew.

The second incident took place around midnight and involved four Roma (two males and two females) who decided to leave after waiting for fourteen hours to get admitted. They left the waiting room swearing, saying bad words about the doctor, and stating the intention to file a complaint. The men warned the security guard that they might return for a fight later than night. Outside, they tried to destroy the beacon light of an ambulance, but only managed to dislocate it. The ambulance doctor asked Nurse Andra if "The West's most noble flower"[11] were going to come back, to which the nurse replied that they wouldn't because they were not angry enough.

However, the observational data reveals that most of the Roma do not engage in disputes with the staff, and most of the people who engage in disputes are not Roma.[12] Thus, a question that begs to be answered is how the stereotype of Roma aggression retains its popularity despite evidence contradicting it.

TRIAGE WORKERS' ORIENTATION
TO ROMANI PATIENTS

Before proceeding to data presentation and analysis, a brief note on the usage of ethnicity is necessary. Romania prohibits the collection of ethnic data in the medical sector, and healthcare workers rigorously follow the rule; I have never assisted to any direct question about or allusion to patients' ethnicity during the admission interview.

However, nurses and clerks claim to have little difficulties in deciding who is a Roma. Skin complexion, social and cultural markers of belonging, and practices typified as Roma—only serve as indicators of Romani ethnicity. For instance, wearing traditional dresses or ethnic jewelry, using Romani language, speaking Romanian with an accent, and coming to the ED in large groups are read as proxies for being Roma. When such cues are missing or cannot be interpreted with certainty, the place of living is used to gauge ethnicity because many Roma live in segregated neighborhoods.[13] During fieldwork, I used the same local knowledge to identify "Roma" patients and companions. At various points in this chapter, I distinguish between "traditional" and "assimilated" Roma. The former label describes people who display at least one marker of traditional Romani culture (e.g., wearing traditional attire). The latter is used for those who have a darker skin complexion and live in segregated settlements or in villages or town districts with a known Roma presence but lack any display of traditional Romani culture. It goes without saying that some individuals referred to here as Roma may not necessarily self-identify as such, while individuals self-identified as Roma may have been misidentified by triage workers. Nevertheless, the degree of congruence between self- and hetero-identification is less relevant for the purpose of this analysis, as the discriminatory practices to which the Roma are subjected are due to their *perceived* ethnicity rather than their self-identification.

Like in the case of other patients, nurses and clerks use the admission interview to verify their assumptions about the Roma. However, there is a particularity of the admission interviews involving the members of this ethnic group. Not only the encounters are almost always confrontational, but the staff's background expectancies about Roma often translate into micro-aggressions, particularly when patients are women. The following situations encountered during fieldwork illustrate the different forms of micro-aggressions to which Romani patients are routinely subjected during the encounter with triage workers:

1. An illiterate female who is asked about her current medication hands the nurse three small bags containing different pills, indicating the ones she is currently taking. The nurse asks her: "Pay attention here, because I'm checking the bag. Don't tell me later [that the medicines] are missing!"
2. Another illiterate adult female reveals during the admission interview that she cannot distinguish the left from the right side of the body. The nurse laughs heartily, and calling the patient by a diminutive name with risible connotations ("Luluța"), invites her to join her son in the preparatory class for primary school.
3. A young woman comes with her son whose face is injured. The nurse scolds her for not having taken proper care of the kid. The mother explains that the injury has occurred in a traffic accident.
4. A middle-aged man exchanges some words in Romani language with a companion while waiting to be seen by the triage nurse. The nurse asks him what he has just said. He explains that he was chatting with his friend in Romani. The nurse exclaims: "I believed I had to understand what you were saying!"
5. A young Romani woman stays in the waiting room, paying attention to what is going on. When a nurse enters the corridor, she jumps in front of her and asks for updates about the situation of her husband. The nurse invites her to check with the triage staff. The woman goes to the triage room and stands there waiting with the hands placed on the counter. Nobody talks to her and after a minute or two the woman leaves and goes to the smoking area outside the main entrance, where she stops another hospital nurse, asking the same question.

These examples show triage workers making explicit the assumptions of dishonesty [1], negligence [3], and poor motherhood [3]; infantilizing patients who lack formal education [2]; engaging in name-calling [2]; responding with sarcasm to the use of Romani language in the public space [4]; withholding information [5]; and treating Roma as non-persons [5]. Through these micro-aggressions, triage workers—wittingly or not—attempt to keep Roma in their place, thus reproducing the wider social order into the microcosm of the ED.

Nurses and clerks orient to Romani patients based on such deeply held assumptions. However, the Roma are not devoid of power during triage encounters. They assert worth by either refuting or creatively exploiting triage workers' ethnic assumptions. In doing so, they adopt three interactional strategies: submission, hard line, and soft resistance.

THE INTERACTIONAL STRATEGIES
OF ROMANI PATIENTS

Submission

Submission consists in acknowledging, accepting, and maximizing the asymmetrical power relation between patients and staff, and avoiding confrontation at all costs. It is accomplished by taking a predominantly reactive stance during verbal exchanges; framing the case in a soft, non-demanding way; limiting eye contact; and not retorting when challenged or affronted. Submission does not imply complete passivity. Many a time I have seen patients engaged in this sort of interactional conduct volunteering an explanation or clarification during the admission interview, making inquiries shortly thereafter, or expressing dissatisfaction with the long waiting time. Nevertheless, the initiative is usually framed timidly, in a way that does not upset the imbalance of power, and almost never escalates to conflict. Submission is used predominantly by traditional Roma females.

The examples below illustrate two cases of submission, showing that some variation exists within this type of interactional strategy. The first one is from a field note, whereas the second comes from a recorded conversation:

A middle-aged Roma woman comes to the triage counter shortly after an admission interview is concluded.

PATIENT: [soft tone] Miss, I'm here and I'm waiting for some lung tests. I've been waiting since nine o'clock [for over twelve hours]. Is anyone coming [to see me]?

CLERK: I DON'T KNOW WHEN COMES, WHO COMES, WHO WILL LET YOU KNOW!

PATIENT: So, what should I do? Wait here?

The clerk does not reply. After a few seconds, the woman returns to the waiting room. After a short while, the clerk gets out and the triage nurse on duty returns to her post. The woman comes back and reiterates the inquiry. This time she mentions having been waiting since 8 instead of 9 a.m. In a polite yet firm way, the nurse tells her that the doctor is in her office seeing other patients. The woman returns to her seat. As she was going back, the nurse shares with me her understanding of the situation: "If she's been waiting since 8, it is obviously not an emergency. Let them alone to grow out of the habit to come to the ED for any kickshaw." (Field note, County)

The second example shows a case of submission in which the patient takes more initiative. The patient, an eighty-seven-year-old Roma female, came to the ED from the railway station, where she suddenly experienced chest pain and a feeling of fainting.

NURSE: Have you gone to the doctor yet?

PATIENT: Yes, I have.

NURSE: Really? Can you show me anything from the previous visits?

PATIENT: I have treatment, everything, but I didn't [bring] them here because I've left from—

NURSE:—well, you have to show them to me, because if I tell you that I show you—I tell you but I cannot prove it, would you trust me?

PATIENT: Mrs.—

NURSE:—Grandma, we need to have the treatment written down somewhere, so that we can see it, right?

PATIENT: Yes. (Audio-recorded conversation, County)

The focus of the interaction is on the patient's illness behavior. The nurse refuses to take the patient's claims at face value, first by expressing doubt ("Really?") and then by making the distrust explicit. While the patient has an explanation for the failure to produce any documentary evidence (the distressing symptoms occurred out of a sudden and the visit to the ED was unplanned), the triage nurse is unwilling to accept it. She interrupts twice the patient's attempt to explain the situation. In the end, the patient gives up and accepts the point made by the nurse.

Although the strategy centers around deference, a value appreciated by nurses and clerks, it rarely leads to the desired outcomes. Romani patients using submission are often criticized, ridiculed, shouted at, or simply ignored. Even when they are treated politely, triage nurses tend to assign them low priority codes that prolong waiting time. A possible explanation for this is that triage workers' deeply held assumption of Roma's dishonesty precludes the success of the strategy.

HARD LINE

Hard line constitutes the interactional opposite of submission. People engaging in this approach are deliberately confrontational and show little concern with saving the face of the interlocutor. To get things done, they break the staff-devised expectations of appropriate patient conduct by questioning triage workers' competence and professionalism, challenging their decisions, outspeaking them, and reacting to criticism with irony and sarcasm. The strategy revolves around claiming respect through carefully organized displays of composure and toughness. However, hard line does not involve threats or allusions to the use of physical violence. Moreover, confrontation is not maintained indefinitely. After a few heated exchanges, patients and triage workers tend to reach surface agreement.

The following excerpt from an audio-recorded conversation illustrates the use of hard line by a young Roma adult accompanying his mother who has cardiac problems:

COMPANION: After the ambulance, there is no one [else]. At least give her a pill or something.

NURSE: Don't tell me—Tell me what the problem of your mother is and—

COMPANION:—you better look here! [He handles her two medical letters] She's really bad. Look at her. [Jenny enters the data into the registry]. She's really bad, what do we do?

NURSE: PLEASE HAVE A SEAT AND GIVE ME A BREAK!

COMPANION: IF I GIVE YOU A BREAK, I GIVE YOU A THREE-HOUR BREAK.

NURSE: I LET—I DECIDE, OK?

COMPANION: I'M JUST ASKING. IT'S YOU WHO DECIDES.

NURSE: I DECIDE. YOU GO THERE ON THE CHAIR AND LET ME GO AND SEE THE PATIENT, YOU LEAVE ME ALONE. I REGISTER THE PATIENT, DO YOU LET ME DO THIS OR NOT?

COMPANION: But, madam—

NURSE:—PLEASE! THAT'S ENOUGH! Does the lady have a job?

COMPANION: She doesn't.

NURSE: No occupation. And what happened to her?

COMPANION: The heart beats over and over, she has high blood pressure.

NURSE: The heart beats over and over because that's how the heart should beat.

COMPANION: Very fast. (Audio-recorded conversation, County)

The man obliquely challenges the decision made by the nurse not to admit the patient right away ("there is no one [else]"), calls into question her professionalism (the reference to the three-hour break), breaks the asymmetry of power relations by suggesting a different course of action ("give her a pill or something"), forces the nurse to end her turn prematurely once, and reciprocates when she raises her voice. All these interactional moves disconcert the interlocutor, who displays hesitation in two non-consecutive turns. After the conflict reaches the apex, however, the companion relents—he lowers his voice, uses the honorific "madam," and does not riposte when interrupted. The next turns are led by the nurse, who attempts to establish the low worth of the patient based on her unemployment status, and of the companion based on his use of an idiom of illness to describe the symptom. It is worth remarking that the question about employment is irrelevant to the formal assessment of the patient's condition. It is used solely to convey moral undeservingness.

Even though it appears that the nurse ultimately won the verbal confrontation, after a few minutes she goes to the waiting room and invites the patient into the adjacent examination room to check her vital signs. Not long after that, she gets admitted. This is not an exceptional situation. Relatively often, patients and companions using the hardline approach manage to shorten considerably their waiting time.

SOFT RESISTANCE

The third interactional strategy consists of a shrewd mélange of compliance and assertiveness through which Roma patients resist micro-aggressions while protecting the face of the interlocutor. Soft resistance bears some similarities with the strategy of submission; in both of them, patients keep a defensive line and avoid challenging triage agents' authority or decisions. However, patients using this strategy do not accept the unfavorable claims made, directly or indirectly, by the interlocutor. Instead, they negotiate the definition of the situation and manage to present themselves as worthy individuals. Soft resistance appears to be used mostly by assimilated Roma and middle-class Roma from both types of communities, males and females alike.

The example below comes from an audio-recorded admission interview with a middle-aged Romani patient experiencing sore throat. The patient has been diagnosed with tonsillitis three weeks earlier and has been scheduled for a surgery. At the moment of the presentation, he experiences severe symptoms:

NURSE: It [the medical letter] says tonsillitis at cold. What did you do? Did you put an ice-cream bolster? By the way, that's interesting. What did you do? To lower your edema, you have to eat something cold, isn't it?

PATIENT: [In resignation] Eat cold . . .

NURSE: What did [the doctor] say?

PATIENT: He said not to eat cold, not to drink, not to [inaudible]

NURSE: Come on! And you, what did you do? [The patient raises his elbows; the nurse laughs] You ate ice-cream and—

PATIENT:—no, I did not eat ice-cream.

NURSE: I will talk to the doctor, and he will come see you.

During the interaction, the nurse tests two assumptions (personal responsibility for the deterioration of health and ignorance) that are consistent with the staff-devised Roma type. The question "what did you do" indicates the expectation of individual agency. This question appears often in interactions with Roma but is much less common with patients of another ethnicity, who tend to be asked the impersonal "what happened"/"how did it happen" instead. The nurse proposes the consumption of ice cream as a mere possibility, and then as a fact despite the patient's opposition. The assumption of ignorance is expressed through the trap question about the need to eat cold items.

The patient refutes these assumptions in a firm yet polite way. He demonstrates a good understanding of the therapeutic indication of not eating anything cold, denies having eaten ice-cream, and suggests having no responsibility for the sore throat that brought him to the ED. In doing so, he maintains a defensive stance and refuses to engage in open confrontation. He communicates disagreement obliquely at first, by repeating in resignation the nurse's words, and then in a straightforward way, by refusing to acknowledge the consumption of ice cream.

The three interactional strategies that emerged from the empirical data are analytical constructs. In practice, there is a porous boundary between submission and soft resistance. For instance, the case of the elderly woman was framed as submission because her attempt to negotiate the definition of the situation was unsuccessful, and she ultimately accepted the point of view of the nurse. The same defensive pattern repeated itself several times during the interaction. If she were allowed to explain the absence of medical documents and challenge the nurses' underlying assumption of misuse of the health system, the interaction would have better fit into the category of "soft resistance." This shows that the strategies are to a certain extent reflective of patients' interactional acumen.

REPRODUCING RACISM

Encouraging Stereotype-Consistent Behavior

The cases discussed in this chapter show an apparent paradox: while nurses and clerks deeply resent patients' alleged "recalcitrance," they tend to reward it with faster admission. Thus, more often than not, displaying composure and toughness and defying the norms of behavior in public places pay off. In the case of Roma, however, the personal benefits come at the cost of staff strengthening their representation of the ethnic group members as ill-tempered, unruly, and aggressive. In other words, Romani patients are incentivized to produce presentations of self that are consistent with, and implicitly legitimize, stereotypes.

Although most people adopting a confrontational stance are not Roma, and most of the Roma do not engage in contentious encounters with triage workers, the stereotype of Roma aggression is supported by the second mechanism, that of ethnicizing violence.

ETHNICIZING VIOLENCE

During fieldwork, I haven't witnessed any situation of overt reference to the patients' ethnicity in the front region of the triage booth. In the back region, however, there were a few cases in which, after some heated encounters, nurses and clerks vented their feelings by using direct references or allusions to the ethnicity of the patients with whom they had interacted. Two features of these negative comments were that the perpetrators did not have the characteristics through which nurses hetero-identify a person as Roma (e.g., residence in a segregated neighborhood, a darker phenotype, wearing traditional dress and ethnic jewelry, etc.) and the word used to refer to them was never "Roma," but "ţigani" or even the English word "gypsy."

> CLERK MARGARETA: To them, you are just someone following orders. They have no respect at all. Everyone coming back from abroad, this sort of gypsies [in English], they ask to be treated like there. But I'm asking them: "What did you bring there? You don't belong anywhere." They have no insurance, but lots of demands. (Informal conversation, City)

The triage clerk made these comments after an encounter with a forty-one-year-old patient and his female companion. As soon as they arrived, the couple started complaining about the aspect of the triage booth, regarding it as the outcome of the hospital management's corruption. Throughout the admission interview, the male treated the clerk with condescendence, calling her "Boss." Neither the patient nor the companion displayed any of the characteristics based on which nurses and clerk infer ethnicity.

In another case, at County hospital, a young male parent came with his infant daughter who had got injured while playing with a spoon.[14] The man was told that he had to wait for at least half an hour, possibly one hour or even longer because the ED was overcrowded, and no orderly was available at that time. He challenged the nurse, rejected her claims, changed the topic, and used sarcasm when she told him not to give a spoon to the child ("What a great advice, thank you. I assume you will write me an invoice for such great advice.") After the patient went to the waiting room, the nurse burst out: "They are from flat nine, and I know that only stupid people and retarded people live there, because I know the flat, it is that one perpendicular to the hospital, in the ghetto."

The mention of the "ghetto" makes a veiled reference to the ethnicity of the person. Nevertheless, the area, which has a significant Roma population, does not qualify as a ghetto because it does not meet the criteria of ethnic segregation, strict boundaries, and development of a collective identity.[15] Instead, it is an inner-city pocket of poverty inhabited by traditional Roma and non-Roma alike. Moreover, the lower-class patient does not have any of the markers of ethnicity, so it is very likely that the ethnic allusion is related to his interactional conduct alone.

Another telling example of ethnicizing violence comes from the interviews and informal discussions with staff members at County. On several occasions, I was told about an act of violence perpetrated on a Christmas day by Romani people:

> NURSE LUCIA: There was a Christmas when they broke screen monitors, broke glasses, they were very aggressive. There have been [CCTV] recordings,

they have been broadcasted by the national television. [. . .] They want to be the first, they want to get admitted before others, but the Roma are not the only ones to do this, there are also Romanians who are like that. (Interview, County)

However, in a later interview, to which two nurses participated, the ethnic identity of the perpetrators was called into question. The conversation reproduced below took place when the interviewees were talking about Roma's alleged "recalcitrance":

INTERVIEWER: Were there any incidents here? And I mean more serious stuff, not just swearing or something like that.

NURSE VERA: Yes, all the time, there are incidents all the time.

INTERVIEWER: I see.

NURSE NINA: Do you know when there was something more serious? One or two years ago, on Christmas. Last year, I think.

NURSE VERA: But those people were not Roma.

NURSE NINA: They were not Roma. (Interview, County)

Although the two triage nurses ultimately agree that the perpetrators were non-Roma, the stereotype-consistent event made it qualify for an illustration of Romani patients' unruly behavior. Other nurses at County also described the event as being committed by Roma, which suggests that the event had been collectively interpreted as ethnical.

CONVENTIONALIZING ROMA AGGRESSION

Complementing the ethnicization of violence, the mechanism of conventionalizing Roma aggression applies the stereotype to situations occurring outside the ED. The following fieldnote describes an event that took place at County:

An ambulance nurse asked the triage nurse if she had some information about a woman who died in the maternity the day before. She added that she heard there was a big scandal there. The triage nurse knew nothing about the case but made an inference regarding the ethnic origin of the deceased: "[If it was a big scandal] It means that she was *țigancă*."[16] Then she made her reasoning clear: "There are people who say: what if she was *țigancă*? Aren't they humans as well? They are, but it is only them who are like this, that the entire clan[17] comes. If this happens to us, it's not that everybody comes."

The event that made the object of the conversation recorded in the fieldnote was the death, in a maternity ward located in another part of the city, of a twenty-four-year-old woman who was four months' pregnant. The local newspaper reported that the death was most likely due to cardiac arrest after a surgical intervention and mentioned that the patient had had the symptoms of an abortion. No details were provided about the nature of the possible abortion.

Remarkable in this encounter is the absence of any direct reference to the ethnicity of the patient in the account provided by the ambulance nurse. However, the triage nurse interprets the scandal as deeply embedded in the Romani culture, and further assumes that the protagonists were the extended family of the deceased. In making her point clear, she mobilizes practical knowledge acquired as a hospital worker (the observed tendency of Roma to come accompanied by several relatives) and uses it in conjunction with the stereotype of Roma recalcitrance.

This is not the only stereotype that is conventionalized through storytelling. One day, one of the nurses at County shared an amusing personal story of pickpocketing going wrong. Earlier that day, as she was standing in the bus, the nurse saw a man's hand getting into her jacket's pocket. She had nothing of value inside, so she decided not to confront the thief. Instead, she stepped on his foot and let her entire weight on him. As she was a woman of large build, she could see the thief silently enduring excruciating pain. In her account, she gave no direct or indirect indication of the thief's ethnic origin. Later that day, another nurse shared the story with her husband during a phone conversation. She began by saying, "when a *țigan* tried to steal from her pocket . . . "

CONCLUSIONS

The exclusion of Roma at the ED is a subtle process that occurs at the intersection between staff-devised assumptions about Roma, the social characteristics of Roma patients, and their interactional conduct. Triage workers translate lay beliefs about the alleged moral character of Roma into background expectations about their use of the service and social worth. While these expectations inform staff's interactional stances and often lead to micro-aggressions during the admission interview, they do not act deterministically. Triage workers seek to test their ethnic assumptions, whereas Roma patients use their creative agency to challenge, refute, or exploit them in order to get access to emergency care. However, the three interactional strategies used by Roma—submission, hard line, and soft resistance—contribute in variegated ways to the reproduction of staff's stereotypes about the Roma.

The study shows that the everyday Roma exclusion at the ED takes covert forms. The staff's deeply entrenched ethnic assumptions are never made explicit during the triage interactions, even though they are instrumental to the moral evaluation of cases. Moreover, the ethnic exclusion does not involve denying access to the service. All Roma get admitted, but their waiting time is generally longer than that of other patients and their likelihood of exposure to micro-aggressions is much higher. In this respect, the ED is not different from other state agencies with which Roma routinely interact,[18] which suggests that the findings of this study may also hold true in other organizational contexts.

Examining the microsocial foundations of ethnic exclusion in organizations can complement studies focusing on large scale policy processes. In a recent paper, Margareta Matache[19] convincingly argued that the reproduction of ethnic inequities in European societies is linked to inadequately planned and implemented policies to improve the situation of Roma, and insufficient commitment to Roma issues on the part of policymakers. The findings of my study indicate that, at the other end of the policy spectrum, street-level bureaucrats also have the potential to undermine inclusive policies. Triage workers engage in ethnic exclusionary practices by mobilizing lay representations about Roma and their culture in the decision-making. In this way, they reproduce and reinforce the wider social order at the ED.

The findings suggest the need for delivering culturally competent emergency healthcare services, improving triage workers' structural competency, and devising organizational mechanisms to investigate and sanction discriminatory practices. Many prejudiced views inherent to the Roma type and many interactional misunderstandings originate in nurses' and clerks' lack of familiarity with Romani culture. Including intercultural education into the curricula of nursing schools and providing the ED staff with continuous training on cultural diversity and Romani culture are some practical solutions for reducing the bias. Another possible intervention is the extension of health mediation[20] to emergency services. Improving structural competency is equally important. Currently, triage workers are inclined to blame the Roma for their socio-economic situation, attributing it to personal flaws and cultural backwardness. The recognition of structural forces that impact in multifaceted ways Romani people's lives and decisions can erode their representation as morally undeserving of care. Finally, the establishment of a functional mechanism for investigating allegations of discrimination at the ED would increase triage workers' accountability and would create disincentives for engaging in ethnic exclusion.

NOTES

1. This does not mean to say that the triage workers' claim of treating everybody the same is necessarily deceptive. While there is often a clear gap between what nurses and clerks say they do and how they actually handle patients, I could find no means to determine whether they were aware of the exclusionary dimension of the moral evaluation process.

2. The nurse uses the word "țigani(i)," which, similar to the English word *gypsies*, is a heavily value-laden ethnonym without any correspondent in the Romani language. However, the equivalence is not perfect. Because "țigan" is an "extremely derogatory" term, etymologically linked to the idea of moral impurity and associated with the historical experience of slavery, its connotations go beyond those conveyed by "Gypsy." See Ian Hancock, "A Glossary of Romani Terms," *Source: The American Journal of Comparative Law*, vol. 45, 343. Nicolae Gheorghe and Iulius Rostas, "Roma or Țigan: The Romani Identity—Between Victimisation and Emancipation," *Roma Rights* 18, no. 1: 43–66.

3. Alexandra Oprea and Margareta Matache, "Reclaiming the Narrative: A Critical Assessment of Terminology in the Fight for Roma Rights," in *Dimensions of Antigypsyism in Europe*, ed. Ismael Cortés Gómez and Markus End (Brussels: European Network Against Racism and Central Council of German Sinti and Roma, 2019), 276–300; Gheorghe and Rostas, "Roma or Țigan: The Romani Identity—Between Victimisation and Emancipation"; Alexandra Oprea, "Romani Feminism in Reactionary Times," *Signs: Journal of Women in Culture and Society* 38, no. 1: 11–21.

4. Nadia Kaneva and Delia Popescu, "'We Are Romanian, Not Roma': Nation Branding and Postsocialist Discourses of Alterity," *Communication, Culture & Critique* 7, no. 4: 506–23; Shannon Woodcock, "Romania and EUrope: Roma, Rroma and Tigani as Sites for the Contestation of Ethno-National Identities," *Patterns of Prejudice* 41, no. 5: 493–515.

5. Rupert Wolfe Murray, "Romania's Government Moves to Rename the Roma," *Time*.

6. This was an unprompted response. The question was "In what respects are they [the Roma] different as patients?"

7. The trope of "Roma clans" or the "Roma underworld" was only encountered at City, where it constituted a key part of the staff's discourse on Roma.

The lack of health insurance is irrelevant for access to the ED because emergency healthcare services are provided free of charge. However, since all formally employed people are covered by the national health insurance, lacking insurance stands as a proxy for unemployment and alludes to the stereotypes of laziness and parasitic lifestyle.

8. Ioana Szeman, *Staging Citizenship: Roma, Performance, and Belonging in EU Romania* (New York and Oxford: Berghahn, 2018), 118.

9. The practice of early marriages is still encountered in some traditional Roma communities, but it is not normative in the Romani culture. The extensive and biased reporting of some cases of early marriage, such as the arranged marriage of the daughter of a Roma informal leader in 2005, gave the phenomenon a large visibility

and reinforced negative stereotypes surrounding the Roma culture. See Nicoleta Bițu and Crina Morteanu, *Drepturile Copilului Sunt Negociabile? Cazul Mariajelor Timpurii În Comunitățile de Romi Din RomâNia* (București: Romani CRISS, 2009); Alexandra Oprea, "The Arranged Marriage of Ana Maria Cioaba, Intra-Community Oppression and Romani Feminist Ideals," *European Journal of Women's Studies* 12, no. 2: 133–48.

10. Both EDs are serviced by security guards. They are in charge with protecting the staff and preventing unauthorized persons from entering the ED proper. The security guards are stationed in close proximity to the triage booths, but they rarely intervene in situations of verbal conflicts between staff and patients.

11. This is a verse from *Scrisoarea III (The Third Letter),* a classical Romanian poem written in the second half of the 19th century by Mihai Eminescu. The doctor alludes to the non-Western origin of the Roma and, possibly, to the recent migration of many Eastern European Roma to Western Europe.

12. While Roma people can be found every day at the two EDs, they represent a tiny minority of patients.

13. It is not uncommon for ambulance crew to inform triage workers that they picked the patient up at the "gypsy quarter" (*țigănie*). This information is important when the patient is brought from rural areas with whom the nurses and clerks are less familiar. For urban patients, this information is superfluous, as triage workers recognize the segregated communities based on the address printed on the ID card.

14. The case was discussed in the previous chapter.

15. See Wacquant, 2013.

16. Roma woman.

17. *Tot neamul.*

18. Szeman, *Staging Citizenship: Roma, Performance, and Belonging in EU Romania*; Iulius Rostas, "ID Checks and Police Raids: Ethnic Profiling in Central Europe," in *Ethnic Profiling by Police in Europe* (Budapest: Open Society Justice Initiative, 2005), 26–31.

19. "Biased Elites, Unfit Policies: Reflections on the Lacunae of Roma Integration Strategies," *European Review* 25, no. 04: 588–607.

20. Marius Wamsiedel, *Roma Health Mediation in Romania: Case Study* (Copenhagen: World Health Organization—Regional Office for Europe, 2013).

Conclusions

I started this project with the intention to approach moral evaluation through an interactionist lens. My aim was to highlight the patients' active contribution to the moral evaluation by examining their strategies of self- and case-presentation, and the interactional negotiation of admission to the emergency service. However, once I got in the field and became familiar with the social world of triage workers, I realized that emphasizing the interactions alone would ineluctably lead to a partial, decontextualized, and thereby distorted representation of what was going on at the triage.

To avoid such pitfalls, I took an analytical detour through the collective habitus of triage workers as members of a community of practice, as articulated in verbal accounts and manifested in the handling of cases. This detour allowed me to grasp how nurses and clerks defined the triage situations, what meanings they attached to the triage work and the users, and how these meanings impacted their subsequent actions.[1] These considerations made the substance of the first three chapters, which exposed the staff's variegated beliefs, expectations, assumptions, and conjectures that precede actual interactions and inform their structure and content. The last three chapters shifted the attention to the interactional accomplishment of the moral evaluation. By looking to the interplay between staff's frames of reasoning and patients' interactional strategies, I showed that moral evaluation is irreducible to the application of pre-defined ideas and schemes of reasoning. Instead, it is a fluid, multifaceted, situational, and, to a certain extent, negotiable process. This "categorization in action"[2] approach avoids the peril of determinism and patient objectification to which many early studies of moral evaluation fell prey.

As moral evaluation occurs at the intersection between medicine and society, this study contributes to the understanding of the interplay between the clinical and the social in the triage processing of patients. It shows that structural conditions create the conditions of possibility for the existence of moral evaluation, whereas dominant values and beliefs shape triage workers' approach to patients and cases. At the same time, the moral evaluation unwittingly reproduces and reinforces stereotypes, contributing to the social marginalization of vulnerable groups and the inequity of access to emergency care.

MORAL EVALUATION AS AN INFORMAL PRACTICE

The moral evaluation of ED patients is a practical necessity. It is an organizational response to three structural conditions: the mismatch between the demand of emergency healthcare and the available resources; the formal obligation to provide access to emergency medicine to all persons demanding it; and the poor organization of the health system, which restricts access to primary care for many.

The process has both exclusionary and inclusionary dimensions, which are reflected in the ways triage nurses and clerks make sense of the crisis of the ED. On the one hand, they tend to blame the patients for the overcrowding of the ED, a condition that leads to numerous problems, including the limited time available for caring for the people with severe, potentially life-threatening conditions; draining of resources; high workload for staff members; and stressful work conditions. Were the patients with trivial medical problems or long-term symptoms to seek care elsewhere, at the family doctor's office or in the polyclinic, the demand of care at ED would decrease significantly. Doing nothing is not a viable solution because further increasing the number of presentations would ultimately suffocate the emergency service. At the same time, there is little triage workers can do in restricting access to persons regarded as subthreshold for admission, as this goes against the current regulations, whose enforcement is closely monitored by health authorities. The triage workers' solution is to play by the rules while skillfully subverting them. By taking advantage of the discretionary power they enjoy as street-level bureaucrats, nurses and clerks educate patients who are not "real" emergencies about the pathway to care, subject them to unpleasant experiences and, in the case of nurses at County, extend their waiting time. Thus, without breaking the formal rule of admitting everyone, triage workers handle patients in a way that is expected to reduce their propensity to use the ED again for health concerns that could be adequately handled in the primary care sector.

On the other hand, triage workers concede that the deficiencies in the organization of the primary care prevent many patients from getting the medical assistance they need. For instance, if the family doctor is on leave, skips work, or is fully booked for many days, the patients on their roll are left without options. The situation is even more pronounced in some remote rural communities, where the provision of family medicine is uneven, and the performance of practitioners is loosely monitored. Triage workers find this situation morally unacceptable and consider that patients should not pay for a fault that is not their own. Therefore, they often deal with situations of this sort by admitting without any sanction people whose health condition itself would not warrant a visit to the ED. However, such favorable treatment is not extended to people whose lack of alternatives is regarded as result of personal flaws or whose condition has deteriorated as a result of personal actions.

The moral evaluation of patients stems not only from staff members' preoccupation with the smooth functioning of the emergency system, but also from lay concerns. The scrutiny of patients' social and moral characteristics reflects the triage workers' desire to apportion care based on individuals' integration in and contribution to the society. Unlike formal entitlement to emergency healthcare, which is universal by policy fiat, deservingness is something that patients achieve or not during triage encounters. To assess worth, nurses and clerks engage in an active, yet discrete, examination of patients' social characteristics, personal accomplishments, and demeanor.

In short, the moral evaluation is an informal social process through which triage workers attempt to make the handling of patients consistent with the mission of the ED and the socially dominant values and norms. The criteria of legitimacy, reasonableness, and social worth reflect the endeavor to protect the service from unwarranted use, the patients from institutional malfunctioning, and the society from cultural transgressors, respectively.

The moral evaluation criteria, discussed in chapter 2, are consistent with the distinction between legitimacy and deservingness, identified long ago by Julius Roth[3] and recently reiterated by Alexandra Hillman.[4] Nevertheless, there are some notable differences between what I have found at County and City, and the extant scholarship on non-clinical evaluation.

First, previous works[5] have documented occasional departures from the rule of legitimacy in the case of economically and socially vulnerable patients. Hospital workers treated some of the patients experiencing severe economic hardship, domestic problems, or difficulties in accessing other therapeutic agencies as if they had met the criteria of eligibility for emergency care, even though they had blatantly failed to do so. The positive discrimination, albeit recurrent, was not an organizationally ratified way of handling patients in dire straits, but a practice selectively used by a few hospital workers. At the EDs in which I carried out fieldwork, reasonableness is a standalone criterion whose conditions of applicability are tacitly agreed upon by all triage agents. It does not cater to the social problems of the patients, but to their inability of attending other healthcare facilities for reasons independent of themselves. Moreover, the lack of enrollment with a general practitioner or the lack of health insurance do not qualify the patient for exemption from the legitimacy rule, since triage workers assume these conditions to be related to individual flaws rather than to structural conditions.

It is not easily apparent why the reasonableness of the visit features so prominently in the categorization practices occurring in Romanian EDs while it is undocumented in other countries. A plausible explanation lies in the structural differences in the provision of healthcare in the primary sector. Since the repeated reforms of the Romanian medical system have led to major shortcomings in the functioning of family medicine, many people find themselves in the practical impossibility of accessing this service despite being formally entitled for it. Therefore, this is a social problem that triage workers cannot ignore in their day-to-day practice. The better access to general practitioners in other countries may explain the lack of similar provisions there. However, cultural explanations for this difference cannot be discounted either.

Second, many studies focusing on doctors' evaluation of the clientele[6] discuss legitimacy in relation to the practical benefits the case brings to staff, such as expanding knowledge, showing prowess, and preparing for examinations. This assumes that legitimacy follows the clinical framing of the case. For the triage agents in my study, legitimacy means determining the nature and the severity of the health condition. Thus, it precedes and anticipates the clinical framing. Moreover, albeit medical in orientation, legitimacy is inferred from various non-clinical considerations, including timing of the presentation, patient's purported credibility, and patient's embodiment of distress. This shows that the same criterion carries different meanings and implications for members of various occupational groups.

Third, I have found that triage workers in this study conduct the assessment of deservingness by taking into consideration not only the overall worth, but also the situational merit of the patient. While the overall worth refers to the relation of individuals with the society at large, delineated in terms of contribution to the general welfare and compliance with the dominant norms, the situational worth describes their relationship with the triage staff, particularly the ability to disrupt in a pleasant way the work routine. Situational worth is to overall worth what reasonableness is to legitimacy—a warranted suspension of its applicability. It is difficult to say whether this constitutes a local variant of the deservingness criterion, or it is a more general phenomenon that previous studies have, for some reason, overlooked.

PATIENT TYPES AND INTERACTIONAL NEGOTIATION

The typification of patients constitutes an important, yet too often overlooked, dimension of the non-clinical evaluation. It is the missing link between classification schemes and interactional negotiation, because through typification triage agents turn the abstract criteria of categorization into specific expectations for many users of the emergency service. It is based on these very expectations that they choose the format of the interaction and decide how to conduct the admission interview.

The typifying activities, which are common to decision-making in everyday life,[7] are salient in triage encounters due to the brevity of interactions, the limited stock of precise knowledge about patients, and the diversity of the clientele. Triage workers at the EDs that I have studied use complex, coherent, and subtle patient types that consist of a combination of presumed health complaints and social characteristics. Although the typifying work applies only to patients the staff regard as problematic, not all members of a patient type are negatively viewed. In fact, with the notable exceptions of "Roma," all other types comprise two mutually exclusive sub-types: the "inebriated" includes "occasionally drunk" and "drunkards," the "advanced age" includes "elderly" and "very elderly," the "social case" includes "the morally flawed" and "the victim of unfortunate circumstances," the "mentally ill" includes "the severely mentally ill" and the "NVDists," and the "people attempting suicide" includes "real suicidees" and "fake suicidees." Nurses and clerks attribute to each sub-type a specific configuration of legitimacy, reasonableness, and social worth. In each of the pairs above, the first sub-type fares better than the second with respect to the non-clinical classification.

Previous studies[8] have emphasized the process of typifying and its impact on the assessment of clientele in emergency healthcare units, but have given scarce attention to the actual types, the underlying assumptions on which they are based, and the specific expectations associated to them. I have endeavored to cover this gap by examining six patient types and showing what nurses and clerks expect to find when they begin the admission interview.

Useful as they are, patient types do not act deterministically. In the moral evaluation process, triage workers use them to delineate a horizon of expectation regarding patients and cases. The constant comparison of admission interviews and their outcomes reveals that many people belonging to negatively typified groups gain smooth access to emergency care, whereas people for whom there is no background expectancy of low legitimacy, reasonableness, and worth sometimes end up being subjected to staff's disciplining actions. This shows that the moral evaluation is a dynamic and interactional process. The admission interview represents the social arena in which participants negotiate meanings; triage agents put their background assumptions about the patient to test, whereas patients endeavor to put on a favorable presentation of self and a convincing presentation of the case.

In the case of patients belonging to negatively typified groups, a pre-condition for negotiating legitimacy, reasonableness, and worth is to dissociate themselves from the type to which they have been assigned. This separation can be achieved by resisting the triage workers' attempts to impose their expectations as real, and by volunteering information that, albeit not necessarily clinically relevant, sets them apart from the group. Once they achieve this, their assessment is largely similar to that of other patients.

The interactional negotiation concerns the issues of credibility, responsible use of the service, and worth. By taking a proactive stance, constructing a simple yet coherent story, and maintaining the initial claims throughout the conversation, patients increase their chances of passing as credible. To appear as responsible users, they embody distress, demonstrate understanding and acceptance of the staff-devised mission of the ED, and stress out the responsibility for the health problem. Patients manufacture worth through the pattern of interactional conduct adopted and the rhetorical maneuvers of projecting a favorable self-presentation.

THE SOCIAL EMBEDDEDNESS OF
MORAL EVALUATION

The moral evaluation of patients is informed by organizational concerns but also by lay beliefs, values, and norms. As members of the society, nurses and clerks share the dominant social representations and use them to sort patients out. Unwittingly, their work serves to the reproduction and reinforcement of such views and the making of inclusion and exclusion along gender, class, and ethnic lines in medical settings. In this sense, the ED can be regarded as a microcosm of the Romanian society and a vantage point for observing it.

Like other ceremonial occasions, the admission interview facilitates "an expressive rejuvenation and reaffirmation of the moral values of the community."[9] This can be clearly seen when it comes to gender. Triage nurses encourage and reward presentations of self that exhibit the traditional delineation of gender roles, with men displaying equanimity, courage, and self-control, and women embodying emotional weakness, fragility, and vulnerability. The brave female and the poltroon male constitute anomalies in dominant gender regime, and their transgression of gender norms is often sanctioned.

Class constitutes an important social characteristic of ED users. Triage workers usually attend to the economic and social situation of their clientele and make use of the available cues to situate the patients in terms of worth. However, unlike gender and ethnicity, social class does not constitute a master status, and the staff's positioning toward it is not homogeneous. Usually, the demeanor of the person matters at least as much as their presumed position in the social hierarchy, which makes the interactional dimension of the assessment more prone to negotiations. Some of the working-class unemployed and retirees receive negative treatment, while others enjoy benevolent treatment even if they fail to meet the legitimacy criterion. The same thing happens with middle-class individuals. On the one hand, their "decent" life and high education are hold in high regard by nurses and clerks. On the other hand, by possessing health insurance and affording to pay the cost of diagnosis and treatment in the private sector if the family doctor is unavailable, they are more likely than indigent patients to be admonished when the presentation is deemed unreasonable. However, there is some degree of disagreement among staff about the middle-class patients' entitlement to and deservingness of care, which stands in contrast with the orientation to blue collar workers and farmers. Interestingly, nurses and clerks acknowledge in the interviews that structural conditions in post-socialist times turned many "decent"[10] people into poverty. However, they obliterate such considerations when interacting with patients. As indicated in chapter 5, poverty is generally not considered an acceptable reason to go to the ED instead of seeing the family doctor.[11]

Ethnicity is a major factor in the moral evaluation of patients. Triage workers at both hospitals meet Romani people with strong aversion and distrust. The staff-devised Roma type is the most homogeneous one, which indicates a dominant narrative supporting little internal variation. However, the triage workers' positioning toward Roma does not come from direct contact but is rather an import from the society at large, most likely through the intermediation of media. Recent examinations of various outlets including newspapers,[12] television programs,[13] reality TV shows,[14] and social media[15] concur in showing that the representations of the Roma are strongly biased. They tend to essentialize ethnicity and associate Romani people with deviance, criminality, tastelessness, and other repugnant characteristics. Such accounts depict the Roma as culturally different and physically and morally dangerous: they allegedly threaten the safety of ordinary people, the orderliness of the neighborhoods they live or spend time in, and ultimately the moral fabric of the society. Even apparently innocuous media depictions of "ordinary" Roma acquire, if interpreted in a specific knowledge context, an unmistakable othering function.[16] While the negative characteristics inherent to the 'Roma' type do not necessarily translate into sanctions when accessing emergency care, patients believed to be Roma face important obstacles in eliciting the staff's favorable treatment. This indicates that the moral evaluation is, unintendedly, a racial project.

The systematic examination of Romani patients' handling at the triage reveals that ethnic stereotypes are pervasive and endure even when there is little empirical evidence to support them. The reproduction of the widespread belief that Roma have a penchant for physical violence, verbal aggression, and unruly conduct, documented in chapter 6, is telling in this respect.

At the beginning of this book, I have mentioned *The Death of Mr. Lazarescu*, the semi-fictional film documenting the most extreme and visible consequences of the social categorization of patients at the ED. Fortunately, the denial of access to emergency care is so rare that it can be regarded as an anomaly in the working of the emergency service rather than its byproduct. Nevertheless, the systematic investigation of the triage decision-making practices reveals subtler forms of exclusion that are not devoid of health consequences.

The moral evaluation of patients is a Procrustean bed, an arbitrary and inconsistent solution to the deep crisis of the Emergency Department and the uneven access to primary care in Romania, that reduces some inequities in the access to healthcare while amplifying others. The nature of the study makes it impossible to assess the success of triage workers' maneuvers to dissuade the misuse of the service and the distal consequences of these maneuvers. However, the use of protracted waiting, scolding, and reprimands to sanction patients whose case is deemed inconsistent with the mission of the ED is likely to deter many from returning to the hospital for any health concern, no matter how urgent. Thus, the exclusionary dimension of the gatekeeping practice has the potential to exacerbate medical vulnerability, reduce the use of emergency services by people needing immediate care, and indirectly contribute to health inequities.

NOTES

1. I did not examine the social worlds of the patients for three main reasons. First, the heterogeneity of the patient population would have made this a daunting task. Secondly, patients were in a situation of health-related vulnerability that the interview situation could have amplified. I wanted to avoid any non-negligible risk for the participants. Thirdly, dividing the field time between triage workers and patients could have made the former question my allegiances. Given the staff's representation of the ED as a besieged fortress, discussed in the introduction, this option could have jeopardized my position in the field.

2. Lesley Griffiths, "Categorising to Exclude: The Discursive Construction of Cases in Community Mental Health Teams," *Sociology of Health & Illness* 23, no. 5: 680.

3. "Some Contingencies of the Moral Evaluation and Control of Clientele: The Case of the Hospital Emergency Service."

4. "Why Must I Wait?"

5. Dodier and Camus, "Openness and Specialisation: Dealing with Patients in a Hospital Emergency Service," 426; Vassy, "Categorisation and Micro-Rationing: Access to Care in a French ED," 428–30.

6. Mannon, "Defining and Treating 'Problem Patients' in a Hospital Emergency Room"; Dodier and Camus, "Openness and Specialisation: Dealing with Patients in a Hospital Emergency Service"; Jeffery, "Normal Rubbish"; Nurok and Henckes, "Between Professional Values and the Social Valuation of Patients: The Fluctuating Economy of Pre-Hospital Emergency Work."

7. Schütz, "Common-Sense and Scientific Interpretation of Human Action"; Kwang-ki Kim and Tim Berard, "Typification in Society and Social Science: The Continuing Relevance of Schutz's Social Phenomenology," *Human Studies* 32, no. 3: 263–89; Thomas Luckmann, "On Meaning in Everyday Life and in Sociology," *Current Sociology* 37, no. 1: 17–29.

8. E.g., Sbaih 1998; Sudnow 1967.

9. Goffman, *The Presentation of Self in Everyday Life*, 23.

10. That is, industrious, responsible, and not complacent.

11. The homeless people, who are in a situation of extreme destitution and subjected to stigma, constitute the only exception to this rule.

12. Angéla Kóczé and Márton Rövid, "Roma and the Politics of Double Discourse in Contemporary Europe," *Identities* 24, no. 6: 684–700; Petre Breazu and Göran Eriksson, "Romaphobia in Romanian Press: The Lifting of Work Restrictions for Romanian Migrants in the European Union," *Discourse & Communication*, 175048132098215.

13. Petre Breazu and David Machin, "How Television News Disguises Its Racist Representations: The Case of Romanian *Antena 1* Reporting on the Roma," *Ethnicities* 20, no. 5: 823–43.

14. Annabel Tremlett, "Demotic or Demonic? Race, Class and Gender in 'Gypsy' Reality TV," *The Sociological Review* 62, no. 2: 316–34; Emma Bell, "'A Thousand Diamonds': Gypsies, Romanies and Travellers and 'Transgressive Consumerism' in Reality Television," in *Consumerism on TV: Popular Media from the 1950s to the Present*, ed. Alison Hulme (Farnham: Ashgate, 2015), 127–46.

15. Jan Chovanec, "'Re-Educating the Roma? You Must Be Joking . . . ': Racism and Prejudice in Online Discussion Forums," *Discourse & Society* 32, no. 2: 156–74.

16. Markus End, "Subtle Images of Antigypsyism: An Analysis of the Visual Perception of 'Roma,'" *Identities* 24, no. 6: 668–83.

Bibliography

Ábrán, Ágota. 2016. "'I Was Told to Come Here in the Forest to Heal': Healing Practices Through the Land in Transylvania." *Transylvanian Review* 25: 91–106.

Allen, Davina. 2001. "Narrating Nursing Jurisdiction: 'Atrocity Stories' and 'Boundary-Work.'" *Symbolic Interaction* 24 (1): 75–103.

Anspach, Renee R. 1988. "Notes on the Sociology of Medical Discourse: The Language of Case Presentation." *Journal of Health and Social Behavior* 29 (4): 357–75.

Barany, Zoltan D. 1994. "Living on the Edge: The East European Roma in Postcommunist Politics and Societies." *Slavic Review* 53 (2): 321–44.

Battistella, Roger M. 1983. "Health Services in the Socialist Republic of Romania: Structural Features and Cost-Containment Policies." *Journal of Public Health Policy* 4 (1): 89–106.

Becker, Howard S. 1967. "Whose Side Are We On?" *Social Problems* 14 (3): 239–47.

Bell, Emma. 2015. "'A Thousand Diamonds': Gypsies, Romanies and Travellers and 'Transgressive Consumerism' in Reality Television." In *Consumerism on TV: Popular Media from the 1950s to the Present*, edited by Alison Hulme, 127–46. Farnham: Ashgate.

Bezzina, Andrew J., Peter B. Smith, David Cromwell, and Kathy Eagar. 2005. "Primary Care Patients in the Emergency Department: Who Are They? A Review of the Definition of the 'Primary Care Patient' in the Emergency Department." *Emergency Medicine Australasia* 17 (5–6): 472–79.

Bițu, Nicoleta, and Crina Morteanu. 2009. *Drepturile Copilului Sunt Negociabile? Cazul Mariajelor Timpurii În Comunitățile de Romi Din România*. București: Romani CRISS.

Borcea, Hadrian. 2007. *Triajul În Structurile Pentru Primirea Urgențelor [The Triage in Emergency Receiving Structures]*. Unpublished document.

Breazu, Petre, and Göran Eriksson. 2020. "Romaphobia in Romanian Press: The Lifting of Work Restrictions for Romanian Migrants in the European Union." *Discourse & Communication*, 175048132098215.

Breazu, Petre, and David Machin. 2020. "How Television News Disguises Its Racist Representations: The Case of Romanian *Antena 1* Reporting on the Roma." *Ethnicities* 20 (5): 823–43.

Buchbinder, Mara. 2017. "Keeping out and Getting in: Reframing Emergency Department Gatekeeping as Structural Competence." *Sociology of Health & Illness* 39 (7): 1166–79.

Buţiu, Călina Ana. 2016. "Healthcare Policy in Romania. Frameworks and Challenges." *Social Change Review* 14 (1): 3–23.

Buus, Niels. 2011. "Categorizing 'Frequent Visitors' in the Psychiatric Emergency Room: A Semistructured Interview Study." *Archives of Psychiatric Nursing* 25 (2): 101–108.

Camus, Agnès, and Nicolas Dodier. 1997. "L'admission Des Malades. Histoire et Pragmatique de l'accueil à l'hôpital [Patient Admission. History and Pragmatics of Hospital Admission]." *Annales. Histoire, Sciences Sociales [Annals. History, Social Sciences]* 52 (4): 733–63.

Carel, Havi, and Ian James Kidd. 2014. "Epistemic Injustice in Healthcare: A Philosophial Analysis." *Medicine, Health Care and Philosophy* 17 (4): 529–40.

CBC. 2019. "Family Calls for Inquest into Suicide of Indigenous Teen in Government Care." CBC. 2019. https://www.cbc.ca/news/canada/hamilton/devon-freeman-1 .5389028.

Cereseto, Shirley, and Howard Waitzkin. 1989. "Capitalism, Socialism and the Physical Quality of Life." *Medical Anthropology* 11 (2): 151–66.

Chovanec, Jan. 2021. "'Re-Educating the Roma? You Must Be Joking . . . ': Racism and Prejudice in Online Discussion Forums." *Discourse & Society* 32 (2): 156–74.

Chukwuma, Adanna, Radu Comsa, Dorothee Chen, and Estelle Gong. 2021. *Provider Payment Reforms for Improved Primary Health Care in Romania*. Washington, DC: World Bank Publications.

Cockerham, William C. 1999. *Health and Social Change in Russia and Eastern Europe*. New York and London: Routledge.

Constantinescu, Cris. 2012. "'My Child Died after Being Shuttled between Hospitals.'" Click. 2012. https://www.click.ro/news/national/mi-au-plimbat-copilul-intre -spitale-pana-murit-0.

Corman, Michael K. 2017. *Paramedics On and Off the Streets: Emergency Medical Services in the Age of Technological Governance*. Toronto: University of Toronto Press.

Cousineau, Matthew J. 2016. "Accomplishing Profession through Self-Mockery." *Symbolic Interaction* 39 (2): 213–28.

Danta, Darrick. 1993. "Ceausescu's Bucharest." *Geographical Review* 83 (2): 170–82.

Derlet, Robert W., and John R. Richards. 2000. "Overcrowding in the Nation's Emergency Departments: Complex Causes and Disturbing Effects." *Annals of Emergency Medicine* 35 (1): 63–68.

Dingwall, Robert. 1977. "'Atrocity Stories' and Professional Relationships." *Sociology of Work and Occupations* 4 (4): 371–96.

Dingwall, Robert, and Topsy Murray. 1983. "Categorization in Accident Departments: 'Good' Patients, 'Bad' Patients and 'Children.'" *Sociology of Health & Illness* 5 (2): 127–48.

Dingwall, Robert, and Phil M. Strong. 1985. "The Interactional Study of Organizations A Critique and Reformulation." *Journal of Contemporary Ethnography* 14 (2): 205–31.

Dodier, Nicholas, and Agnès Camus. 1998. "Openness and Specialisation: Dealing with Patients in a Hospital Emergency Service." *Sociology of Health & Illness* 20 (4): 413–44.

Dodier, Nicolas. 1998. "Clinical Practice and Procedures in Occupational Medicine: A Study of the Framing of Individuals." In *Differences in Medicine*, edited by Marc Berg and Annemarie Mol. Durham and London: Duke University Press.

Dudwick, Nora. 2000. "Postsocialism and the Fieldwork of War." In *Fieldwork Dilemmas: Anthropologists in Postsocialist States*, edited by Hermine G. de Soto and Nora Dudwick, 13–30.

Dumitrache, Liliana, Mariana Nae, Daniela Dumbrăveanu, Gabriel Simion, and Bogdan Suditu. 2016. "Contrasting Clustering in Health Care Provision in Romania: Spatial and Aspatial Limitations." *Procedia Environmental Sciences* 32: 290–99.

Dumitrache, Liliana, Mariana Nae, Gabriel Simion, and Ana-Maria Taloş. 2020. "Modelling Potential Geographical Access of the Population to Public Hospitals and Quality Health Care in Romania." *International Journal of Environmental Research and Public Health* 17 (22): 8487.

Edwards, Bernie, and David Sines. 2008. "Passing the Audition—the Appraisal of Client Credibility and Assessment by Nurses at Triage." *Journal of Clinical Nursing* 17 (18): 2444–51.

End, Markus. 2017. "Subtle Images of Antigypsyism: An Analysis of the Visual Perception of 'Roma.'" *Identities* 24 (6): 668–83.

European Commission. 2014. "Patient Safety and Quality of Care." Eurobarometer. 2014. http://ec.europa.eu/public_opinion/archives/ebs/ebs_411_fact_ro_en.pdf.

European Roma Rights Center. 2006. *Ambulance Not on the Way: The Disgrace of Health Care for Roma in Europe.* Budapest: European Roma Rights Center.

Félix-Brasdefer, J. César. 2015. *The Language of Service Encounters*. Cambridge: Cambridge University Press.

Field, Mark G. 1990. "Noble Purpose, Grand Design, Flawed Execution, Mixed Results: Soviet Socialized Medicine after Seventy Years." *American Journal of Public Health* 80 (2): 144–45.

———. 1995. "The Health Crisis in the Former Soviet Union: A Report from the 'Post-War' Zone." *Social Science & Medicine* 41 (11): 1469–78.

Fleck, Gábor, and Cosima Rughiniş. 2008. *Come Closer: Inclusion and Exclusion of Roma in Present Day Romanian Society.* Bucharest, Romania: Human Dynamics.

"Fondurile pentru analize compensate, epuizate în câteva zile. Explicaţiile medicilor [The Funds for Subsidized Lab Tests, Exhausted in a Few Days. The Doctors' Explanations]." 2016. Digi 24. https://www.digi24.ro/magazin/stil-de-viata/viata-sanatoasa/fondurile-pentru-analize-compensate-epuizate-in-cateva-zile-explicatiile-medicilor-505034.

FRA. 2016. *Second European Union Minorities and Discrimination Survey Roma—Selected Findings.* Vienna: European Union Agency for Fundamental Rights. https://fra.europa.eu/en/publication/2016/eumidis-ii-roma-selected-findings.

Friedman, Jack R. 2006. "The Challenges Facing Mental Health Reform in Romania." *Eurohealth* 12 (3): 36–39.

———. 2008. "Ambivalent and Manichean: Moral Disorder Among Romania's Downwardly Mobile." *The Annual Review of the George Barițiu History Institute, Series Humanistica* 6 (1): 133–58.

———. 2009. "The 'Social Case': Illness, Psychiatry, and Deinstitutionalization in Postsocialist Romania." *Medical Anthropology Quarterly* 23 (4): 375–96.

———. 2012. "Thoughts on Inactivity and an Ethnography of "Nothing": Comparing Meanings of 'Inactivity' in Romanian and American Mental Health Care." *North American Dialogue* 15 (1): 1–9.

Gal, Susan, and Gail Kligman. 2000. *The Politics of Gender After Socialism: A Comparative-Historical Essay.* Princeton, NJ: Princeton University Press.

Garfinkel, Harold. 1956. "Conditions of Successful Degradation Ceremonies." *American Journal of Sociology* 61 (5): 420–24.

Gates, D. M. 2004. "The Epidemic of Violence against Healthcare Workers." *Occupational and Environmental Medicine.*

Geest, Sjaak van der, and Kaja Finkler. 2004. "Hospital Ethnography: Introduction." *Social Science & Medicine*, Hospital Ethnography, 59 (10): 1995–2001.

George, Siân, Katy Daniels, and Evridiki Fioratou. 2018. "A Qualitative Study into the Perceived Barriers of Accessing Healthcare among a Vulnerable Population Involved with a Community Centre in Romania." *International Journal for Equity in Health* 17 (41): 1–13.

Gheorghe, Nicolae, and Iulius Rostas. 2015. "Roma or Țigan: The Romani Identity—Between Victimisation and Emancipation." *Roma Rights* 18 (1): 43–66.

Glaser, Barney G., and Anselm L. Strauss. 1964. "The Social Loss of Dying Patients." *The American Journal of Nursing* 64 (6): 119–121.

Glaser, Barney, and Anselm Strauss. 1965. *Awareness of Dying: A Study of Social Interaction.* Chicago: Aldine.

———. 1971. *Status Passage.* London: Routledge & Kegan Paul.

Glenn, Phillip. 2003. *Laughter in Interaction.* Cambridge: Cambridge University Press.

Goffman, Erving. 1953. "Community Conduct in an Island Community." University of Chicago.

———. 1956. *The Presentation of Self in Everyday Life.* Edinburgh: University of Edinburgh Social Science Research Center.

———. 1967. "On Face-Work: An Analysis of Ritual Elements in Social Interaction." In *Interaction Ritual: Essays in Face-to-Face Behavior*, 5–46. New York: Anchor Books.

———. 1997. "On Cooling the Mark Out: Some Aspects of Adaptation to Failure." In *The Goffman Reader*, edited by Charles Lemert and Anne Branaman, 3–20. Oxford: Blackwell.

Gordon, Deborah R. 1988. "Tenacious Assumptions in Western Medicine." In *Biomedicine Examined*, 19–56. Dordrecht: Springer Netherlands.

Gordon, J. A. 1999. "The Hospital Emergency Department as a Social Welfare Institution." *Annals of Emergency Medicine* 33 (3): 321–25.

Griffiths, Lesley. 2001. "Categorising to Exclude: The Discursive Construction of Cases in Community Mental Health Teams." *Sociology of Health & Illness* 23 (5): 678–700.

Guțoiu, Giorgian. 2021. "Development Inequalities of Romanian Physical Public Healthcare Infrastructure: The Case of Hospital Beds." *Human Geographies* 15 (1): 37–52.

Hackenberg, Elisa A. M., Ville Sallinen, Lauri Handolin, and Virve Koljonen. 2019. "Victims of Severe Intimate Partner Violence Are Left Without Advocacy Intervention in Primary Care Emergency Rooms: A Prospective Observational Study." *Journal of Interpersonal Violence*, March, 1–23.

Hadfield, Jo, Dora Brown, Louise Pembroke, and Mark Hayward. 2009. "Analysis of Accident and Emergency Doctors' Responses to Treating People Who Self-Harm." *Qualitative Health Research* 19 (6): 755–65.

Hancock, Ian. 1997. "A Glossary of Romani Terms." *The American Journal of Comparative Law*. Vol. 45.

Hasenfeld, Yeheskel. 2000. "Organizational Forms as Moral Practices: The Case of Welfare Departments." *Social Service Review* 74 (3): 329–51.

Have, Paul Ten. 1995. "Formatting the Consultation: Communication Formats and Constituted Identities." In *Artikelen van de Tweede Sociolinguïstische Conferentie*, edited by Erica Huls and Jetske Klatter-Folmer, 245–68. Delft: Eburon.

———. 2006. "On the Interactive Constitution of Medical Encounters." *Revue Française de Linguistique Appliquée [French Journal of Applied Linguistics]* 11 (2): 85–98.

Henderson, Gail, and Myron Cohen. 1984. *The Chinese Hospital: A Socialist Work Unit*. New Haven: Yale University Press.

Heritage, John. 2004. "Conversation Analysis and Institutional Talk." In *Handbook of Language and Social Interaction*, edited by Kristine L. Fitch and Robert E. Sanders, 103–47. Manwah, NJ: Lawrence Erlbaum.

Heritage, John, and Jeffrey D. Robinson. 2006. "Accounting for the Visit: Patients' Reasons for Seeking Medical Care." In *Communication in Medical Care: Interaction between Primary Care Physicians and Patients*, edited by John Heritage and Douglas W. Maynard, 48–85. Cambridge: Cambridge University Press.

Hillman, Alexandra. 2014. "'Why Must I Wait?' The Performance of Legitimacy in a Hospital Emergency Department." *Sociology of Health & Illness* 36 (4): 485–99.

Hochschild, Arlie R. 2008. *The Managed Heart: Commercialization of Human Feeling*. 2nd ed. Berkeley, CA: University of California Press.

Holloway, Immy, Beatrice Sofaer-Bennett, and Jan Walker. 2007. "The Stigmatisation of People with Chronic Back Pain." *Disability and Rehabilitation* 29 (18): 1456–64.

Horodnic, Adrian V. 2021. "Trends in Informal Payments by Patients in Europe: A Public Health Policy Approach." *Frontiers in Public Health* 9 (November): 1–9.

Hughes, David. 1988. "When Nurse Knows Best: Some Aspects of Nurse/Doctor Interaction in a Casualty Department." *Sociology of Health and Illness* 10 (1): 1–22.

———. 1989. "Paper and People: The Work of the Casualty Reception Clerk." *Sociology of Health & Illness* 11 (4): 382–408.

Hughes, David, and Lesley Griffiths. 1997. "'Ruling in' and 'Ruling out': Two Approaches to the Micro-Rationing of Health Care." *Social Science & Medicine* 44 (5): 589–99.

Hughes, Everett Cherrington. 2009. *The Sociological Eye: Selected Papers*. New Brunswick, NJ: Transaction Publishers.

Huschke, Susann. 2014. "Performing Deservingness. Humanitarian Health Care Provision for Migrants in Germany." *Social Science & Medicine* 120 (11): 352–59.

Iancu, Alice, Oana Băluță, Alina Dragolea, and Bogdan Florian. 2012. "Women's Social Exclusion and Feminisms: Living in Parallel Worlds? The Romanian Case." In *Gendering Post-Socialist Transition: Studies of Changing Gender Perspectives*, edited by Krasimira Daskalova, Caroline Hornstein Tomić, Karl Kaser, and Filip Radunović, 183–216. Münster: LIT Verlag.

Jackson, Kenneth. 2019. "Death as Expected: Inside a Child Welfare System Where 102 Indigenous Kids Died over 5 Years." APTN News. 2019. https://www .aptnnews.ca/national-news/inside-a-child-welfare-system-where-102-indigenous -kids-died-over-5-years/.

Jeffery, Roger. 1979. "Normal Rubbish: Deviant Patients in Casualty Departments." *Sociology of Health & Illness* 1 (1): 90–107.

Johannessen, Lars E.F. 2018. "Narratives and Gatekeeping: Making Sense of Triage Nurses' Practice." *Sociology of Health & Illness* 40 (5): 892–906.

———. 2019a. "The Commensuration of Pain: How Nurses Transform Subjective Experience into Objective Numbers." *Social Science & Medicine* 233: 38–46.

———. 2019b. "Negotiated Discretion: Redressing the Neglect of Negotiation in 'Street-Level Bureaucracy.'" *Symbolic Interaction* 42 (4): 513–38.

Kaneva, Nadia, and Delia Popescu. 2014. "'We Are Romanian, Not Roma': Nation Branding and Postsocialist Discourses of Alterity." *Communication, Culture & Critique* 7 (4): 506–23.

Kim, Kwang-ki, and Tim Berard. 2009. "Typification in Society and Social Science: The Continuing Relevance of Schutz's Social Phenomenology." *Human Studies* 32 (3): 263–89.

Kirkup, Kristy. 2020. "How Devon Freeman Died: An Ontario Teen's Suicide Raises Hard Questions about Child Welfare and Indigenous Youth." The Globe and Mail. February 13, 2020. https://www.theglobeandmail.com/politics/article-how-devon -freeman-died-an-ontario-teens-suicide-raises-hard/.

Kóczé, Angéla, and Márton Rövid. 2017. "Roma and the Politics of Double Discourse in Contemporary Europe." *Identities* 24 (6): 684–700.

Kovács, Borbála. 2013. "Nannies and Informality in Romanian Local Childcare Markets." In *The Informal Post-Socialist Economy: Embedded Practices and Livelihoods*, edited by Jeremy Morris and Abel Polese, 67–84. London and New York: Routledge.

Kühlbrandt, Charlotte, Katharine Footman, Bernd Rechel, and Martin McKee. 2014. "An Examination of Roma Health Insurance Status in Central and Eastern Europe." *The European Journal of Public Health* 24 (5): 707–12.

Lara-Millán, Armando. 2014. "Public Emergency Room Overcrowding in the Era of Mass Imprisonment." *American Sociological Review* 79 (5): 866–87.

Law 95. 2006. *Legea Nr. 95/2006 privind reforma în domeniul sănătăţii [Law 95/2006 Regarding Healthcare Reform]*. Bucharest, Romania: Monitorul Oficial [Official Gazzette of Romania].

Li, Sarah, and Anne Arber. 2006. "The Construction of Troubled and Credible Patients: A Study of Emotion Talk in Palliative Care Settings." *Qualitative Health Research* 16 (1): 27–46.

Liu, Jianxin, Yong Gan, Heng Jiang, Liqing Li, Robyn Dwyer, Kai Lu, Shijiao Yan, et al. 2019. "Prevalence of Workplace Violence against Healthcare Workers: A Systematic Review and Meta-Analysis." *Occupational and Environmental Medicine* 76 (12): 927–937.

Long, Debbi, Cynthia Hunter, and Sjaak van der Geest. 2008. "When the Field Is a Ward or a Clinic: Hospital Ethnography." *Anthropology & Medicine* 15 (2): 71–78.

Lorber, Judith. 1975. "Good Patients and Problem Patients: Conformity and Deviance in a General Hospital." *Journal of Health and Social Behavior* 16 (2): 213–25.

Luckmann, Thomas. 1989. "On Meaning in Everyday Life and in Sociology." *Current Sociology* 37 (1): 17–29.

Maanen, John van. 1979. "The Fact of Fiction in Organizational Ethnography." *Administrative Science Quarterly* 24 (4): 539–50.

Malone, Ruth E. 1995. "Heavy Users of Emergency Services: Social Construction of a Policy Problem." *Social Science & Medicine* 40 (4): 469–77.

———. 1998. "Whither the Almshouse? Overutilization and the Role of the Emergency Department." *Journal of Health Politics, Policy & Law* 23 (5): 795–832.

Mannon, James M. 1976. "Defining and Treating 'Problem Patients' in a Hospital Emergency Room." *Medical Care* 14 (12): 1004–13.

Marrow, Helen B. 2012. "Deserving to a Point: Unauthorized Immigrants in San Francisco's Universal Access Healthcare Model." *Social Science & Medicine* 74 (6): 846–54.

Matache, Margareta. 2017. "Biased Elites, Unfit Policies: Reflections on the Lacunae of Roma Integration Strategies." *European Review* 25 (04): 588–607.

May, David, and Michael P. Kelly. 1982. "Chancers, Pests and Poor Wee Souls: Problems of Legitimation in Psychiatric Nursing." *Sociology of Health & Illness* 4 (3): 279–301.

McArthur, Margaret, and Phyllis Montgomery. 2004. "The Experience of Gatekeeping: A Psychiatric Nurse in an Emergency Department." *Issues in Mental Health Nursing* 25 (5): 487–501.

McKeganey, Neil. 1989. "On the Analysis of Medical Work: General Practitioners, Opiate Abusing Patients and Medical Sociology." *Sociology of Health & Illness* 11 (1): 24–40.

McKinney, John C. 1969. "Typification, Typologies, and Sociological Theory." *Social Forces* 48 (1): 1–12.

Messing, Vera. 2014. "Methodological Puzzles of Surveying Roma/Gypsy Populations." *Ethnicities* 14 (6): 811–29.

Metzl, Jonathan M., and Helena Hansen. 2014. "Structural Competency: Theorizing a New Medical Engagement with Stigma and Inequality." *Social Science & Medicine* 103 (Supplement C): 126–33.

Metzl, Jonathan M., JuLeigh Petty, and Oluwatunmise V. Olowojoba. 2017. "Using a Structural Competency Framework to Teach Structural Racism in Pre-Health Education." *Social Science & Medicine* 199: 189–201.

Mihalache, Iuliana-Claudia, Felicia-Cătălina Apetroi, and Mihaela Tomaziu-Todosia. 2019. "Equity in Financing the Health Sector: An Important Aspect in Reducing Inequalities in Accessing Health Services. Romania in the European Context." In *European Union Financial Regulation and Administrative Area*, edited by Mihaela Tofan, Irina Bilan, and Elena Cigu, 563–74. Iași: Alexandru Ioan Cuza University Press.

Mishler, Elliot George. 1984. *The Discourse of Medicine: Dialectics of Medical Interviews*. Norwood, NJ: Ablex Publishing Corporation.

Mixich, Vlad. 2012. "Corupția din sistemul medical - protejată sau exorcizată de noua lege a sănătății? [The Corruption in the Medical System - Protected or Exorcised by the New Healthcare Law?]." Hotnews. 2012. https://www.medlife.ro/articole -medicale/coruptia-din-sistemul-medical-protejata-sau-exorcizata-de-noua-lege-a -sanatatii.html.

Mizrahi, Terry. 1985. "Getting Rid of Patients: Contradictions in the Socialisation of Internists to the Doctor-Patient Relationship." *Sociology of Health & Illness* 7 (2): 214–35.

Morris, David M, and James A Gordon. 2006. "The Role of the Emergency Department in the Care of Homeless and Disadvantaged Populations." *Emergency Medicine Clinics of North America* 24: 839–48.

Murakami, Ryu. 2003. *Almost Transparent Blue*. Translated by Nancy Andrew. Tokyo; New York: Kodansha USA.

Murray, Rupert Wolfe. 2010. "Romania's Government Moves to Rename the Roma." Time. 2010. http://content.time.com/time/world/article/0,8599,2035862,00.html.

National Anti-corruption Directorate. 2015. "Bilanț 2014 [Annual Review 2014]." 2015. http://www.pna.ro/comunicat.xhtml?id=5982.

National Institute of Statistics [Romania]. 2013. "The Stable Populations (Residents) - Demographic Structure." Final Results of the 2011 Census of Population and Households. 2013. https://www.recensamantromania.ro/rpl-2011/rezultate-2011/.

———. 2021. "Earnings since 1938 - Annual Series." 2021. https://insse.ro/cms/en/ content/earnings-1938-annual-series-0.

Neghina, Raul, Adriana M. Neghina, Iosif Marincu, and Ioan Iacobiciu. 2011. "Malaria and the Campaigns toward Its Eradication in Romania, 1923–1963." *Vector Borne and Zoonotic Diseases* 11 (2): 103–10.

Nurok, Michael, and Nicolas Henckes. 2009. "Between Professional Values and the Social Valuation of Patients: The Fluctuating Economy of Pre-Hospital Emergency Work." *Social Science & Medicine* 68 (3): 504–10.

OECD, and European Observatory on Health Systems and Policies. 2019. *Romania: Country Health Profile 2019*. Paris: OECD Publishing.

———. 2021. *Romania: Country Health Profile 2021*. Paris: OECD Publishing.

Oleszczyk, Marek, Igor Švab, Bohumil Seifert, Anna Krztoń-Królewiecka, and Adam Windak. 2012. "Family Medicine in Post-Communist Europe Needs a Boost. Exploring the Position of Family Medicine in Healthcare Systems of Central and Eastern Europe and Russia." *BMC Family Practice* 13 (1): 15.

Olsson, M., and H. Hansagi. 2001. "Repeated Use of the Emergency Department: Qualitative Study of the Patient's Perspective." *Emergency Medicine Journal* 18 (6): 430–34.

Oprea, Alexandra. 2005. "The Arranged Marriage of Ana Maria Cioaba, Intra-Community Oppression and Romani Feminist Ideals." *European Journal of Women's Studies* 12 (2): 133–48. https://doi.org/10.1177/1350506805051234.

———. 2012. "Romani Feminism in Reactionary Times." *Signs: Journal of Women in Culture and Society* 38 (1): 11–21. https://doi.org/10.1086/665945.

Oprea, Alexandra, and Margareta Matache. 2019. "Reclaiming the Narrative: A Critical Assessment of Terminology in the Fight for Roma Rights." In *Dimensions of Antigypsyism in Europe*, edited by Ismael Cortés Gómez and Markus End, 276–300. Brussels: European Network Against Racism and Central Council of German Sinti and Roma.

Parekh, Nikesh, and Tamsin Rose. 2011. "Health Inequalities of the Roma in Europe: A Literature Review." *Central European Journal of Public Health* 19 (3): 139–42.

Parsons, Talcott. 1951a. "Illness and the Role of the Physician: A Sociological Perspective." *The American Journal of Orthopsychiatry* 21 (3): 452–60.

———. 1951b. *The Social System*. Glencoe, IL: Free Press.

Pasquini, Mirko. 2022. "Like Ticking Time Bombs. Improvising Structural Competency to 'Defuse' the Exploding of Violence against Emergency Care Workers in Italy." *Global Public Health*, November, 1–12.

Peneff, Jean. 1992. *L'hôpital En Urgence: Étude Par Observation Participante [The Hospital in Emergency: A Study by Participant Observation]*. Paris: Métailié.

Rechel, Bernd, and Martin McKee. 2009. "Health Reform in Central and Eastern Europe and the Former Soviet Union." *The Lancet* 374 (9696): 1186–95.

Reeves, Carla L. 2010. "A Difficult Negotiation: Fieldwork Relations with Gatekeepers." *Qualitative Research* 10 (3): 315–31.

Rey Pino, Juan M., Gonzalo Sánchez Gardey, and Ingunn Hagen. 2008. "When Staff Create the Organisational Culture: A Case Study in the Spanish Emergency Health Care System." *Journal of Health Management* 10 (2): 163–89.

Rhodes, Karin V., James A. Gordon, and Robert A. Lowe. 2008. "Preventive Care in the Emergency Department, Part I: Clinical Preventive Services-Are They Relevant to Emergency Medicine?" *Academic Emergency Medicine* 7 (9): 1036–41.

Ringold, Dena, Mitchell Alexander Orenstein, and Erika Wilkens. 2005. *Roma in an Expanding Europe: Breaking the Poverty Cycle*. Washington, DC: World Bank Publications.

Rivkin-Fish, Michele. 2005. "Bribes, Gifts and Unofficial Payments: Rethinking Corruption in Post-Soviet Russian Health Care." In *Corruption. Anthropological Perspectives*, edited by Dieter Haller and Cris Shore, 47–64. London and Ann Arbor, MI: Pluto Press.

Romanian Ministry of Health. 2009. *Ordinul Nr. 48/2009 privind aprobarea proto-colului naţional de triaj al pacienţilor din structurile pentru primirea urgenţelor [Order 48/2009 Regarding the Approval of the National Protocol for the Triage of Patients in Emergency Units]*. Bucharest, Romania: Monitorul Oficial [Official Gazzette of Romania].

Roscoe, Lori. A., Eric M. Eisenberg, and Colin Forde. 2016. "The Role of Patients' Stories in Emergency Medicine Triage." *Health Communication* 31 (9): 1155–64.

Rostas, Iulius. 2005. "ID Checks and Police Raids: Ethnic Profiling in Central Europe." In *Ethnic Profiling by Police in Europe*, 26–31. Budapest: Open Society Justice Initiative.

Roth, Julius. 1963. *Timetables*. Indianapolis: Bobbs-Merrill.

Roth, Julius A. 1972a. "Staff and Client Control Strategies in Urban Hospital Emergency Services." *Journal of Contemporary Ethnography* 1 (1): 39–60.

———. 1972b. "Some Contingencies of the Moral Evaluation and Control of Clientele: The Case of the Hospital Emergency Service." *American Journal of Sociology* 77 (5): 839–56.

Rowland, Diane. 1991. "Health Status in East European Countries." *Health Affairs* 10 (3): 202–15.

Sampson, Steven. 1981. "Muddling through in Rumania (or: Why the Mamaliga Doesn't Explode)." *International Journal of Rumanian Studies* 3: 165–85.

———. 1983. "Bureaucracy and Corruption as Anthropological Problems: A Case Study from Romania." *Folk. Dansk Ethnografisk Tidsskrift Kobenhavn* 25: 63–96.

Sanders, Julie. 2000. "A Review of Health Professional Attitudes and Patient Perceptions on 'Inappropriate' Accident and Emergency Attendances. The Implications for Current Minor Injury Service Provision in England and Wales." *Journal of Advanced Nursing* 31 (5): 1097–1105.

Sbaih, L. 1998. "Initial Assessment: Gaining Impressions and 'Normal Cases.'" *Accident and Emergency Nursing* 6 (2): 70–74.

Schütz, Alfred. 1953. "Common-Sense and Scientific Interpretation of Human Action." *Philosophy and Phenomenological Research* 14 (1): 1–38.

Scîntee, Gabriela, and Cristian Vlădescu. 2012. "Primary Health Care in Romania after 20 Years of Reforms." In *Health Reforms in South-East Europe*, edited by William Bartlett, Jadranka Božikov, and Bernd Rechel, 262. Houndmills, Basingstoke, Hampshire: Palgrave Macmillan.

Seim, Josh. 2020. *Bandage, Sort, and Hustle: Ambulance Crews on the Front Lines of Urban Suffering*. Oakland, CA: University of California Press.

Siân, George, Katy Daniels, and Evridiki Fioratou. 2018. "A Qualitative Study into the Perceived Barriers of Accessing Healthcare among a Vulnerable Population

Involved with a Community Centre in Romania." *International Journal for Equity in Health* 17 (1): 1–13.

Sotiropoulos, Dimitri A., Ileana Neamtu, and Maya Stoyanova. 2003. "The Trajectory of Post-Communist Welfare State Development: The Cases of Bulgaria and Romania." *Social Policy & Administration* 37 (6): 656–73.

Spânu, Florina, Adriana Băban, Mara Bria, and Dan L. Dumitrascu. 2013. "What Happens to Health Professionals When the Ill Patient Is the Health Care System? Understanding the Experience of Practising Medicine in the Romanian Socio-Cultural Context." *British Journal of Health Psychology* 18 (3): 663–79.

Stan, Sabina. 2012. "Neither Commodities nor Gifts: Post-Socialist Informal Exchanges in the Romanian Healthcare System." *Journal of the Royal Anthropological Institute*, no. 18: 65–82.

———. 2018. "Neoliberal Citizenship and the Politics of Corruption: Redefining Informal Exchange in Romanian Healthcare." In *Economy, Crime and Wrong in a Neoliberal Era*, edited by James G. Carrier, 172–94. New York and Oxford: Berghahn Books.

Stan, Sabina, and Valentin-Veron Toma. 2019. "Accumulation by Dispossession and Public–Private Biomedical Pluralism in Romanian Health Care." *Medical Anthropology* 38 (1): 85–99.

Stillo, Jonathan. 2015. "'We Are the Losers of Socialism!' Tuberculosis, the Limits of Bio-Citizenship and the Future of Care in Romania." *Anthropological Journal of European Cultures* 24 (1): 132–40.

Stoica, Cătălin Augustin. 2012. "Old Habits Die Hard? An Exploratory Analysis of Communist-Era Social Ties in Post-Communist Romania." *European Journal of Science and Theology* 8 (1): 171–93.

Strong, Philip M. 2006a. "Minor Courtesies and Macro Structures." In *Sociology and Medicine: Selected Essays by P.M. Strong*, edited by Anne Murcott, 37–56. Aldershot: Ashgate.

———. 2006b. "The Rivals: An Essay on the Sociological Trades." In *Sociology and Medicine: Selected Essays by P.M. Strong*, edited by Anne Murcott, 119–36. Aldershot: Ashgate.

———. 2006c. "Two Types of Ceremonial Order." In *Sociology and Medicine: Selected Essays by P.M. Strong*, edited by Anne Murcott, 57–81. Aldershot: Ashgate.

Suciu, Şoimita Mihaela, Codruta Alina Popescu, Mugur Daniel Ciumageanu, and Anca Dana Buzoianu. 2017. "Physician Migration at Its Roots: A Study on the Emigration Preferences and Plans among Medical Students in Romania." *Human Resources for Health* 15 (1): 1–9.

Sudnow, David. 1967. *Passing on: The Social Organization of Dying*. Englewood Cliffs, NJ: Prentice-Hall.

Szeman, Ioana. 2018. *Staging Citizenship: Roma, Performance, and Belonging in EU Romania*. New York and Oxford: Berghahn.

Taekema, Dan. 2020. "Inquest into Death of 16-Year-Old Devon Freeman Announced." CBC. 2020. https://www.cbc.ca/news/canada/hamilton/devon-freeman-inquest-announced-1.5462832.

Teşliuc, Emil, Vlad Grigoras, and Manuela Sofia Stănculescu. 2016. *The Atlas of Rural Marginalized Areas and of Local Human Development in Romania.* Bucharest: World Bank.

Timmermans, Stefan. 1998. "Social Death as Self-Fulfilling Prophecy: David Sudnow's 'Passing On' Revisited." *The Sociological Quarterly* 39 (3): 453–72.

Tiron, Mirabela. 2018. "Anomaliile din sănătate: Spitalele de stat sunt gazde pentru laboratoare private, fondurile Casei se duc la privați, dar pacienții sunt plimbați de la un laborator la altul pentru că nu există fonduri pentru analize gratuite [Anomalies in the Healthcare S." Ziarul Financiar. 2018. https://www.zf.ro /eveniment/anomaliile-sanatate-spitalele-stat-gazde-laboratoare-private-fondurile -casei-duc-privati-pacientii-plimbati-laborator-exista-fonduri-analize-gratuite -17345071.

Toye, Francine, and Karen Barker. 2010. "'Could I Be Imagining This?'—the Dialectic Struggles of People with Persistent Unexplained Back Pain." *Disability and Rehabilitation* 32 (21): 1722–32.

Tremlett, Annabel. 2014. "Demotic or Demonic? Race, Class and Gender in 'Gypsy' Reality TV." *The Sociological Review* 62 (2): 316–34.

UNAIDS. 2004. "Romania: Epidemiological Fact Sheets." https://data.unaids.org/ publications/fact-sheets01/romania_en.pdf.

Vassy, Carine. 2001. "Categorisation and Micro-Rationing: Access to Care in a French Emergency Department." *Sociology of Health and Illness* 23 (5): 615–32.

———. 2004. "L'Organisation Des Services d'urgences, Entre Le Social et Le Sanitaire [The Organization of Emergency Services, between Social and Sanitary]." *Mouvements* 32 (2): 67–74.

Vlădescu, Cristian, Silviu Rădulescu, and Sorin Cace. 2005. "The Romanian Health Care System: Between Bismark and Semashko." In *Decentralization in Healthcare: Analyses and Experiences in Central and Eastern Europe in the 1990s,* edited by George Shakarishvili, 437–85. Budapest: Open Society Institute.

Vlădescu, Cristian, Gabriela Scîntee, and Victor Olsavszky. 2008. "Romania: Health System Review." *Health Systems in Transition* 10 (3): 1–172.

Voicu, Mălina, and Paula Andreea Tufiş. 2012. "Trends in Gender Beliefs in Romania: 1993–2008." *Current Sociology* 60 (1): 61–80.

Wacquant, Loïc. 2013. "A Janus-Faced Institution of Ethnoracial Closure: A Sociological Specification of the Ghetto." In *Spaces of the Poor: Perspectives of Cultural Sciences on Urban Slum Areas and Their Inhabitants,* edited by Hans-Christian Petersen, 15–46. Bielefeld: Transcript Verlag.

Wamsiedel, Marius. 2013. *Roma Health Mediation in Romania: Case Study.* Copenhagen: World Health Organization - Regional Office for Europe.

———. 2016a. "Lay Values, Organizational Concerns, and the Handling of 'Social Cases' in Romanian Emergency Departments." *Transylvanian Review* 25 (S1): 61–76.

———. 2016b. "Accomplishing Public Secrecy: Non-Monetary Informal Practices and Their Concealment at the Emergency Department." *Journal of Contemporary Central and Eastern Europe* 24 (3): 307–20.

———. 2017. "Approaching Informality: Rear-Mirror Methodology and Ethnographic Inquiry." In *The Informal Economy in Global Perspective: Varieties of Governance*, edited by Abel Polese, Colin C. Williams, Ioana A. Horodnic, and Predrag Bejakovic, 97–115. London: Palgrave Macmillan.

———. 2018. "Reasonableness: Legitimate Reasons for Illegitimate Presentations at the ED." *Sociology of Health and Illness* 40 (8): 1347–60.

———. 2020. "Credibility Work and Moral Evaluation at the ED." *Social Science and Medicine* 248 (112845): 1–8.

———. 2022a. "The Meanings and Consequences of Informal Payments in the Romanian Healthcare Sector." *Economic Sociology* 23 (3): 5–9.

———. 2022b. "Temporal Typifications as an Organizational Resource: Experiential Knowledge and Patient Processing at the Emergency Department." *Time & Society* 31 (2): 157–76.

Wamsiedel, Marius, Eniko Vincze, and Iustina Ionescu. 2012. *Roma Health: The Perspective of Actors Involved in the Health System—Doctors, Health Mediators and Patients*. Bucharest: Romani CRISS.

Wang, Huihui, Adanna Chukwuma, Radu Comsa, Tania Dmytraczenko, Estelle Gong, and Lidia Onofrei. 2021. "Generating Political Priority for Primary Health Care Reform in Romania." *Health Systems & Reform* 7 (2): 1–11.

Wang, Zhen, Xiaying Xiong, Shuang Wang, Junguo Yan, Martin Springer, and R P Dellinger. 2018. "Causes of Emergency Department Overcrowding and Blockage of Access to Critical Services in Beijing: A 2-Year Study." *The Journal of Emergency Medicine* 54 (5): 665–73.

Weber, Gerard A. 2009. "Forsaken Generation: Stress, Social Suffering and Strategies among Working-Class Pensioners in Post-Socialist Moldova, Romania." The City University of New York.

———. 2015. "'Other Than a Thank-You, There's Nothing I Can Give': Managing Health and Illness among Working-Class Pensioners in Post-Socialist Moldavia, Romania." *Human Organization* 74 (2): 115–24.

———. 2016. "'Please Ask the Priest to Pray for Dana, the Sick One': Health-Seeking, Religion and Decline of the Public Sector in Post-Communist Romania." *Transylvanian Review* 25: 77–90.

Wendt, Claus, Lorraine Frisina, and Heinz Rothgang. 2009. "Healthcare System Types: A Conceptual Framework for Comparison." *Social Policy & Administration* 43 (1): 70–90.

Werner, Anne, Lise Widding Isaksen, and Kirsti Malterud. 2004. "'I Am Not the Kind of Woman Who Complains of Everything': Illness Stories on Self and Shame in Women with Chronic Pain." *Social Science & Medicine* 59 (5): 1035–45.

Werner, Anne, and Kirsti Malterud. 2003. "It Is Hard Work Behaving as a Credible Patient: Encounters between Women with Chronic Pain and Their Doctors." *Social Science & Medicine* 57 (8): 1409–19.

———. 2005. "'The Pain Isn't as Disabling as It Used to Be': How Can the Patient Experience Empowerment Instead of Vulnerability in the Consultation?" *Scandinavian Journal of Public Health* 33 (66 suppl): 41–46.

Williams, Colin C., Ioana Horodnic, and Adrian Horodnic. 2016. "Who Is Making Informal Payments for Public Healthcare in East-Central Europe? An Evaluation of Socio-Economic and Spatial Variations." *Eastern Journal of European Studies* 7 (1): 49–61.

Wind, Gitte. 2008. "Negotiated Interactive Observation: Doing Fieldwork in Hospital Settings." *Anthropology & Medicine* 15 (2): 79–89.

Winkelman, Michael. 2009. *Culture and Health: Applying Medical Anthropology.* San Francisco, CA: Jossey-Bass.

Womack, Mari. 2010. *The Anthropology of Health and Healing.* Lanham, MD: Altamira Press.

Woodcock, Shannon. 2007. "Romania and EUrope: Roma, Rroma and Tigani as Sites for the Contestation of Ethno-National Identities." *Patterns of Prejudice* 41 (5): 493–515.

World Bank. 2022. "Rural Population (% of Total Population) - European Union." World Data Indicators [Data File]. 2022. https://data.worldbank.org/indicator/SP .RUR.TOTL.ZS?locations=EU&most_recent_value_desc=true.

World Health Organization. 2012. *Evaluation of Structure and Provision of Primary Care in Romania.* Copenhagen: World Health Organization.

Zaman, Shahaduz. 2008. "Native among the Natives: Physician Anthropologist Doing Hospital Ethnography at Home." *Journal of Contemporary Ethnography* 37 (2): 135–54.

Index

alcohol intoxication:
  acute. *See* "occasionally drunk";
  chronic. *See* "drunkards";
  and moral evaluation, 75–80
ambulance:
  and access to emergency care, 10,
    22, 46, 50, 132;
  and moral evaluation, 57, 77–78,
    100, 145, 154–55, 158n13;
  and paperwork, 143–44;
  patients brought by, 46, 55,
    77–78, 82, 85, 100, 131–32;
  and transportation of psychiatric
    patients, 81

Buchbinder, Mara, 60, 61

child patients, 45, 136n18, 129–
  30, 146, 153
constant comparative method, 64n14
Corman, Michael, 6

deservingness. *See* social worth
diabetes, 126
dirty work, 12, 77, 91n27
domestic violence, 42, 50, 59
"drunkards":
  attribution of responsibility, 76;
  challenges to the ED, 77;

legitimacy of, 77–78, 124;
reasonableness of, 77–78, 124;
Romani patients as, 88, 142;
sanctioning of, 79;
social class and, 78;
social worth of, 76–79;
staff's interaction with,
  76–77, 77–78

elderly patients:
  classification of, 68;
  economic situation of, 68;
  family relationship of, 69;
  as problem patients, 69;
  social status of, 68;
  tentative moral evaluation of, 68;
  as worthy patients 45
Emergency Departments:
  crisis of, 28–29;
  overcrowding, 5, 36, 160;
  perceived misuse of, 21, 27, 33;
  reorganization of, 28, 48n62;
  staff in, 9–10
Emergency Severity Index. *See*
  triage algorithm
epidemiologic transition, 22

family medicine:

as a determinant of the ED
      crisis, 51–52
filial piety, 48, 56, 68, 69, 90n5

gatekeeping role of the triage:
      inclusionary function, 60–62;
      exclusionary function, 62
gender, 9, 100, 101, 114n19,
      139, 143, 164
Goffman, Erving, 74, 136–37n21

healthcare system in Romania:
      during socialism, 22–23;
      financing, 23;
      formal costs, 25;
      informal costs. *see*
         informal payments;
      migration of doctors and
         nurses, 24;
      post-socialist reforms, 23–24;
      primary healthcare, 23, 26;
      rural-urban disparities, 25–26;
      social health insurance, 23–25;
      staff shortage, 29
high blood pressure, 42n73, 51, 70,
      103–4, 150
Hillman, Alexandra, 6, 17n20, 112,
      124, 134, 161
homeless. *See* Social case
humor:
      as sanction, 79, 85–86;
      situational worth and, 58, 59,
         60, 101, 132

informal payments, 20n3, 25,
      34, 39–40n36
interactional despotism, 36

Johannessen, Lars, 6, 114n14

kinship language, 68–69, 70, 91n10

legitimacy of the case, assessment of:
      background assumptions 46–47;

clinical and non-clinical
      considerations in, 49;
      duration of illness and, 47;
      frequency of ED visits and, 48;
      patients' talk and demeanor
         and, 48–49;
      patients' familiarity with the
         triage and, 48;
      timing of arrival and,
         47–48, 63n3;
      trustworthiness and, 49

memorable cases, 45
mental illness:
      mild. *See* "NVDists";
      moral evaluation of, 80–84;
      severe. *See* "severely mentally ill"
MESRE. *See* Mobile Emergency
      Service for Resuscitation and
      Extrication
methodology:
      constant comparative method,
         64n14, 124, 163;
      ethnography, 5–6, 7, 11, 13,
         19n48, 20n52;
      positionality, 20n54;
      selection of hospitals, 7–8;
      triangulation of methods, 20n54
Mobile Emergency Service
      for Resuscitation and
      Extrication, 10, 19n47
moral evaluation of patients:
      consequences of, 32–36;
      structural determinants of, 36;
      theory of, 3–5

neuro-vegetative dystonia. *See* NVDists
"occasionally drunk":
      attribution of responsibility, 79;
      legitimacy of, 124;
      reasonableness of, 124;
      social class and typification
         as, 78, 79;
      social worth of, 79;
      staff's interaction with, 79–80

Parsons, Talcott, 3–4, 53, 60, 128
patients:
    denied access to emergency
      care, 42–43n73;
    presumed dishonesty of, 46;
    sanctioning of, 34–36, 37;
    socialization of, 33–34, 37, 49–50
Peneff, Jean, 91n27
"Problem patients," 67, 69, 90nn2–3

racism:
    color-blind, 140–41;
    explicit, 140–41;
    reproduction of, 152–55;
    systemic, 2
"Real" emergencies, 21, 26, 30, 31, 32,
    37, 41n57, 45, 50, 62n2, 64n14, 119,
    124, 137nn27–28, 160
reasonableness of the visit,
    assessment of:
      criteria in, 50–52;
      domestic violence and, 50;
      drinking-related
        conditions and, 51;
      homelessness and, 53–54;
      lack of access to primary care
        and, 51–52, 54;
      perceived legitimacy and, 52–53,
        54, 64n15;
      positive discrimination
        and, 52, 60;
      Romani patients and, 54;
      structural competence and, 61;
      structural conditions and, 51–52;
      traffic accidents and, 50
regular users of the ED, 58, 59, 60
Roma in Romania:
    access to healthcare
      services of, 26;
    discrimination in the healthcare
      system of, 26;
    health insurance status of, 38n24;
    socio-economic status
      of, 26, 41n51
Romani culture, staff perception of the:

determinant of poverty, 73;
determinant of social
    exclusion, 89;
resource for getting faster
    access, 74;
source of trouble at the ED, 73–74
Romani patients:
    assimilated Roma, 145, 150;
    female Roma, 129–30, 146–
      47, 148, 150;
    male Roma, 114n20, 125,
      143, 144, 150;
    traditional Roma, 91n24, 145, 150
Romani patients, moral evaluation of:
    background expectations, 54,
      72–74, 88–89, 107, 124;
    consequences of, 74, 155–56;
    derogatory language, 91n20, 146;
    microaggressions,
      135n15, 146–47;
    practical accomplishment, 74–75,
      85–86, 91n24, 107–11, 125,
      129–30, 146–47, 148, 151
Romani patients, typification of the:
    aggressiveness, 140–45;
    disreputable characteristics,
      72–73, 89, 107, 110, 142;
    improper use of the ED, 72,
      140, 142–43;
    lack of health insurance, 72–73;
    overuse of the ED, 72;
    positive characteristics, 140;
    "problem patients," 88;
    unemployment, 73;
    unhealthy lifestyle, 88;
    untrustworthiness, 129;
    welfare benefits, 73
Roth, Julius, 161
rural areas:
    health care in, 22–26,
      40nn41–42, 160;
    moral evaluation of patients
      from, 52, 61, 70, 74, 131,
      158n13, 160;
    mortality rate in, 41n46;

population of, 40n40

Seim, Josh, 5–6
sick role model, 3, 4
situational worth, 58–60
sixth sense, 98, 112, 114n17
SMURD. *See* Mobile Emergency
  Service for Resuscitation and
  Extrication
social case, 1, 60, 81, 87, 90n4, 107, 110
social class, 21, 22, 24, 56, 68, 78, 79,
  84, 86, 111, 129, 130, 131, 150,
  153, 164–65
social worth of the patient,
  assessment of:
    criteria in, 54–56;
    family life and, 55–56, 57;
    formal education and, 55;
    patient's age and, 56;
social class and, 165;
    unemployment and, 55, 57, 150
street-level bureaucracy, 5, 33, 67,
  112, 156, 160
structural competence, 60, 61, 156
suicide attempts:
    "blackmail suicide." *See* "staged
      suicide attempt";

handling of, 85, 131–32;
lay explanations for, 85–88;
moral evaluation of, 45, 64n15;
"real suicide attempt," 84, 88,
  131–32, 163;
"staged suicide attempt," 84,
  85–86, 163

traffic accidents, 50, 129–30, 146
triage algorithm:
    informal, 10, 34–35, 114n17;
    in practice, 47, 70, 149;
    priority codes, 10,
      18–19n46, 34–35;
    posters of, 34
triage assessment of patients:
    subjectivity of, 45–46
triage workers:
    perceived mission of
      the ED, 30–32
typification work:
    patient types, 67;
    structural determinants of, 67
"țigan":
    contested term, 141, 157n2;
    use by staff of, 73, 140, 141,
      152, 154, 155

About the Author

Marius Wamsiedel is a sociologist by training and an assistant professor of global health at Duke Kunshan University. His work examines the social categorization of patients, the emergency triage decision-making process, the economy of favors in healthcare settings, and the access to health services by vulnerable populations.

Ingram Content Group UK Ltd.
Milton Keynes UK
UKHW012017140323
418579UK00003B/62